# Java™ RMI: Remote Method Invocation

# Java™ RMI: Remote Method Invocation

## Troy Bryan Downing

IDG Books Worldwide, Inc.
An International Data Group Company

Foster City, CA ◆ Chicago, IL ◆ Indianapolis, IN ◆ Southlake, TX

Java™ RMI: Remote Method Invocation

Published by
**IDG Books Worldwide, Inc.**
An International Data Group Company
919 E. Hillsdale Blvd., Suite 400
Foster City, CA 94404
www.idgbooks.com (IDG Books Worldwide Web site)

Library of Congress Catalog Card No.: 97-73632

ISBN: 0-7645-8043-4

Printed in the United States of America

10 9 8 7 6 5 4 3 2 1

1E/QX/QR/ZY/FC

Distributed in the United States by IDG Books Worldwide, Inc.

Distributed by Macmillan Canada for Canada; by Transworld Publishers Limited in the United Kingdom; by IDG Norge Books for Norway; by IDG Sweden Books for Sweden; by Woodslane Pty. Ltd. for Australia; by Woodslane Enterprises Ltd. for New Zealand; by Longman Singapore Publishers Ltd. for Singapore, Malaysia, Thailand, and Indonesia; by Simron Pty. Ltd. for South Africa; by Toppan Company Ltd. for Japan; by Distribuidora Cuspide for Argentina; by Livraria Cultura for Brazil; by Ediciencia S.A. for Ecuador; by Addison-Wesley Publishing Company for Korea; by Ediciones ZETA S.C.R. Ltda. for Peru; by WS Computer Publishing Corporation, Inc., for the Philippines; by Unalis Corporation for Taiwan; by Contemporanea de Ediciones for Venezuela; by Computer Book & Magazine Store for Puerto Rico; by Express Computer Distributors for the Caribbean and West Indies. Authorized Sales Agent: Anthony Rudkin Associates for the Middle East and North Africa.

For general information on IDG Books Worldwide's books in the U.S., please call our Consumer Customer Service department at 800-762-2974. For reseller information, including discounts and premium sales, please call our Reseller Customer Service department at 800-434-3422.

For information on where to purchase IDG Books Worldwide's books outside the U.S., please contact our International Sales department at 415-655-3200 or fax 415-655-3295.

For information on foreign language translations, please contact our Foreign & Subsidiary Rights department at 415-655-3021 or fax 415-655-3281.

For sales inquiries and special prices for bulk quantities, please contact our Sales department at 415-655-3200 or write to the address above.

For information on using IDG Books Worldwide's books in the classroom or for ordering examination copies, please contact our Educational Sales department at 800-434-2086 or fax 817-251-8174.

For press review copies, author interviews, or other publicity information, please contact our Public Relations department at 415-655-3000 or fax 415-655-3299.

For authorization to photocopy items for corporate, personal, or educational use, please contact Copyright Clearance Center, 222 Rosewood Drive, Danvers, MA 01923, or fax 508-750-4470.

# ABOUT IDG BOOKS WORLDWIDE

Welcome to the world of IDG Books Worldwide.

IDG Books Worldwide, Inc., is a subsidiary of International Data Group, the world's largest publisher of computer-related information and the leading global provider of information services on information technology. IDG was founded more than 25 years ago and now employs more than 8,500 people worldwide. IDG publishes more than 275 computer publications in over 75 countries (see listing below). More than 60 million people read one or more IDG publications each month.

Launched in 1990, IDG Books Worldwide is today the #1 publisher of best-selling computer books in the United States. We are proud to have received eight awards from the Computer Press Association in recognition of editorial excellence and three from *Computer Currents'* First Annual Readers' Choice Awards. Our best-selling *...For Dummies*® series has more than 30 million copies in print with translations in 30 languages. IDG Books Worldwide, through a joint venture with IDG's Hi-Tech Beijing, became the first U.S. publisher to publish a computer book in the People's Republic of China. In record time, IDG Books Worldwide has become the first choice for millions of readers around the world who want to learn how to better manage their businesses.

Our mission is simple: Every one of our books is designed to bring extra value and skill-building instructions to the reader. Our books are written by experts who understand and care about our readers. The knowledge base of our editorial staff comes from years of experience in publishing, education, and journalism — experience we use to produce books for the '90s. In short, we care about books, so we attract the best people. We devote special attention to details such as audience, interior design, use of icons, and illustrations. And because we use an efficient process of authoring, editing, and desktop publishing our books electronically, we can spend more time ensuring superior content and spend less time on the technicalities of making books.

You can count on our commitment to deliver high-quality books at competitive prices on topics you want to read about. At IDG Books Worldwide, we continue in the IDG tradition of delivering quality for more than 25 years. You'll find no better book on a subject than one from IDG Books Worldwide.

*John Kilcullen*
John Kilcullen
CEO
IDG Books Worldwide, Inc.

*Steven Berkowitz*
Steven Berkowitz
President and Publisher
IDG Books Worldwide, Inc.

Eighth Annual
Computer Press
Awards ≥1992

Ninth Annual
Computer Press
Awards ≥1993

Tenth Annual
Computer Press
Awards ≥1994

Eleventh Annual
Computer Press
Awards ≥1995

# Credits

ACQUISITIONS EDITOR
John Osborn

DEVELOPMENT EDITOR
Stefan Grünwedel

TECHNICAL EDITOR
Jon Meyer

COPY EDITORS
Robert Campbell
Carolyn Welch

PRODUCTION COORDINATOR
Susan Parini

COVER DESIGNER
Cyndra Robbins

GRAPHICS AND PRODUCTION
SPECIALISTS
Shannon Miller
Maureen Moore

QUALITY CONTROL SPECIALIST
Mark Schumann

ILLUSTRATOR
Greg Maxson

PROOFREADER
Christine Sabooni

INDEXER
Sherry Massey

# About the Author

**Troy Bryan Downing** is Vice President of Production at WebCal Corporation, an Internet and intranet software development company and content provider. Downing is also an adjunct faculty member at New York University's Information Technology Institute, where he lectures on Java and various Internet-based technologies, as well as develops curricula. He has written and coauthored a number of Web-related books.

*For my family—*
*my wife, Laura, for her eternal love and understanding;*
*my daughter, Morgan, for her crazy distractions;*
*and Dylan for keeping us all in shape*

# Preface

*Java RMI: Remote Method Invocation* is both a how-to and a reference guide on using RMI for creating distributed applications in Java. RMI is a Java-specific implementation of a distributed object model. There are more general approaches to developing distributed applications using implementations of the Common Object Request Broker Architecture (CORBA), but these generally require writing language-neutral interfaces in a ternary Interface Description Language (IDL) that must be compiled separately from your application. This adds to the complexity of developing distributed applications. By contrast, RMI provides you with a simple, elegant interface to distributing objects that are implemented in the Java language.

Recently, Javasoft has announced the support of the Internet Inter-Orb Protocol (IIOP) to deal with RMI-to-CORBA applications development. This will enable programmers to write distributed applications in Java, using the RMI architecture, yet still include CORBA-based connectivity to their non-Java applications. Currently, RMI/IIOP connectivity hasn't been implemented, but Javasoft has announced that it will be included in the next major release of the Java Development Kit.

As this is an advanced how-to guide and reference, I assume that you are already a programmer and have written Java applets and applications. For those who are not yet familiar with the Java programming language, I suggest obtaining a copy of a Java programming book that includes a reasonable reference section to supplement this book—for example, *Java™ Master Reference* by Arthur Griffith from IDG Books Worldwide (ISBN: 0-7645-3084-4).

This reference is for programmers who are interested in building distributed applications for Java-centric environments. I assume that your distributed objects are written in Java and interact with other objects that are also written in Java. This reference is also intended for programmers who want to compare and contrast RMI with other ORB architectures for evaluating the pros and cons of using these different object models.

# Requirements

Most of the examples in this book use classes and methods that were introduced with the Java Development Kit (JDK) version 1.1. One of the main goals of the Java architecture is to be platform-neutral. Unfortunately, this goal is not always met. Many of the late APIs and enhancements to Java are available for Solaris and Windows 95/NT long before they are available in the embedded Java Virtual Machines (JVMs) of popular Web browsers—or in JDKs for other platforms. As of this writing, the Sunsoft version of JDK 1.1 is available for Solaris and Windows 95/NT, and the JVM is running under the current release of the HotJava browser. Netscape Communications Corporation plans to support JDK 1.1 in its next release of Netscape Communicator, and Microsoft Corporation has similar plans for its Microsoft Internet Explorer. The applets in this book were all tested using the appletviewer application that comes with the JDK 1.1 for Solaris and appletviewer for Windows 95.

With that understood, all you need for developing applications and compiling the source examples that come with this book is a system that supports JDK 1.1 (or later) and the appropriate Java compiler (such as javac, which comes with the JDK).

# What's in This Book?

This book is divided into two chapters and three parts.

Part I, "Overview of Java RMI," covers the building blocks of the RMI system, as well as background information about network computing in general. This includes high-level descriptions of the classes and interfaces used to create RMI-based applications. The overview also covers the RMI Name Service, or "Registry," and gives simple examples of how to build and deploy simple RMI applications.

Part II, "Advanced Java RMI Concepts," moves forward into more detailed information about distributing objects using RMI. The basics of object distribution, complex parameter passing, and object serialization are covered, as well details about the RMI architecture.

Part III, "Real-World Applications of Java RMI," jumps forward into actual RMI application code. This section contains lots of source code and commentary. The applications cover client- and server-side code for building a "Chat" system and RMI-based database access system.

Part IV, "Java API Quick Reference," consists of six mini references to the packages and classes that are related to RMI and object serialization. This is not intended to be a complete Java API reference, but as a supplement to a reference to the standard Java class libraries. Each reference section contains the methods and interfaces for a particular package: java.rmi, java.rmi.dgc, java.rmi.registry, java.rmi.server, and java.io. RMI exception classes appear in the last reference section.

Finally, Appendix A discusses miscellaneous security issues, such as using RMI through firewalls, and configuring and dealing with default browser restrictions, such as the "Applet Host" network restriction. Appendix B contains the thrown-by index (methods that throw certain exceptions) and Appendix C contains the defined-in index (methods defined in the classes of the java.rmi.* packages). Appendix D describes the contents of the CD-ROM.

# What's on the CD-ROM?

The CD-ROM that accompanies this book contains all of the source code contained in the text. The source code examples in the book are drawn directly from these source files with only minor modification. (The CD-ROM source code is sometimes more heavily commented.)

The CD-ROM also contains the Java Development Kit version 1.1.4 from Sun Microsystems. Read Appendix D for more information about the contents of the CD-ROM.

# Conventions Used in This Book

All code samples found in this book can also be found on the accompanying CD-ROM that comes with this book. Code samples will have the following style:

```
public class Hello
extends Applet
  implements Runnable {

public void init() {
   //do something
  }
}
```

All user input will be in boldface as follows:

```
javac -d /temp *.java
```

Any text that is output to the console will be in a monospaced font and appear as follows:

```
Error: NoSuchMethodException thrown by rmibook.util.foo()
```

# Request for Comments

If you find any errors, find something in this book confusing, incorrect, misleading, or extremely insightful, please let me know. I will try to respond in a reasonable amount of time and will definitely take your comments into consideration when logging errata or working on subsequent editions of this book. The best way to contact me is by e-mail at downing@webcal.com. There is also an HTML form you can fill out that is connected to my Web page at http://www.webcal.com/downing/. Of course, you should let the publisher know what you think of this book by going to http://my2cents.idgbooks.com.

# Acknowledgments

I would like to thank Jon Meyer for his hard, detailed work with the technical edits. Jon's efforts and insights were a great help in putting this book together. Acknowledgments are also due to Pedro Casals and the staff at Waterside Productions, Zia Khan at Xenosys Corporation for the news feeds and access to source code, the NYU Media Research Lab for being such an interesting place to work at and being mostly responsible for exposing me to these exciting technologies, and the staff at IDG Books Worldwide (see their names on the credits page) for putting this all together.

# Contents at a Glance

# Contents

## Part II Advanced Java RMI Concepts

## Part III Real-World Applications of Java RMI

## Part IV Java API Quick Reference

# Part 1

## Overview of Java RMI

Chapter 1: Overview of Network
Programming

Chapter 2: Overview of RMI Architecture

Chapter 3: Using the Registry

# Chapter 1

# Overview of Network Programming

## IN THIS CHAPTER

- ◆ Basic network support in Java
- ◆ Low-level network programming in Java
- ◆ Network programming protocols
- ◆ Remote procedure calls
- ◆ Network objects
- ◆ Remote Method Invocation

*Remote Method Invocation (RMI) enables the programmer to create distributed Java-to-Java applications, in which the methods of remote Java objects can be invoked from other Java virtual machines, possibly on different hosts. A Java program can make a call on a remote object once it obtains a reference to the remote object, either by looking up the remote object in the bootstrap naming service provided by RMI or by receiving the reference as an argument or a return value. A client can call a remote object in a server, and that server can also be a client of other remote objects. RMI uses Object Serialization to marshal and unmarshal parameters and does not truncate types, supporting true object-oriented polymorphism.*
—Java Distributed Systems Web page

PROGRAMMERS OFTEN CONSIDER NETWORK programming to be cryptic and unapproachable. Not that the application programming interfaces (APIs) are difficult to understand (although some are pretty hard to look at due to the complexity of the code), but more because the programmer is forced to implement protocols on top of these APIs. Unless you are trying specifically to write a network protocol, the low-level "nuts and bolts" aren't really that interesting. As a programmer you want to focus on the task at hand, which may require communicating or sending data to remote processes. If transmission of the data is handled invisibly and reliably, it is much easier to spend your energies perfecting your application and not worrying about what's under the hood. It's a lot like driving a car. It's possible to build a special-purpose engine for every trip that you want to take, but normally, all you want to do is climb in and drive. Of course, you may want to know if the engine is reliable, or powerful, but unless you are an engine designer, you're not going to be rebuilding engines.

Many network programmers still use the BSD (Berkeley Systems Design) socket API. This API has been around for years on BSD UNIX systems, and many newer versions of UNIX now emulate this API, allowing programmers to maintain access to it. Newer network technologies have appeared such as TLI and, of course, non-UNIX APIs such as Winsock and MacOS sockets. The main problem with these interfaces is that they require the programmer to design complex communications protocols at the application level. Using the BSD API, a programmer has to decide how to moderate data transmission and check for platform-dependent changes in data representation (such as byte order as well as size and representation differences in integral and floating-point data types). In essence, as a programmer, you must worry about packaging and unpacking data that you send and receive, in essence, converting it from local representation to network representation and then converting it back to the local representation. These issues generate a lot of overhead for the programmer, as well as problems that develop from the complexity of the code necessary to implement simple transmission protocols.

Some of these problems, especially problems associated with implementing transmission protocols, have been addressed with a mechanism called Remote Procedure Call (RPC). RPC allows programmers to register their applications with a special port mapper that maps these programs to a network address. Once registered, procedures in these applications can be called from remote clients as if they were local procedures, without the programmer worrying about encoding or decoding the data for transmission over the network. The service addresses that are assigned to these procedures are normally called port numbers. Every network application that exists on a single host has a unique port number. The unique network number of the host machine, coupled with this port number, make up the complete network address of the service. Locating and binding to an available port number is taken care of automatically. RPC makes it easier to develop network applications because it adds a level of abstraction that allows a programmer to call a procedure on a remote application in much the same way that a procedure is called within the same application. This level of abstraction enables programmers to concern themselves with the actual system design with little or no concern for data transmission or communication protocols.

# Basic Network Support in Java

When Java was first released, it had basic support for TCP and UDP sockets. It is actually much easier to write network applications using the Java socket classes than using the equivalent BSD library functions, since most of the work of setting up the structures that these sockets depend on is taken care of for you in the Java class libraries. There is still one problem: Java has a nice interface for establishing sockets and reading/writing data on these sockets, but it is still up to the programmer to implement communications protocols to pack and unpack data sent over a network connection, and there is no easy way to send complex data such as an arbitrary object through a socket connection.

RPC is a reasonable model for distributed procedural code, but it falls apart with object-oriented code because many of the arguments and return values sent to "procedures" in Java are in fact objects. RPC supports only a fairly limited set of basic data types. In response to this, the designers of Java added support that was very similar to RPC, called *remote method invocation* (RMI).

RMI allows Java programs to register their class methods with a server that does the port arbitration in much the same way that RPC does. Once this has been set up, sending messages, or invoking methods on remote processes, is as simple as invoking a method on a local object. This functionality facilitates rapid development of distributed applications, saving you the need to implement data conversion or transmission protocols.

RMI is dependent on the ability to "serialize" objects—to turn an object into a serial representation that is suitable for transmission over a network connection, and then to reconstruct it upon receipt. This is necessary for remote methods that take objects as their parameters as well as methods that have objects as their return values.

In order to facilitate *object serialization* (OS), an interface, Serializable, was created. Virtually any object that implements this interface can be written to and read from a stream. In the Java Developer's Kit (JDK) version 1.1, all of the core classes in java.util and java.lang implement this interface, so types such as `Strings` and `Floats` can easily be sent as objects over a socket connection. A more interesting property, however, is the capability to create arbitrary objects that can be sent over a socket connection and reconstructed by the receiver.

# Low-Level Network Programming in Java

When I first tried writing a network application in Java, I was pleasantly surprised at how simple it was. It had been my experience that learning to write network applications in any new toolkit was a tedious and confusing exercise. I've been using the Berkeley Socket API for UNIX for years, and I have built a library of simple, general-purpose wrappers around that API that I've used for developing 90 percent of the UNIX network applications that I've written. The first time I looked at the Java networking API, I found it to be very similar to the wrappers that I had been using in C, and just as easy to use.

Java's networking support is built around sockets. Sockets are generally of two types, either connection-based or connectionless. A connection-based socket can be thought of as a phone call. A number is dialed, someone (or something) picks up the phone on the other end, and both sides have the exclusive use of that circuit until one of the parties breaks the connection. TCP is a connection-based protocol. In fact, it is the connection-based protocol used for Java sockets establishing "virtual circuit" connections.

A connectionless communications protocol, or *datagram,* is more like sending a postcard. You write an address on the front of a card, write a message on the back, and then drop it in a mailbox and hope it gets where it's supposed to. Because there is no connection during communication, state (that is, the current "state" of the system) must be maintained separately. This is normally done by the client. Each "postcard" is numbered and contains any state information that the server needs in order to process the data. If cards are lost in the mail or are received out of order, it is up to the client to re-request lost cards and put out-of-order cards into their proper order. In other words, the server simply fills requests that the client must ask for and verify. The standard connectionless protocol with the TCP/IP protocol suite is the User Datagram Protocol (UDP). This protocol is used by the connectionless sockets in the Java libraries. It's interesting to note that TCP is actually a higher-level abstraction built on top of UDP. TCP presents a stream-based abstraction to the programmer but uses its own logic on top of UDP to communicate with another machine.

There are reasons for both TCP and UDP. In general, TCP is more robust and easier to write applications around, but UDP is much faster. (That pretty much blows away the telephone/postcard comparison, but you should get the idea.)

# Network Programming Protocols

Let's take a quick look at some of the components that make up the application, session, and transport layers of a network communications model.

Some of the more common network protocols in use today are the File Transfer Protocol, the Simple Mail Transfer Protocol, the Remote Shell protocol, the Telnet protocol, and the Hypertext Transfer Protocol. Most of these are high-level protocols that sit on a lower-level transport protocol such as the Transmission Control Protocol (TCP) or the User Datagram Protocol (UDP). Because TCP is one of the most common of these, let's take a closer look at what you get from TCP.

Historically, programmers have written network applications on top of TCP sockets. A socket is the endpoint of a network connection. This endpoint is often referred to via a file descriptor, and once the connection is established, the application reads and writes data using the descriptor.

# What Is a Protocol?

Before I discuss various network protocols, it is necessary to understand what a protocol is. *Webster's New World Dictionary* describes a protocol as "the ceremonial forms accepted as correct in official dealings." This is not as off-base as it may sound. A network protocol essentially describes a set of official rules that must be obeyed by sender and receiver in order to communicate. I guess these rules could be considered *ceremonial.* In any case, let's take a look at a very simple, everyday protocol, making a phone call. Certain rules must be followed to use a telephone, and in general, these rules must be followed in order:

1. The caller must determine the phone number of the person he wishes to call. If the number is unknown, a directory service is consulted.

2. The caller picks up the receiver on the telephone.

3. The caller waits for the dial tone.

4. The caller dials the phone number.

5. The caller listens for either a busy signal or a ringing tone. If there is a busy signal, the caller hangs up and jumps back to step 2.

6. The caller waits for an answer. If the phone call is answered, communication begins; otherwise, the caller determines how long to wait before timing out and hangs up.

7. The caller verifies that the receiver is the one intended. If so, communication continues; otherwise, the caller hangs up and verifies the phone number, jumping back to step 1.

8. Once communication is complete, the caller hangs up the phone.

The receiver has the following protocol:

1. Wait for the phone to ring.

2. Pick up the receiver.

3. Verify that the call was intended for the receiver. If not, hang up; otherwise, communication continues.

4. Once communication is complete, the receiver hangs up the phone and jumps back to step 1.

This may seem like a silly example, but it demonstrates a simple communications protocol. If steps aren't carried out in order, you get undefined behavior. For example, the caller can't dial the phone number before the phone is taken off the hook, and the receiver generally can't answer the phone before it has started ringing. Let's map this

*continued*

## What Is a Protocol? *(Continued)*

same idea to a high-level network protocol, namely the Hypertext Transfer Protocol (HTTP).

In HTTP the server will take on the role of the receiver, and arbitrary client browsers will take on the roll of callers. The HTTP server will never initiate a call on its own, but it will answer calls from other callers. Let's look at the browser side of this protocol:

1. A user types a URL (Uniform Resource Locator) into the browser; the URL could look like this: `http://foo.com/index.html`.

2. The browser extracts the server name from the URL, in this case `foo.com`.

3. The browser tries to locate the IP address (corresponding to the phone number in the previous example) for the server. Normally, a *domain name server* (DNS) is queried. If the DNS can locate the IP address of the machine, the number is returned in the form, for example, "128.122.129.65"; otherwise, the lookup fails and the browser displays an error message.

4. The browser connects to port 80 (the standard HTTP port number) on the machine at address 128.122.129.65. If the connection is not successful, an error message is produced by the browser stating "Service not Available."

5. Once the connection is established, the browser sends an HTTP header that requests the document described in the URL (in this case, the file index.html). The header is structured as follows: a command directive such as PUT, GET, POST, or HEAD followed by the name of the document in question, followed by the version of HTTP that the browser is using. So in order to get the index.html document, the following header would be sent to the HTTP server: `GET /index.html HTTP/1.0`.

6. Once the request has been made, the browser waits for a response header. The response header will contain an HTTP status code such as "200 Document Follows" or "404 Document not Found." If the status code indicates that a document follows, the browser then reads the document data from the connection and kills the connection once the document is received. Otherwise, the browser takes some alternate action depending on the status code that was received.

The server has a much simpler set of rules with this protocol:

1. Wait for a connection on port 80.

2. Accept the connection.

> 3. Wait for the browser to request something by sending an HTTP header. If anything is received over the connection that is not a valid HTTP header, send an error message and close the connection.
>
> 4. Locate the document that was requested. If it is found, send an HTTP status code "200 Document Follows" and then send the document data. Otherwise, send the appropriate error, relocation, or security status code.
>
> 5. Wait for the client to terminate the connection.
>
> 6. Jump back to step 1.
>
> This is an example of a high-level protocol. The lower-level protocols that can be found at the transport layer (the underlying delivery system, such as TCP/IP) and below are very similar but not as human readable. All these protocols define a set of rules that dictate how two or more entities interact with each other. One of the most common protocols I will discuss is the *Transmission Control Protocol/Internet Protocol* (TCP/IP), which is the basic communications protocol for nearly every Internet application. HTTP, for example, sits on top of TCP/IP. TCP/IP handles all of the low-level transport of the data, and HTTP handles the higher-level communication between a Web server and a browser.

Programmers find that one of the more tedious parts of writing TCP-based applications is setting up the connections. The programmer must fill in exhaustive data structures that describe the type of socket connection before calling procedures to connect to services, listen for connections, accept connections, bind to available port numbers, and so on. Using the socket data structures directly gives the programmer the freedom to customize the type of connection, although often all you want is a connection to another machine that you can simply read from and write to. Once this part has been accomplished, then comes the next layer, in which the programmer must define the higher-level communications protocol and handle data transmission and representation between machines (marshaling). Not all machines represent data in the same way, so conversions are often necessary. In Listing 1-1, I use the Berkeley Systems API to create a server socket in C.

**Listing 1-1. A BSD server implementation (sock_lib.c on the CD-ROM)**

```
#include <signal.h>
#include <ctype.h>
#include <sys/types.h>
#include <sys/time.h>
#include <sys/socket.h>
#include <netinet/in.h>
#include <arpa/inet.h>
```

```c
#include <netdb.h>
#include <errno.h>

#define stderr 2

#define DEFAULT_PROTOCOL    0

int initserver(int *port)
/* Initialize a server on the given port return a file
   descriptor */
{
    int serverFd, serverLen; /*file descriptors for
                                socket connections */
    int maxtries = 10;
    /*Structure for holding a socket address */
    struct sockaddr_in serverINETAddress;
    struct sockaddr* serverSockAddrPtr;

    /* used to allocate space for the structure */
    serverLen = sizeof (serverINETAddress);
    serverSockAddrPtr = (struct sockaddr*) &serverINETAddress;

    /* zero out the memory to clear any garbage */
    memset(&serverINETAddress,0,serverLen);
    serverINETAddress.sin_family = AF_INET;
    /*The htonl() procedure converts from host
      to network representation of a long int */
    serverINETAddress.sin_addr.s_addr = htonl(INADDR_ANY);
    serverINETAddress.sin_port = htons(*port);

    /* set up file descriptor and prepare comm port */
    if(!(serverFd = socket(AF_INET, SOCK_STREAM, DEFAULT_PROTOCOL))){
        perror("socket failed\n");
        exit(1);
    }

/* keep trying to bind to the given address, return upon success */
  while(bind(serverFd,serverSockAddrPtr,serverLen)) ;
    serverINETAddress.sin_port = htons(*port);

    /* listen for connections on the given port */
    if(listen(serverFd,5)) {
        perror("Listen Failed.\n");
        exit(1);
    }
    /* upon success, this returns the file descriptor used for
  accepting socket connections*/
    return(serverFd);
}

/* This will wait for the client, and return a
   descriptor for the client upon success */
```

```
int get_connection(int serverFd)
{
   struct sockaddr_in clientINETAddress;
   struct sockaddr* clientSockAddrPtr;
   int clientFd,clientLen;
   clientSockAddrPtr = (struct sockaddr*) &clientINETAddress;
   clientLen = sizeof(clientINETAddress);
   clientFd = accept(serverFd,clientSockAddrPtr,&clientLen);
   return(clientFd);
}

/* used by a client to make a connection to
   another host on the network */
int make_connection(int port,char* host)
{
   unsigned long getINETAddress(char*);
   int clientFd, serverLen, result, times=20;
   struct sockaddr_in serverINETAddress;
   struct sockaddr* serverSockAddrPtr;
   unsigned long inetAddress;

   serverSockAddrPtr = (struct sockaddr*) &serverINETAddress;
   serverLen = sizeof (serverINETAddress);

   inetAddress = getINETAddress(host);
   memset(&serverINETAddress,0,sizeof(serverINETAddress));
   serverINETAddress.sin_family = AF_INET;
   serverINETAddress.sin_addr.s_addr = inetAddress;
   serverINETAddress.sin_port = htons(port);

   clientFd = socket(AF_INET, SOCK_STREAM, DEFAULT_PROTOCOL);

       do
       {
   serverINETAddress.sin_port = htons(port++);
         result = connect(clientFd, serverSockAddrPtr, serverLen);
         if (result == -1) sleep(1);
       }  while ((result == -1)&& times--);

   return(clientFd);
}

/* Convert a name to an IP address */
unsigned long getINETAddress(char* name)
{
   unsigned long nameToAddr(char* name);
   unsigned long inetAddress;

   inetAddress = nameToAddr(name);
   if (inetAddress == 0) {
 fprintf (stderr,"\nHostname not found\n");
 exit(1);
```

```
    }
    return inetAddress;
}

/* used by getINETAddress */
unsigned long nameToAddr(char* name)
{

    char hostName[100];
    struct hostent* hostStruct;
    struct in_addr* hostNode;

    if(isdigit(name[0])) return(inet_addr(name));

    if (strcmp(name,"s")==0)
    {
        gethostname(hostName,100);
    }
    else
        strcpy (hostName, name);

    hostStruct = gethostbyname(hostName);
    if (hostStruct == NULL) return 0;
    hostNode = (struct in_addr*) hostStruct->h_addr;

    return(hostNode->s_addr);
}
```

All this code did was give you a handful of procedures that could be used to create a server socket, connect to a server, and accept a connection from a client. This could be abstracted to a set of library functions:

```
int initserver(int *port);
int get_connection(int serverFd);
int make_connection(int port, char* hostname);
```

So any connection-based network server could simply call the initserver() function and then call the get_connection() procedure any time it wanted to wait for a client to connect. Once a connection was made, the file descriptor returned by get_connection() could be used to read and write data to the client. Likewise, a client need only call make_connection() with the appropriate port number and host name to get a file descriptor that it can use to read and write data to the server. This library works fine as long as you only want to use blocking TCP sockets (sockets that halt all other processing until they are finished accepting data). The underlying library would have to be modified for any other type of connection.

The next step would be to implement a communications protocol. Often, you can't assume a homogeneous computing environment, so you will also have to deal with data representation. The common way to address this problem is to format all data into big-endian, or "most significant byte first," byte order. Then any machine accessing the data will know to convert data between its local representation and the network representation of MSB-LSB, or "most significant byte–least significant byte." The size of data types must also be addressed, because some machines store integers as 16-bit quantities, while others may store them as 32-bit or 64-bit quantities. You can see that this can get messy pretty quickly.

Next, order of operations must be considered. For example, does a client connect and say "hello" before transmitting data, does the server wait for a request, how is the communication moderated? All we are getting with the preceding code is a simple file descriptor that represents a connection to another machine. We still have to deal with how data is read and written from and to this connection.

What would be nice would be a very simple abstraction where you could simply write something like

```
answer = query(server, querydata)
```

and all of the connection internals, data representation, and network transmission would be handled for you. This would facilitate creating network applications quickly with the focus on the application rather than on the network. Better yet, it would be nice to simply distribute procedures on various machines but have them look like local procedures to the application developer. This would allow the programmer to worry about the application design rather than network protocols.

# Remote Procedure Calls

Remote procedure calls (RPCs) provide a system that enables an application to call procedures that exist on another machine. This system is a network abstraction that gives the impression that one is calling standard procedures in a local application. In fact, the RPC system bundles the parameters, ships them off to another machine, passes them to an application running on that machine, takes the results, packages them, and ships them back to the application that made the call in the first place.

This system greatly simplifies marshaling parameters back and forth and relieves the programmer of the task of implementing protocols for packaging and sending parameters as well as unpacking values returned from the procedure calls. The system has a couple of drawbacks, among which are the necessity of creating interface descriptions in a special interface description language, and that of running a compiler independent of your application compiler to generate all of the "glue" code that makes this work.

RPC applications must register themselves with a port mapper that maps them to anonymous ports on the machine. When an application requests a service from this port mapper, it then returns the address of the service being sought. This allows a single port mapper running on a well-defined port number, or "address" to be used for an arbitrary number of services that are all running on anonymous ports. For the most part, this is a powerful and useful architecture that is still used for many services today. The big problem with RPC is that RPC is really intended for procedurally oriented applications and doesn't have some of the functionality that you would expect of an object-oriented system such as Java.

RPC introduces an abstraction model for easily distributing applications over a network. There are a few drawbacks, such as the need to learn a special interface definition language (IDL) for defining the procedures and mapping these interfaces to the language that you are using to develop your application in, but for the most part, RPC simplifies the communications part of a distributed application.

# Network Objects

Currently, there is a lot of interest in distributed objects for object-oriented applications. We want the same level of abstraction we have with RPC, but applied to accessing objects that may exist on different machines, on remote networks. One such architecture that is being deployed today is the Common Object Request Broker Architecture (CORBA). CORBA is a specification for distributing objects on a network. The idea behind CORBA is to define a language-neutral *interface description language* (or IDL) that can be used to define the interaction of objects distributed over a network. The interface allows you to send objects to remote methods as parameters, by passing either the actual object or a copy of it, and defines the interaction of remote code with local code. One thing that makes CORBA a powerful specification is that it is not linked directly with any programming language. CORBA objects can be written in C, Ada, Java—you name it. The one drawback is that CORBA is not as simple to use as an *object request broker* (ORB), or distributed object system, that is language specific, such as the Distributed Component Object Model (DCOM) for Microsoft applications, and remote method invocation (RMI) for Java.

To summarize, the various distributed systems abstractions that have been mentioned include RPC for procedurally based distributed applications, CORBA for a language-neutral object-oriented specification, DCOM for an object-oriented implementation specific to ActiveX and various Microsoft applications, and RMI as an object-oriented implementation for distributing Java applications.

# Remote Method Invocation

RMI facilitates rapid prototyping and deployment. There is no need to learn another language for the IDL component, and all of the code that handles the communication is generated for you directly from your class files.

RMI uses a registry server, similar to a port mapper in RPC, for registering and locating objects, but it can then use handles on objects to locate subsequent objects, so accessing remote systems is relatively simple. All marshaling of parameters and return values is taken care of by the system, so you can focus on the application design without too much concern for the communication.

Calls to remote methods look the same as calls to local methods. The only difference is getting an initial reference to an object (that is normally done through a registry service), and the fact that objects passed as parameters or returned as return values are passed by value rather than passed by reference: An object that is returned by a remote method call and then modified locally will not affect the original object that exists on the server that implemented the remote methods. This abstraction makes RMI extremely simple to work with.

# Summary

A number of methods exist for developing network applications, ranging from raw sockets on up to CORBA. All of these have distinct benefits and drawbacks in areas ranging from program complexity, to performance, to cross-platform compatibility. This chapter has highlighted some of the advantages and disadvantages of each of these methods.

RMI is a simple abstraction that makes programming distributed systems in an all-Java environment as simple as writing standalone Java applications. The main benefit of RMI is ease of use for rapid prototyping and deployment.

In the following chapters, I will discuss the RMI architecture, examine the registry that is used for name service for an RMI system, and finally work through some more complicated applications of RMI.

# Chapter 2

# Overview of RMI Architecture

## IN THIS CHAPTER

- ◆ Remote object structure
- ◆ The stub and skeleton layers
- ◆ The object hierarchy
- ◆ Garbage collection and security

REMOTE METHOD INVOCATION (RMI) is a pure-Java answer to remote procedure calls (RPC), and in some sense to the Distributed Component Object Model (DCOM) and the Common Object Request Broker Architecture (CORBA). It is important to note that as of this writing, Javasoft has made an announcement that RMI will support the Object Management Group's Internet InterOrb Protocol. This announcement was made after industry pressure to have CORBA support in the RMI system. So far, no announcements have been made as to when the specifications will be available. All of these models are abstractions of distributing programs across the memory address space of a single machine, across multiple processors in a single machine, or across many machines on a network.

RMI can happen between virtual machines on a single machine, or it can be distributed over a network. There are actually reasons for either approach. For example, an application that is distributed among many objects on the same machine allows for a very modular application design approach. Let's assume that you have a well-defined set of interfaces that objects in your system use to communicate with each other. The design of objects that implement these interfaces can be invisible outside of the individual objects. Essentially, interaction with an object is entirely described by the interface. Using this model, any object can be replaced individually without having to worry about the rest of the system. The only requirement is that the interface doesn't change.

Still, the network is an integral part of all of these systems, including RMI. Separating components of your system and spreading them out among distant machines allows you to easily build client-server, as well as peer-to-peer network, applications. What RMI gives you is a high-level interface for building network applications. All of the dirty work is done for you, and you can concentrate on the design and functionality of your applications rather than on how they communicate. Using the RMI interfaces, you can quickly and easily build powerful network applications that aren't prone to the bugs and design flaws that tend to creep in when you are developing low-level network protocols.

In this chapter you are going to take a look at the lower-level interfaces for communicating via sockets. I will discuss API and structure used to create basic network applications using the standard Java network libraries. Next, I will discuss the RMI architecture and how it builds on top of that underlying support.

The RMI model attempts to make designing distributed applications as simple and straightforward as designing nondistributed applications. The programmer doesn't need to worry about sending data or translating data into objects, or any of the ugly stuff that the communication level is responsible for. The only concern is solid application design with minor attention paid to locating objects, as well as to handling some exceptions that are specific to network applications. The communication elements of the program have been abstracted to the point of seeming local. This abstraction frees you from the drudgery of writing low-level protocols and building objects based on data that you are reading over the network, but it can also be a little misleading.

It is, in fact, so simple to write an application that uses objects on remote machines, that you can easily forget that the application is distributed across a network. But even though the programming interface has made it seem as if programming an application with access to remote objects is exactly the same as programming an application that uses only local objects, this is not true. An application that uses remote objects is inherently different from an application that is entirely local. Some of the differences are increased latency (which can be several orders of magnitude slower), network failure, and partial failure due to network or remote machine problems. It is left to the programmer to deal with all of these issues.

Latency can be dealt with, to some degree, by carefully designing an application so that only those calls that must be made to a remote object are remote calls. In other words, methods that can remain local are not gratuitously distributed. Other than this, it is impossible for a call to an object that is not only in a different name space, but perhaps in a different city altogether, to respond as quickly as a call to an object that is running on the same processor in the same name space. This will always be true.

The problems of full and partial failures can be dealt with only by giving careful consideration to exceptions and possible exceptional conditions that may arise during run time, and by dealing with them appropriately in the design of the application.

It is obvious that RMI was designed to make the design and implementation of network distributed applications almost like that of stand-alone object-oriented programs. No separate interface description language (IDL) or funky "programming language-neutral" development language is used to glue the parts together. Everything is written in pure Java; actually, RMI is a Java-specific model for writing distributed applications, unlike CORBA, which is intended to be language-neutral, or DCOM, which was designed with Microsoft's ActiveX architecture in mind.

What you give up in language neutrality, you make up in simplicity. A call to a remote object using RMI is identical to a call to a local object, with the following exceptions:

◆ An object passed as a parameter to a remote method or returned from the method must be serializable or be another Remote object (see Chapter 6).

◆ An object passed as a parameter to a remote method or returned from the method call is passed by value rather than by reference. The only exception to this is a remote object that is passed to a remote method or returned by it. In this case, a reference to the remote object is used.

◆ A client always refers to a remote object through one of the Remote interfaces that it implements. A remote object can be cast to any of the interfaces that it implements.

◆ The equals(), hashCode(), and toString() methods, usually inherited by all objects in Java, have been overridden by java.rmi.RemoteObject. These methods have been modified to deal appropriately with a remote object. For example, the equals() method checks if two object references are equal, not whether the contents are equal. Also, the hashCode() method returns the same key for any references that refer to the same remote object. The toString() method has been modified to include information about the transport of the object, such as the underlying network protocol, host name, and port number the object is coming from.

# Remote Object Structure

A remote method invocation is made through a reference to a remote object. The object is exported via a server application, and a handle to the object is obtained by a remote client either by looking up the object by name with a *registry* (see Chapter 3) or by checking the return value from another remote method call.

This object must implement at least one interface that extends the java.rmi.Remote interface. All interaction with the remote object will be performed through this interface. Essentially, the interface describes the methods that can be invoked remotely, and the remote object implements them.

When a reference to a remote object is obtained, the object is not sent over the network to the client requesting it. In its place is a proxy object or stub that is the client-side proxy for the remote object. All interactions by the client will be performed with this stub class. The stub is responsible for handing off data between the local system and the remote one. Many clients can have references to a single remote object. Each client will have its own stub object that represents the remote object, but the remote object will not be replicated.

On the server side a skeleton class is responsible for handing off the method calls and data to the actual object being referenced. This is the server-side proxy for the object being exported. The complete system can be thought of as a four-layer model (see Figure 2-1):

◆ Layer 1 is the application layer, the actual implementation of your client and server applications. Here the high-level calls are made to access and export remote objects.

◆ Layer 2 is the proxy layer or the stub/skeleton layer. This layer is what the application deals with directly. All calls to remote methods and the marshaling of parameters and return objects are done through these proxies.

◆ Layer 3 is the remote reference layer; it is responsible for dealing with the semantics of remote invocations. This layer is responsible for handling replicated objects and for performing implementation-specific tasks with remote objects.

◆ Layer 4 is the transport layer. This layer is responsible for actually setting up connections and handling the transport of data from one machine to another.

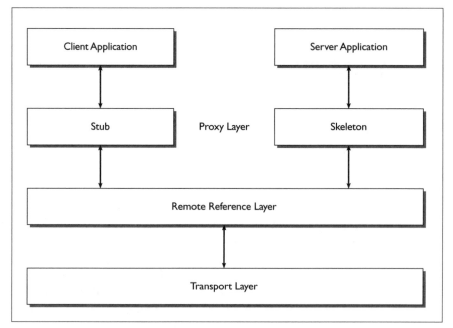

Figure 2-1. A four-layer RMI system

# Interface Description

In many distributed programming models, you must define an interface to your remote objects in an *interface description language* (IDL) and then run a special compiler or generator on the IDL files that generates the files that your objects use to define their remote methods. This requires you not only to implement your application in your language of choice but also to use a secondary language and compiler for generating the glue.

In the RMI model, all interfaces are described in pure Java. There is no need for a separate IDL. The necessary files are generated directly from the compiled object code that implements remote interfaces. Namely, the RMI stub compiler (RMIC) is used to generate the special objects that are needed to connect remote server objects to clients. I will go into a little more detail about RMIC in Chapter 4. For now, I will focus on the system layers, and the stub and skeleton files that are generated using RMIC.

# The Application Layer

An application that makes some of its methods available to remote clients must declare the methods in an interface that extends java.rmi.Remote. The java.rmi.Remote interface is an empty interface that declares no methods. Essentially it is used to flag an object as being remotely accessible. When you want to define a set of methods that will be remotely called, they must be declared in one or more interfaces that extend the java.rmi.Remote interface.

You implement a Remote interface in the same way that you implement any other Java interface. The only difference is some added exception handling for dealing with RemoteExceptions. These are specific to remote calls and can be thrown if a problem arises in contacting or interacting with a remote application.

Once the methods described in the remote interfaces have been implemented, the object must be exported. This can be done implicitly if the object extends the UnicastRemoteObject class of the java.rmi.server package, or it can be done explicitly with a call to the exportObject() method of that same package.

Finally, the application will normally register itself with a name server, or registry. This is used to make first contact with the application and obtain a reference to its remote objects. Once first contact is made, any other remote object references that the server may want to export may be returned by method calls from the first object. Because of this, name service is generally only necessary upon application start-up.

On the client side, a client simply requests a remote object from either a registry or a remote object that it has already obtained. The reference to the remote object is cast to one of its Remote interfaces, and any calls to remote methods can be made directly through this interface.

# The Stub and Skeleton Layers

The stub and skeleton classes are generated using the RMI stub compiler (RMIC). Use of the stub compiler is covered in Chapter 4. These are simply class files that do the client- and server-side representations of a remote object.

## The Stub Class

The *stub* is the client-side proxy for the remote object. The stub is the applications interface to the remote object; it is responsible for initiating a call to the remote object that it represents by way of the remote reference layer. The stub is also responsible for marshaling method arguments to a marshal stream that is also acquired through the remote reference layer. A *marshal stream* is simply a stream object that is used to transport parameters, exceptions, and errors needed for method dispatch and returning the results. The stub and skeleton classes both use these streams for communicating with each other. The stub unmarshals values that have been returned by the remote object. This is also by way of the marshal stream. Finally, the stub class informs the remote reference layer that a call is complete.

Since the stub class must implement all of the same interfaces as the remote object that it represents, it can be cast as any of those remote interfaces. A remote object may contain nonremote methods and fields, but these are not defined in any of the remote interfaces. This design effectively allows a stub to have type equivalency to any of the remote interfaces of a remote object. The interfaces implemented by a stub can be checked with the built-in `instance of` operator. This can be used to test whether a remote object implements a given interface.

Listing 2-1 shows the source code for a typical stub class. This code was automatically generated using the RMIC but is interesting to study; it will help you gain a better understanding of how the system works.

**Listing 2-1. Generated stub source** (`ChatImpl_Stub.java`)

```
// Stub class generated by rmic, do not edit.
// Contents subject to change without notice.

package rmibook.chat;

public final class ChatImpl_Stub
    extends java.rmi.server.RemoteStub
    implements rmibook.chat.Chat
{
    private static java.rmi.server.Operation[] operations = {
        new java.rmi.server.Operation("void
 chatNotify(rmibook.chat.Message)"),
        new java.rmi.server.Operation("java.lang.String getName()")
    };

    private static final long interfaceHash = -1970090836367953198L;
```

```
    // Constructors
    public ChatImpl_Stub() {
        super();
    }
    public ChatImpl_Stub(java.rmi.server.RemoteRef rep) {
        super(rep);
    }
    // Methods from remote interfaces

    // Implementation of chatNotify
    public void chatNotify(rmibook.chat.Message $_Message_1) throws
java.rmi.RemoteException {
        int opnum = 0;
        java.rmi.server.RemoteRef sub = ref;
        java.rmi.server.RemoteCall call =
sub.newCall((java.rmi.server.RemoteObject)this, operations, opnum,
interfaceHash);
        try {
            java.io.ObjectOutput out = call.getOutputStream();
            out.writeObject($_Message_1);
        } catch (java.io.IOException ex) {
            throw new java.rmi.MarshalException("Error marshaling
arguments", ex);
        };
        try {
            sub.invoke(call);
        } catch (java.rmi.RemoteException ex) {
            throw ex;
        } catch (java.lang.Exception ex) {
            throw new java.rmi.UnexpectedException("Unexpected
exception", ex);
        };
        sub.done(call);
        return;
    }

    // Implementation of getName
    public java.lang.String getName() throws
java.rmi.RemoteException {
        int opnum = 1;
        java.rmi.server.RemoteRef sub = ref;
        java.rmi.server.RemoteCall call =
sub.newCall((java.rmi.server.RemoteObject)this, operations, opnum,
interfaceHash);
        try {
            sub.invoke(call);
        } catch (java.rmi.RemoteException ex) {
            throw ex;
        } catch (java.lang.Exception ex) {
            throw new java.rmi.UnexpectedException("Unexpected
exception", ex);
        };
```

```
        java.lang.String $result;
        try {
            java.io.ObjectInput in = call.getInputStream();
            $result = (java.lang.String)in.readObject();
        } catch (java.io.IOException ex) {
            throw new java.rmi.UnmarshalException("Error
unmarshaling return", ex);
        } catch (java.lang.ClassNotFoundException ex) {
            throw new java.rmi.UnmarshalException("Return value
class not found", ex);
        } catch (Exception ex) {
            throw new java.rmi.UnexpectedException("Unexpected
exception", ex);
        } finally {
            sub.done(call);
        }
        return $result;
    }
}
```

# The Skeleton Class

Much like the stub classes, the skeleton classes marshal parameters to and from a marshal stream. The difference is that the skeleton class stays on the server side of the connection and deals directly with the implementation classes of the Remote methods being exported. The skeleton is responsible for sending parameters to the method implementation and for sending return values and exceptions back to the client that made the call. Essentially, the skeleton is responsible for receiving method calls from a stub class, marshaling any necessary parameters, and dispatching the actual methods being exported. This is the server-side proxy for the remote object.

Listing 2-2 is the source code for a generated skeleton class that is the server-side proxy for the stub class from Listing 2-1.

**Listing 2-2. Generated skeleton class** (ChatImpl_Skel.java)

```
// Skeleton class generated by rmic, do not edit.
// Contents subject to change without notice.

package rmibook.chat;


public final class ChatImpl_Skel
    extends java.lang.Object
    implements java.rmi.server.Skeleton
{
    private static java.rmi.server.Operation[] operations = {
        new java.rmi.server.Operation("void
chatNotify(rmibook.chat.Message)"),
```

```
        new java.rmi.server.Operation("java.lang.String getName()")
    };

    private static final long interfaceHash = -1970090836367953198L;

    public java.rmi.server.Operation[] getOperations() {
        return operations;
    }

    public void dispatch(java.rmi.Remote obj,
java.rmi.server.RemoteCall call, int opnum, long hash) throws
java.rmi.RemoteException, Exception {
        // Exceptions pass through, to be caught, identified and
marshaled

        if (hash != interfaceHash)
            throw new
java.rmi.server.SkeletonMismatchException("Hash mismatch");
        rmibook.chat.ChatImpl server = (rmibook.chat.ChatImpl)obj;
        switch (opnum) {
        case 0: { // chatNotify
            rmibook.chat.Message $_Message_1;
            try {
                java.io.ObjectInput in = call.getInputStream();
                $_Message_1 = (rmibook.chat.Message)in.readObject();
            } catch (java.io.IOException ex) {
                throw new java.rmi.UnmarshalException("Error
unmarshaling arguments", ex);
            } finally {
                call.releaseInputStream();
            };
            server.chatNotify($_Message_1);
            try {
                call.getResultStream(true);
            } catch (java.io.IOException ex) {
                throw new java.rmi.MarshalException("Error
marshaling return", ex);
            };
            break;
            }

        case 1: { // getName
            call.releaseInputStream();
            java.lang.String $result = server.getName();
            try {
                java.io.ObjectOutput out =
call.getResultStream(true);
                out.writeObject($result);
            } catch (java.io.IOException ex) {
                throw new java.rmi.MarshalException("Error
marshaling return", ex);
            };
            break;
```

```
            }
        default:
            throw new java.rmi.RemoteException("Method number out of
    range");
        }
    }
}
```

# The Remote Reference Layer

The *remote reference layer* is effectively the abstraction between the stub and skeleton classes and the actual communications protocols that are handled by the transport layer. The remote reference layer expects to get a stream-oriented connection from the transport layer. The actual transport may take place using a non-connection-based protocol, but interaction between the remote reference layer and the transport layer will take place as if it involved a stream, or connection-based, protocol.

The remote reference layer will be used to handle replicated objects, once this feature is incorporated into the RMI system. Replicated objects will allow simple dispatch to many programs that are exporting substantially the same Remote objects. This layer will also be responsible for establishing persistence semantics and strategies for recovery of lost connections.

# The Transport Layer

The *transport layer* is responsible for handling the actual machine-to-machine communication. Because this communication is abstracted in this way, it allows system implementors to replace the low-level communications protocols with alternatives.

By default, communication will take place through a standard TCP/IP connection. The transport layer creates a stream that is accessed by the remote reference layer to send and receive data to and from other machines. The transport layer sets up connections to remote machines, manages the connections, monitors the connections to make sure that they are all "live," and listens for connections from other machines.

The transport layer can be modified to handle encrypted streams, compression algorithms, and a number of other security- or performance-related enhancements. Because this layer is independent of the reference layer, the stub/skeleton layer, and the application layer, an RMI application does not need to know the specifics of any changes made to the transport layer.

# The Object Hierarchy

Most objects that are exported as remote objects either directly or indirectly subclass the RemoteObject class and implement at least one Remote interface. This could be the java.rmi.Remote interface or an extension class of the java.rmi.Remote interface. In any case, it is possible to export an object that does not subclass java.rmi.server.RemoteObject, but the object must then be explicitly exported by passing a reference to the remote object to the exportObject() method of the UnicastRemoteObject class in the java.rmi.server package.

Most objects that are remotely accessible implement the RemoteObject class indirectly by extending the java.rmi.server.UnicastRemoteObject class. The java.rmi.Remote interface does not define any methods, and so, in order to export any remote methods, a subclass of java.rmi.Remote must define the methods that will be remotely available. An application that implements a Remote interface and either extends java.rmi.server.UnicastRemoteObject or exports itself with the exportObject() method is effectively set up to serve remote methods to client applications.

The base object of all remote objects is effectively java.rmi.RemoteObject, although java.lang.Object literally plays that role. In other words, the RemoteObject class overrides certain methods in the java.lang.Object class in order to make sense in the context of distributed objects. The UnicastRemoteObject class indirectly subclasses the RemoteObject class via the java.rmi.server.RemoteServer class. Required semantic changes to a few of the methods of the java.lang.Object class make this hierarchy necessary. Accordingly, the java.rmi.server.RemoteObject class overrides the java.lang.Object methods in order for the object to make sense when it is being referenced by a remote machine.

Figure 2-2 demonstrates the hierarchy and dependencies of an exportable remote object, which are detailed in the list that follows:

- ◆ java.lang.Object is the base class

- ◆ The java.rmi.server.RemoteObject interface extends Object and implements java.rmi.Remote

- ◆ The java.rmi.server.RemoteServer class extends RemoteObject

- ◆ The java.rmi.server.UnicastRemoteObject class extends RemoteServer

- ◆ Any user-defined Remote object usually extends UnicastRemoteObject and implements a user-defined interface that extends java.rmi.Remote

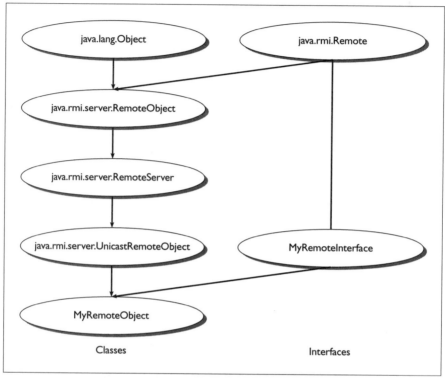

Figure 2–2. The Remote object hierarchy

# Name Service

In general, it is necessary to bootstrap an application that uses RMI. A server will register any remote objects that it is exporting with a name server called a *registry*. When a client wishes to obtain a reference to a remote object, a URL-based lookup is performed on a well-known registry, and a reference to the remote object is returned if the lookup succeeds.

There are two ways of using the registry services. The first is to follow the RPC model and maintain a registry server that is running on a well-known port number. Any number of applications that export objects can register with this registry as long as they are running on the same physical machine. A client can then look up the registered services via URLs passed to certain lookup() and list() methods that query the registry. The second method consists of an application running its own registry services. This allows the application to have complete control over the registry but makes it more difficult to define a well-known port that will be used to access remote objects.

Remote methods can be designed to return other remote objects. Because of this, it is generally necessary to contact a registry server only when making initial contact with an application. Once one of the remote objects on a server has been located, references to others can be obtained via method calls to the first object. The Registry application and API are discussed in detail in Chapter 3.

# Garbage Collection

One of the great things about developing applications in Java is the fact that the programmer is freed from the drudgery of memory management. No more memory leaks! This is due to the fact that garbage collection is an integral component to the Java environment. The garbage collection algorithm is implementation-specific but guaranteed to be there.

A general-purpose mark-and-sweep garbage collector running on a local machine is an entirely different beast from a garbage collector that is running on a distributed application that may be linking many Java machines. Problems arise out of the complexity of checking for references to objects. It's no longer a local problem, and reference counts must be maintained for all remote machines that have a reference to a local object. As long as a reference to an object exists, local or remote, that object cannot be garbage-collected.

The distributed garbage collection algorithm used by the RMI system is a reference-counting algorithm similar to the Network objects in the Modula-3 programming and runtime environment. When a client first receives a reference to a remote object, a "referenced" message is sent to the server that is exporting the object. Every subsequent reference within the client's local machine causes a reference counter to be incremented. As a local reference is finalized, the reference count is decremented, and once the count goes to zero, an "unreferenced" message is sent to the server. Once the server has no more live references to an object and there are no local references, it is free to be finalized and garbage collected.

If a remote object implements the java.rmi.server.Unreferenced interface, it must implement a body for the unreferenced method. This method will be called once the object is no longer referenced. This allows you to write code that is called whenever an object becomes unreferenced. The unreferenced method may be called more than once as the set of references are removed. The object won't be finalized and collected until all references are removed, including both local and remote references.

It is also important to note that, under certain circumstances such as network failure, an object may be collected prematurely, because the transport layer may think that a connection to a machine containing a reference to the object is no longer live. The host, therefore, believes that the client no longer maintains a reference to the object. In this case, the object may be collected even though a remote reference still exists. If this happens, attempts by the client to access the remote object will result in a RemoteException being thrown.

# Class Loaders

In Java, a class loader is responsible for dynamically loading the classes necessary for an application as they are needed. This includes locating the files, locally or remotely, and retrieving them.

There are different class loaders for different types of applications. For example, a default class loader is used to load locally run files. If an application is run as a stand-alone application, and if it defines a `main()` method, the default class loader will be used to load any classes that the application needs in order to execute from the local file system. Applets have special security and class loader needs, so an `AppletClassLoader` is used to load the classes necessary for an applet to execute. Remote method invocation also has special requirements and normally employs the `RMIClassLoader`. The `RMIClassLoader` is responsible for loading the stub and skeleton classes used by the RMI system, as well as any utility classes necessary for these stubs and skeletons. In general, the `RMIClassLoader` will first attempt to load classes that can be found on the local file system via the CLASSPATH environment variable. If the classes cannot be found locally, the `RMIClassLoader` extracts a URL that is included in a marshal stream of serialized objects. This URL is then used as the codebase for locating the necessary classes. This method is used only for objects passed as parameters or return types, and only if the classes couldn't be found locally. Finally, in the case of stub and skeleton classes, a system property—the `java.rmi.server.codebase` property—is used to locate the necessary class files. This can be set by using the -D flag when you launch the Java interpreter.

The class loader that is used initially to load an application is used to load all subsequent classes. If an application is initially loaded as an applet, all necessary classes will be loaded with the `AppletClassLoader`, and if an application is started as a stand-alone application, all necessary classes will be loaded with the default class loader.

If you want to force RMI to only load classes from the local codebase, the system property `java.rmi.server.useCodebaseOnly` property can be set, effectively forcing all classes to be loaded from the local system. Any classes that are needed but can't be loaded will cause an exception to be thrown.

# Security

The only way to guarantee a secure system, regardless of the system, is to separate it from the network and lock it in a guarded room. Practically speaking, security is based more on risk assessment. A system administrator, or implementor, must decide what security precautions are necessary given the nature of a given application, its vulnerability, and the sensitivity of its systems and data.

The Java security model generally trusts applications that came from the local file system. If fact, the interpreter does not generally verify classes that were loaded from the local file system. It is assumed that the files that you are running from your own machine are safe.

On the other hand, applets are highly mistrusted, as they should be. You don't want to run untested code of unknown origin on your machine without taking some precautions. You have no way of knowing whether the code is unintentionally damaging, or outright malicious.

Most of the concerns over security are closely associated with network applications. The possibility exists that malicious code will be loaded onto your system, or that someone will be listening in on your conversations as they are transmitted over the network.

The first problem can be dealt with by installing a security manager. The RMI run time requires that a security manager be explicitly set. In the case of an applet, the `AppletSecurityManager` is automatically set for you, but in the case of a stand-alone application, the default security manager will prevent the system from loading classes from anywhere but the local file system. The `RMISecurityManager` is a direct descendant of `java.lang.SecurityManager`. It is used to set the security policies used to govern the behavior of the stub and skeleton classes.

The security manager is set using `System.setSecurityManager` (new `RMISecurityManager()`) and must be set before any remote stub classes are loaded over the network. The `RMISecurityManager` essentially prohibits the stub classes from doing anything but loading necessary class files over the network. Even with `RMISecurityManager` set, network loading of stub classes will still be prevented if the `java.rmi.server.useCodebaseOnly` property is set.

As for eavesdroppers, since the transport layer abstracts the communication used by the RMI system, new transport mechanisms can be slipped into place that are built upon the Secure Sockets Layer (SSL) or other encryption techniques.

# Performance

RMI gives you a nice, simple, easy-to-use interface for writing network applications. With this comes a price. RMI will never be as fast as local procedure calls, and it will generally be slower than optimized, special-purpose communications protocols built directly on top of the transport layer. Overhead incurred in sending objects back and forth to remote procedures can bog your system down even more.

If you intend to write video streaming applications, or other applications that require high network performance, RMI is probably not going to satisfy your needs. If you want to rapidly develop network applications and you can deal with increased latency, RMI is the way to go.

# Summary

The RMI system is made up of a series of layers. On the application side, you have a remote interface that is implemented by a class that is exported in one of two ways—either by extending `UnicastRemoteObject` or by passing a reference of itself to `UnicastRemoteObject.exportObject()`.

The next layer down is the stub/skeleton layer, which is generated from your compiled remote object using the RMIC. This generates a stub class to act as a client-side proxy and a skeleton class to act as a server-side proxy, handling the work of dispatching the actual method calls. Finally you have an underlying transport layer that uses socket-based communications protocols to send data over the network.

The system works with a registry name server for bootstrapping connections and has various facilities for RMI-specific class loading and security mechanisms.

Remote method invocation describes a simple method for writing applications that can be distributed locally and over networks. Any object that is to be exported simply implements a `Remote` interface, subclasses a `RemoteObject` (or exports itself using the `UnicastRemoteObject.exportObject()` method) and registers itself with a name service.

A client can access a remote object by looking it up in a name service and then essentially working with it as if it were a local object. In the next chapter I will talk about the registry services used to register and look up remote objects, and then you will begin writing some client/server RMI applications.

# Chapter 3

# Using the Registry

IN CHAPTER 2, I DISCUSSED the low-level ideas and protocols of the RMI architecture, one of whose major components is the registry. The registry is a simple server that enables an application to look up objects that are being exported for remote method invocation.

Once you have hold of an object that is being exported by a server using RMI methods, communication is often as simple as calling methods on that object that may exist on an entirely different machine. This setup requires some way of locating these remote objects. An easy way to call the methods of a remote object doesn't do you much good if you can't find the object in the first place. Once an object has been located, using it to pass other remote objects is relatively simple. But to find the initial object, you normally (but not always) require the services of a registry.

In the RPC model, a *port mapper* server runs on a well-known port waiting for connections. A number of applications that implement certain remote procedures may be sitting idle, but their port numbers are chosen somewhat randomly. The port mapper keeps a table of all the available services and the port numbers that they are listening to. A caller need only know the port number for the RPC server and the name of the service that it requires. The port mapper attempts to locate the service requested in its tables, and if it finds that particular service, it returns the address so that the client can then connect directly to that service and execute normally. Using this model, a client only needs to know the name of the service and the well-defined address of the port mapper in order to access a remote procedure.

RMI, being somewhat similar to RPC, uses a service similar to the port mapper, called the registry. The registry simply keeps track of the addresses of remote objects that are being exported by their applications. All objects are assigned unique names that are used to identify them. Certain methods can be called from the `rmi.registry.Registry` interface, or from the `rmi.Naming` class, that allow applications to add, remove, and access remote objects in the registry's table of objects and associated names. Simply stated, a server registers one of its objects with a registry by a calling a `bind()` or `rebind()` method on a registry instance, passing it a String that uniquely identifies the object and a reference to an instance of the object that is being exported. Since all objects must have a unique name, a `bind()` call to a registry that contains a name `String` that is already registered will result in an exception being thrown. Alternatively, `rebind()` replaces an old object with a given name with a new object.

# The RMI Registry

There are two ways to start a registry. Using the `java.rmi.*` registry, classes and interfaces, you could write and start your own registry, adding registry service directly to your application, or, because most sites will require only a single registry, you can use the RMI registry application (rmiregistry) that comes with the Java Developer's Kit.

The RMI registry application is normally started as a background application and then left alone. By default, it will run on port number 1099, but alternative ports can be selected at launch time. To start the RMI registry in UNIX, use the following command line:

```
rmiregistry &
```

Optionally, a port number can be supplied on the command line:

```
rmiregistry 2099 &
```

If you are running the registry on a Windows machine, you can start it in the same manner from a DOS prompt, but omitting the ampersand (&), which is a special character that causes the application to be run in the background on a UNIX box. Essentially, RMI registry will load as a TSR application in Windows. If you wish to run the RMI registry in a separate DOS shell, you can start the registry with the DOS "start" command. For example:

```
c:\ start rmiregistry
```

# Locating Stub and Skeleton Classes

When the RMI registry is started, it will use the CLASSPATH environment variable to find classes that it needs in order to serve remote objects. The CLASSPATH should contain an entry for the directory to contain the stub and skeleton classes

---

**Superuser Privileges**

In UNIX, port numbers below 1,024 are reserved for system services such as ftp, telnet, smtp, rlogin, and http. In order to prevent casual users from binding to these ports and replacing these standard services, access to these low port numbers is restricted to users with root or *superuser* privileges. Most users will, therefore, start their registry servers on a port number above 1,024 and below 16,000.

---

that I will generate with the RMI stub compiler in the following chapters. If the CLASSPATH does not contain an entry for the class directory for a particular server, a system property that contains the necessary path information must be specified when the server is launched. Normally, you start the Java interpreter with the –D flag followed by the `java.rmi.server.CodeBase` property followed by a URL that is used to load the necessary files. For example, a server that has its stub and skeleton classes stored in a directory that can be accessed with the URL `http://foo.com/MyStubs/` would be launched with the following line:

```
java -Djava.rmi.server.CodeBase=http://foo.com/MyStubs/MyServer
```

This example will set `CodeBase` to the value "`http://foo.com/MyStubs/`." This tells the registry that it can use this URL to load the classes it needs when an object is requested. Obviously, the registry can only pass out references to objects that it can locate. It is assumed that any remote objects exported by `MyServer` and bound in the registry can be referenced by stub and skeleton classes that are accessible by this URL.

# URL Conventions for Accessing the Registry

It seems that just about any object or service on the Internet can be referenced by a URL. This is not surprising, because a Uniform Resource Locator (URL) is nothing more than a naming convention. This convention allows the specification of a protocol, a machine name, a service port number, a file, and various other parameters. A standard HTTP URL, `http://www.foo.com:80/index.html` for example, specifies protocol `http`, machine name `www.foo.com`, and optional service port number 80, as well as document `index.html`.

## Why All the Punctuation?

In HTTP, the first ":" is used to mark the end of the protocol identifier, the "//" is used to note the start of a machine name, and the ":" following the machine name is used to attach the port number.

Because 80 is the standard port number for HTTP services, it is not normally listed. In other words, the default port number is added automatically if no port number is expressly given.

Most Web browsers will also assume the protocol. For example, the URL www.foo.com/index.html will automatically be assumed to use the Hypertext Transfer Protocol (HTTP), since this is the common protocol for Web access.

Registry servers can also be referenced by a URL. Under normal circumstances, a URL will be used to locate a registry server running on a specified port, on a specified machine, and a request will be made "by name" for a specific remote object. The protocol specification for this service is rmi:, and the standard port number is 1099. So when requesting an object that is bound in an rmi registry on the machine www.foo.com under the name "MyRemoteObject," you would reference the URL rmi://www.foo.com/MyRemoteObject (see Figure 3-1).

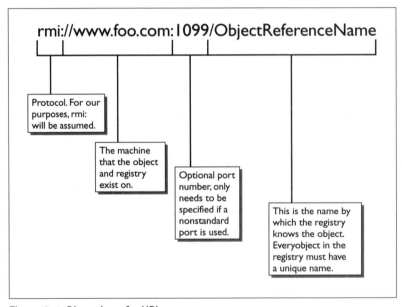

Figure 3-1. Dissection of a URL

Both servers that are using the registry to export objects and clients that are using the registry to look up objects can use URL naming conventions to locate the registry and exported objects that are registered with a particular registry. Many assumptions can be made about URLs that can greatly reduce what you must enter. For example, when using the methods of the `java.rmi.Naming` class, you know that the protocol is assumed to be `rmi`, so you can omit the "`rmi:`" protocol designation. If the registry is running on the standard port, 1099, the port number can be omitted. If the machine name is left off, the local machine is assumed. Thus a server that wants to register an object on a registry that is running on the same machine (as described in the tip that follows) could use a URL that consists of only the name that the object will be bound as. For example, in this case, the URL "`rmi://local-machine.com:1099/MyObject`" would be the same as the URL "`MyObject`."

---

## Binding Tip for RMI Registry

An RMI registry can be queried from any machine that has network access to the machine running the registry. A program that exports objects, however, can *only* bind (or register) with a registry running on the same machine. Therefore, a URL used by a server, to register an object it wishes to export, can always consist of the name of the object with everything else assumed unless a nonstandard port number is used.

---

# Binding an Object to the Registry

Any application can register, or *bind*, an object to a registry provided that the object either extends `UnicastRemoteObject` or extends a Remote interface and is exported with the `UnicastRemoteObject.exportObject()` method. In either case, a registry must be running on the same machine as the application.

When an application binds an object, three things are required:

◆ A reference to an instance of the object being bound

◆ The address of the registry server (including port number)

◆ A name that the object will be registered under (this will be used to locate the object when clients query the registry)

The simplest form used to bind an object in a registry uses the URL conventions discussed in the previous section. A class in the `java.rmi.*` package (the `java.rmi.Naming` class) has several methods that can be used to query a registry as well as register objects with it.

Because an object is requested by the name that it is registered under, all names in a particular registry must be unique. In other words, an object called MyRemoteObject may be registered under the name "RefToMyObject," but it must be the only object in the registry that is known by that name. In order to maintain a large name space, it is often desirable to use package names (MyPackage.RefToMyObject, for example) when registering an object. Because of this need to have a one-to-one mapping of a name to an object, there are two distinct methods in the Naming class for registering an object. One method will throw an exception if it tries to bind a name that already exists, and the other will replace any previously registered objects of the same name. These two methods are called bind() and rebind(), respectively.

The java.rmi.Naming.bind() method takes two arguments: a URL to a registry that includes the "name" of the object and a reference to the object being registered. For example, the following code fragment will register an object MyRemoteObject on the registry that is running on www.foo.com under the name "MyObject." There are several exceptions that may be thrown, such as a MalformedURLException, a RemoteException, an UnknownHostException, or an AlreadyBoundException. This makes it necessary to enclose the bind() and object instantiation in a try/catch phrase. I'll put a generic catch clause here, and deal with particular exceptions later on:

```
try {
   MyRemoteObject ro= new MyRemoteObject();
   java.rmi.Naming.bind("rmi://www.foo.com/MyObject", ro);
} catch (Exception e) {
  //normally we would check for specific Exceptions
  //and make decisions based on these
}
```

The java.rmi.Naming.rebind() method takes the exact same parameters but will not throw an AlreadyBoundException, as any object references that are already in the registry under the name "MyObject" will be replaced.

As I mentioned earlier in this chapter, many parts of the URL can be omitted. In the case of the preceding code fragment, the bind() statement could be replaced with the equivalent statement:

```
java.rmi.Naming.bind("MyObject", ro);
```

This is because the server must be running on the machine www.foo.com in order for the first URL to work. The server and registry must be on the same machine, and then a URL that assumes the same machine is all you need to specify. This also makes the code more portable, because a machine name isn't hard-coded into it.

# Removing an Object from the Registry

Removing an object is just as simple as adding one. In the previous section, the only thing you had to worry about was whether an object was already bound or not, and then deciding whether or not to replace it. When removing an object, you only have to be concerned with whether the object is bound in the registry or not.

Use the same URL conventions for locating an object in the registry as you would for adding a reference as described in the previous section. An application can remove a reference only on a registry that is running on the same machine. Obviously, you don't want anonymous users to access your server over the network and start removing objects from your registry. As I am still using URLs to refer to the remote objects, I will still use the Naming class, which is essentially a URL-based interface for a registry server.

Before removing an object, it might make sense to find out if the object is registered in advance. The java.rmi.Naming.list() method will return an array of Strings that contain all of the names that are currently registered. The following code fragment will query your www.foo.com registry server for all currently registered objects and see if any of them match the name "MyObject." The list() method will throw a RemoteException if the registry can't be located, a MalformedURLException if it can't make sense of the URL that you pass it, and an UnknownHostException if it can't make sense of the host name you pass it:

```
String[] remoteObjects;
PrintStream out = System.out;

try {
   //get list from the registry
   remoteObjects = Naming.list("rmi://www.foo.com/");
} catch (RemoteException e) {
   out.println("Couldn't locate Registry");
} catch (MalformedURLException e) {
   out.println("Couldn't parse URL String");
} catch (UnknownHostException e) {
   out.println("Can't locate the host. Check spelling and make sure
 DNS is running.");
}

for(int c; c < remoteObjects.length; c++)
   //if "MyObject" is found, print a message
   if(remoteObjects[c].equals("MyObject"))
      out.println("MyObject is in the Registry");
```

Once you have determined that the object you are interested in does in fact reside in the list of currently registered objects, you can remove it from the registry with a call to java.rmi.Naming.unbind(). The unbind() method will remove the object that is referenced by a URL passed to the method from the registry determined by the same URL. In other words, `unbind()` will check to see if there is already an object bound in the registry that is referenced by the URL that is passed to the `unbind()` method. If an object is bound by the given URL, it will remove the object from the registry. It will throw the usual exceptions that we've discussed, `MalformedURLException`, `RemoteException`, and `UnknownHostException`, but it might also throw a `NotBoundException` if it can't find the object that you are asking to have removed. As noted before, an application can remove only an object that is bound to a registry that is running on the same machine as the application attempting the `unbind()` call. This feature prevents servers running on other machines from replacing bound objects in your registry, but servers running on the same machine can replace these objects.

The following code fragment will attempt to remove your "MyObject" reference from the registry:

```
String u = "rmi://www.foo.com/MyObject";
    // note that the following String would be equivalent:
    //String u = "MyObject";
    //Since we must be talking about the current machine.
try {
   Naming.unbind(u);
} catch (NotBoundException e )
   out.println("The object requested was not bound in the
 registry");
} catch (RemoteException e) {
   out.println("Couldn't locate Registry");
} catch (MalformedURLException e) {
   out.println("Couldn't parse URL String");
} catch (UnknownHostException e) {
   out.println("Can't locate the host. Check spelling and make sure
 DNS is running.");
}
```

As an exercise, let's recreate the functionality of the `rebind()` method using `bind()` and `unbind()`. You will attempt to bind an object, check to see if an `AlreadyBoundException` is thrown, and if so, unbind the object and try again. This is only an exercise. There is no need to use this code, as you already have a `rebind()` method that implements this functionality:

```
    //create an instance of our remote object
MyRemoteObject ro = new MyRemoteObject();
    //Let's create a name for this object for the registry
final String regName = "MyObject";

    //first attempt to bind our class
try {
   Naming.bind(regName, ro);
} catch (AlreadyBoundException e) {
   //The name we chose was already in the registry, let's
   //get rid of the previous one
```

```
    try {
        Naming.unbind(regName);
        //try to bind again
        Naming.bind(regName, ro);
    } catch(Exception ex) {
            out.println("rebind failed");
    }
} catch (Exception e) {
    //deal with the other possible exceptions, such as
  MalformedURLException, etc.
}
```

# Requesting Objects from the Registry

So far, you've only looked at the server side of registering objects. You must also be able to query a registry for an object, by name, and then get a handle on the remote object that is running in the application that made the registration. In Chapter 2, I talked about the RMI architecture, including the stub and skeleton classes that are used to marshal the execution of remote methods. When a client requests an object from a registry, the registry returns the stub class for that object, not the object itself. The object continues to run in the same name space, on the same machine, in the same virtual machine that it was launched on. The stub is simply a surrogate to this remote object. But as far as the client is concerned, there is really no difference. The stub reference acts as if it were the actual object.

Some of the rules that are in force for binding to a registry go away when you are requesting an object from a registry. For obvious security reasons, you must be a local user to add or remove objects to or from a registry. But in general, anyone can request an object from a registry. The client does not have to be running on the same machine as the registry. If this were the case, this wouldn't be a very useful model for distributed applications, unless your definition of distributed applications implied "distributed on the same machine."

## Applet Security

Applets have special security requirements and, in general, have stricter security policies than full Java applications. One such policy that is enforced by most of the major Web browsers is the inability to establish network connections to any machine other than the one that served the applet. This means that an applet that came from the machine www.foo.com can only connect to a registry that is running on www.foo.com. This is *assuming that the applet is* running in a browser that denies network connections to other machines. This security mechanism is referred to as an Applet-Host security restriction and is the default setting for most browsers.

Now, let's assume that you have an object, MyRemoteObject, that is registered on the machine www.foo.com, registered under the name "MyObject." You will request a reference to that object from the registry using the java.rmi.Naming.lookup() method. This method will take a URL that points to the registry as a parameter and, if it finds that object, will return a reference to it. The lookup() method will throw certain exceptions—MalformedURLException, RemoteException, and UnknownHostException—as they were with previous calls to methods in the Naming class, but it will also throw a NotBoundException if the object being requested is not bound in the registry.

The following code sample will attempt to get a handle on the *MyRemoteObject* that is registered under the name "MyObject":

```
MyRemoteObject o;    //this is where we store the object reference
try {
    //request reference to MyRemoteObject using its URL with the
    //name "MyObject"
    //Note the casting
    o = (MyRemoteObject)Naming.lookup("rmi://www.foo.com/MyObject");
} catch (NotBoundException e) {
    out.println("Couldn't find object in registry");
} catch (RemoteException e) {
    out.println("Couldn't locate Registry");
} catch (MalformedURLException e) {
    out.prinln("Couldn't parse URL String");
} catch (UnknownHostException e) {
    out.println("Can't locate the host. Check spelling and make sure
  DNS is running.");
}
```

If all went well in the preceding example, you now have a handle on the remote object and can refer to it through the variable o. Note that you had to cast the return value of lookup() as a MyRemoteObject object. The lookup() method will return an object of type java.rmi.Remote and must always be cast to the type of object you are expecting to be returned. If different types of objects are possible, you can always store the object as an Object and then determine which type it is by using the instanceof operator.

Once you have a reference to this object, you can call methods on the remote object as if they were methods of a local object. For example, let's assume that the object MyRemoteObject that you have in the variable o has a method called doSomething(). Well, once you have the return value from lookup() stored in o, you can call the doSomething() method with the simple statement:

```
o.doSomething();
```

This will cause the doSomething() method to be executed on the remote machine. All of the network protocol handling is done for us invisibly, and you don't really need to concern yourself with the fact that the method is actually executing somewhere else.

# Using the java.rmi.registry Package

All of the methods that we've used so far to interact with a registry have used URLs with various methods of the java.rmi.Naming class. Also, lower-level calls for doing the same thing are available in the java.rmi.registry package. This package contains an interface, Registry, that defines the method interface for a registry server. The package also contains a class LocateRegistry that can be used to find or create a registry.

The Registry interface is the base interface for objects that create or interact with a registry server. This interface defines methods of the same names that you used with the Naming class, such as bind(), rebind(), list(), and unbind(). The main difference here is that the strings that are passed are not necessarily assumed to be URLs. These methods may be used on a local implementation of the Registry interface.

The most common way that this interface is used is in conjunction with the java.rmi.registry.LocateRegistry class. This class can be used to get a handle on a registry that can then be queried using the methods just mentioned. A code sample that will use the LocateRegistry class to locate a registry and then query the registry for an object registered under the name "MyClass" would look something like this:

```
//Exception handling has been omitted from this example
Registry r =
  java.rmi.registry.LocateRegistry.getRegistry("www.foo.com");
MyRemoteObject o = (MyRemoteObject)r.lookup("MyClass");
```

In this example, the term "MyClass" is not treated as a URL. It is the actual name of the object being queried. Because r contains a reference to an actual registry, there is no need for a URL. The getRegistry() method simply returns a reference to an instance of a registry running on a remote system. There are a number of parameter permutations that can be used for getting a registry. The getRegistry() method with no arguments will attempt to access a registry running on the local machine. When called with an integer parameter, as getRegistry(int), it attempts to access a registry running on the local machine on the port number that matches the integer parameter. As in the preceding example, it can be called with a host name as a parameter, and the final permutation uses both a host name and an integer to access a registry running on a remote machine on a nonstandard port. For more specifics about the LocateRegistry class, turn to the API reference at the back of the book.

Here is a simple example, including exception handling, that will export the object MyRemoteObject on the registry running on the local machine with the standard port number of 1099:

```
Registry reg; //to hold the registry reference
MyRemoteObject ro; //to hold the remote object that will be
  registered
```

```
try {
   //create an instance of the object to export
   ro = new MyRemoteObject();

   //get a handle on the local Registry server
   //note that getRegistry() is called with no parameters.
   //this will cause it to look for a Registry server on the
   //local machine on the standard Registry port
   reg = java.rmi.registry.LocateRegistry.getRegistry();

   //bind our object with the registry we just located
   reg.rebind("MyObject", ro);

//catch exceptions. Note that we don't need
//MalformedURLException
//UnknownHostException since we are operating on the
//local machine and aren't using URLs.
} catch (RemoteException e) {
   out.println("Couldn't locate Registry");
} catch (AccessException e) {
   //the Registry object didn't allow access
   out.println("rebind() access denied.");
}
```

# Implementing the Registry Interface

Any machine that offers RMI services must have at least one registry running in order to bootstrap RMI clients. Often the RMI registry application that comes with the Java Development Kit is all you will need. There are occasions, however, when you may want to run a registry from within your application. In this case, you will want to start a registry on a specified port and maintain a handle on it for dynamically binding and removing methods to that registry. This method guarantees control over the registry for an application, because the application can create its own instance of a registry server. It's important to note that both the registry and the server implementation can exist as the same process, as illustrated in the server that you will build in Chapter 7.

A registry can be started only on the local machine that is hosting the application that starts it. The registry can be started on any available port number above 1024, or on ports below 1024 if it is run with a User ID (UID) that has superuser privileges.

The java.rmi.registry.LocateRegistry class is used to create new instances of a registry. These instances can be referred to with a java.rmi.registry.Registry interface, which is the object type that is returned by a call to the createRegistry() method of the LocateRegistry class. The createRegistry() method takes an integer port number as a parameter and attempts to start a registry server on that port. Upon failure, a RemoteException is thrown, signifying the fact that `createRegistry()` was unable to create a registry on the given port. Upon success, a `Registry` object is returned and the `bind()`, `rebind()`, `list()`, `lookup()`, and `unbind()` methods can be called on that object. Let's take a look at a code fragment that creates a new registry on port 5000:

```
Registry reg;

try {
    reg = java.rmi.registry.LocateRegistry.createRegistry(5000);
} catch (RemoteException e) {
    out.println("Couldn't create Registry, try another port number");
}
```

Now let's extend this code fragment a bit and create an instance of a remote object, and then let's bind it with the registry that you just created:

```
try {
    MyRemoteObject ro = new MyRemoteObject();
    reg.rebind("MyObject", ro);
} catch (RemoteException rx) {
    out.println("error creating remote object, or binding registry");
} catch (AccessException ax) {
    out.println("operation rebind() not permitted");
}
```

You could also extend this code fragment to print a list of all of the names that are currently registered:

```
String list[]; //used to store the list of names
try {
    //get the list of names
    list = reg.list();
} catch (RemoteException rx) {
    out.println("list failed.");
} catch (AccessException ax) {
    out.println("Access denied");
}

//print the list of names
for(int c=0; c< list.length; c++)
    out.println(list[c]);
```

One of the benefits of starting your own server using the `LocateRegistry.createRegistry` mechanism is that an application can check for the existence of a registry at run time. If a registry exists, your application can register its remote objects with that registry. If a registry does not exist, the application can start one itself. This gives you a lot of flexibility when deciding how to run your services.

# Summary

Registry services for RMI are somewhat similar to the port mapping services in RPC. A well-known host name and port number (network address) are used to find things that are running on random, anonymous port numbers on the same machine. In order to bootstrap, a client requesting an object in the RMI model must query a registry that it knows about for the address of the object that it is interested in. In other words, the client will ask the registry for the port number of a specific object knowing, in advance, how to find the registry. Normally, a single registry on a well-defined port will have a table of many available remote objects. Queries for these objects are made by name using either the URL-based methods of the `java.rmi.Naming` class or the lower-level methods of the `java.rmi.registry.Registry` interface. Once a client has a handle on the remote object, the registry is no longer needed for accessing methods from the same application. The registry does not return the actual object that it has registered, but rather a stub class that is the local representation of the remote object. Any operations on the stub class are sent to the matching server-side skeleton class that marshals parameters and method calls to the actual object that is being referred to.

In most cases, the RMI registry application will fill the registration needs of your applications. Both the methods of the `Naming` class and the `Registry` interface can be used to interact with this registry. But in certain cases, you may want an application to start its own registry, in which case, you will use the `java.rmi.registry.LocateRegistry` class to create a new registry server and then interact with that.

This chapter discussed the various methods of registering and gaining access to remote objects. In Chapter 4 you will take a look at the remote objects—how they make their methods remotely accessible, how they register themselves, and how clients interact with them.

# Part II

## Advanced Java RMI Concepts

# Chapter 4

# Pushing Someone Else's Buttons

## IN THIS CHAPTER

♦ Creating and implementing a remote interface

♦ The TimeServer client

♦ RMI stub compiler (rmic)

♦ A punch clock server

IN THIS CHAPTER YOU ARE going to look at the programming interface level of RMI to create an application that exports an object, registers it with an RMI registry server, and sets up a client that queries the registry for a handle to the exported object, calls a method on the object, and receives a return value. In essence, the client application is pushing buttons on the server object and receiving a new object in response. Simply stated, this chapter will explore calling methods on other machines using code samples to demonstrate the main ideas of remote methods.

Think of accessing remote methods as pushing buttons on another machine. Essentially, you are given a handle to an object that is nothing more than a proxy to an object that exists elsewhere. When you call the methods on this object, they are not executing in your local environment. They are in fact being marshaled back and forth between your machine and the machine that is exporting them. All execution happens on the machine that is actually running the remote object's associated application code.

The great part about this is that all you have to do is implement a simple interface, call a few routines to set up the exporting and bootstrapping (that is, initialization) of the client and server applications, and then call the methods as if they were local. Really, for most simple method calls, nothing is noticeably different from a local method call. By simple method calls, I mean calls without any fancy parameters or return types. Most of the standard objects that you will find in `java.lang.*` and `java.util.*` can be passed as parameters and returned from method calls as if they were simple base types. Exceptions are listed in Chapter 6 on object serialization. Obviously, this completely leaves out any user-created types as parameters or return values. In most cases, these objects can also be used if they simply implement the `java.io.Serializable` interface. If you are anxious to read ahead on the semantics and interfaces for object serialization, see Chapter 6.

I've mentioned pushing someone else's buttons, but it is important to note here that RMI allows for a more distributed model than strict client-server systems. In other words, you may want someone to push your buttons. Once your client application bootstraps with another application that is exporting an object, the client may export itself back to the server, enabling the server to call methods on the client. This works great as a callback mechanism for many applications. In other words, it allows a client to mind its own business until the server decides to notify it of new data or a new situation to deal with. In this model, the server can be nothing more than a registry that allows clients to register themselves and get handles on other client applications so that they can all start pushing each other's buttons. Also, because these references are essentially objects that can be passed around, references can be passed to servers with light loads for dynamic load balancing, or clients in a distributed chat application can communicate through a server for general conversations but then get handles on individual clients for private communication with lighter demands on the server and the network channels used to transport the conversations. In other words, there is no need to have your conversation ushered through the server, if it is not meant to be distributed to a list of participants.

In Figure 4-1 the circled letters represent references to remote objects. The S circles are references to server objects and the C circles are references to client objects. This is essentially the stub classes that RMI uses to communicate to remote objects. Figure 4-1 shows how these references interact with their remote objects.

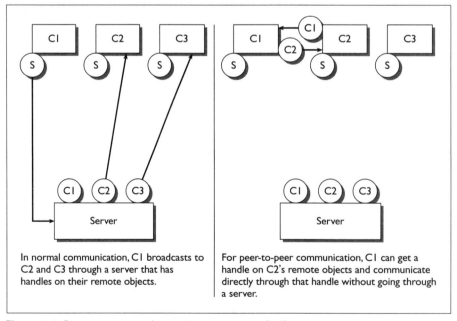

Figure 4-1. Peer-to-server and peer-to-peer communication

In the following sections, you are going to create a time server application to demonstrate exporting an object, looking it up in the registry, and calling its methods. This application will export an object with a single method, `time()`, that will return the system time on the server that is exporting it. This is similar to the time services running on many UNIX systems and is a useful mechanism for synchronizing the system time on a number of other systems via a machine designated as an authority. This is particularly useful when exporting file systems, because the modification dates should all be in sync on the various machines that use the files. (It should be noted that exact synchronization is not possible because of network latency.)

In creating this application, you will first design an interface that defines the remote method signature, then write a server application that implements this interface, and finally write a client that looks up and uses the interface. The final step is to generate the stub and skeleton class files, start the RMI registry, launch your server application, and test it with your client application (covered in the section "Implementing the TimeServer Client").

# Creating a Remote Interface

Any class that exports objects must implement an interface that defines the methods that can be accessed via a remote application. The class may have methods that are not defined in this interface, but these methods will not be available to remote clients. It is also possible for a single class to implement many remote interfaces so that different methods are available depending on which interface the object is being cast as.

Essentially, a client gets a handle to the interface describing the remote methods of an object. This interface must be a derivative of `java.rmi.Remote`. In the current example, your interface will have a single method that takes no parameters but returns the system time for the system running the server.

Using your favorite text editor, create the source file shown in Listing 4-1. Notice the package name `rmibook.timeserver`. As a convention, all code listings in this book will be in a subpackage of the `rmibook` package. This mimics the package setup for the source code that accompanies this book. If you are not using the source code from the CD-ROM, you can omit or change the package names as long as you are consistent throughout the code.

Listing 4-1. The Time Server application (TimeServer.java)

```
package rmibook.timeserver;

public interface TimeServer extends java.rmi.Remote {

      public String getTime()
throws java.rmi.RemoteException;

}
```

Here you have defined a public interface, `TimeServer`, that extends `java.rmi.Remote`. It is important to note that the interface must be public in order to be imported by remote clients. It must also extend the `java.rmi.Remote` interface or a subclass of the `Remote` interface in order to be exported.

For the body of the interface, you have declared one public method that returns a `String`. The `getTime()` method will be called by a client on a server that implements this method. The server will return a `String` object that contains the current date on the server. Essentially any errors produced by the RMI mechanisms will result in a `java.rmi.RemoteException` being thrown. You declare that this method throws a `RemoteException` and that any client that accesses this method must encompass the call in a try/catch clause, or it must declare `RemoteException` in its `throws` clause. The `TimeServer` interface that you just defined will be used by the server that implements the `getTime()` method, and it will be used by the client that you create as a handle to the server object. Essentially, a client will request a reference to a `TimeServer` object and then call the `TimeServer.getTime()` method in order to retrieve the `String` representing the server's system time.

# Implementing a Remote Interface

Now that you have your `TimeServer` interface, you must create a server implementation of it. The server will implement the body of the `getTime()` method and register itself with a local registry in order to be located by prospective clients.

The server implementation, `TimeServerImpl.java`, is part of the same package as the `TimeServer` interface, so you will include the same package statement. Also, in order to keep the code simple, you will import the `java.rmi` package and the `java.rmi.server.UnicastRemoteObject` class:

```
package rmibook.timeserver;

import java.rmi.*;
import java.rmi.server.UnicastRemoteObject;
```

The next step is to create the class. Our class will implement the interface that you created and will extend `java.rmi.server.UnicastRemoteObject`. There are two choices when crafting a remote object: either extend `UnicastRemoteObject` or export the object using one of the member functions of `UnicastRemoteObject`. For this example, you will just extend the class; you will discuss exporting objects by other means a little later, in Chapter 7. Here's the code:

```
public class TimeServerImpl
extends UnicastRemoteObject
        implements TimeServer {
```

The use of `TimeServerImpl` is only a convention. It is not necessary to name the class and the interface with the same root name.

Our next task is to create a body for the `getTime()` function that was declared in the `TimeServer` interface. This function will simply return the local system time as a string:

```
public String   getTime(){
        System.out.println("Sending data...");
        return new java.util.Date().toString();
}
```

As declared in the interface, the method must be public. Just as a diagnostic tool, I've added a `println()` statement so that you can monitor when this method gets called. Any time the method is called, "Sending data..." will be printed on the server's console, not on the console of the client that is actually making the call. The final statement just creates a new `Date` object that will be initialized with the current date by default and returns the value as a string using the `java.util.Date.toString()` method. The `getTime()` method will be called by a remote client and executed on a server; the resulting `String` will be sent over the network and received by the client as if it were a local return value.

The constructor for this class is pretty straightforward. The only reason that it is included is to print a diagnostic message to let us know when it's been instanced:

```
public TimeServerImpl() throws RemoteException {
        System.out.println("Initializing Timeserver");
    }
```

Not much to explain there. Moving along, this server will run as a standard Java stand-alone application. As such it must declare a `main()` method. In `main()`, you will create an instance of an RMI security manager. The RMI mechanisms define a policy of requiring a program that exports remote objects to explicitly set a security manager. If a security manager is not set, no methods will be allowed remote invocation. The system will disallow stub and skeleton loading if there isn't a security manager in place. As a developer, you can create your own security manager, but for most applications, `java.rmi.RMISecurityManager` will do. This sets certain security policies in place that allow methods to be called remotely without compromising too much on the security side. The `RMISecurityManager` is discussed in more detail in the `java.rmi` API section.

After setting a security manager, you will create an instance of your server application that will be the object that you bind with the RMI registry, using a `rebind()` call so that any previous applications in the registry known by the same name will be replaced in the registry. You could use a `bind()` call instead, but then you would have to deal with catching an `AlreadyBoundException` if the name is already in use by a previously launched copy of this application or another one with the same name. The `rebind()` method takes two arguments. The first argument is a URL that points to a registry; this registry must be on the same machine that you are running this application on (an application can only bind with a local registry). The second argument is a reference to the actual object being exported. (See Chapter 3 for more information on the registry.) In this case, you pass a reference to an instance of `TimeServerImpl`.

## URL Naming Tip for Local Servers

The canonical form of an RMI URL is `rmi://rmi-machine-name:port/BindingName`. The port number is necessary only if you are running your registry on a nonstandard port. Also, the `rmi:` part of the URL is normally assumed, and the `BindingName` is the name that your application will be mapped to when other applications query the registry for it. Since an application can only bind on the local host that it is running on, a short form of the RMI URL would consist of only the `BindingName` of the application. For example, when registering an object with a registry, instead of using the URL `"rmi://myhost.com/MyServer,"` you could just use the URL `"MyServer."`

Finally, if there are any problems binding, a `RemoteException` will be thrown, so put the `rebind()` statement in a try/catch phrase and print out an error message if there is a problem. Because one of the parameters to the `rebind()` method is parsed as a URL, there is the possibility of getting a `MalformedURLException`, so catch that and print a message:

```
public static void main(String arg[]) {
    System.setSecurityManager(new RMISecurityManager());
    try {
        //create an instance of the server
        TimeServerImpl TSI = new TimeServerImpl();
        //bind the server with the name "TimeServer"
        Naming.rebind("TimeServer", TSI);
            System.out.println("Registered with registry " );
    } catch (RemoteException e) {
        System.out.println("Error: " + e);
    } catch (java.net.MalformedURLException e) {
        System.out.println("URL Error: " + e);
    }
}
```

Listing 4-2 shows the code you have so far.

Listing 4-2. Implementing the TimeServer interface (TimeServerImpl.java)

```
package rmibook.timeserver;
```

```
import java.rmi.*;
import java.rmi.server.UnicastRemoteObject;

public class TimeServerImpl
        extends UnicastRemoteObject
        implements TimeServer {
   public String   getTime(){
      System.out.println("Sending data...");
      return new java.util.Date().toString();
   }
   public TimeServerImpl() throws RemoteException {
      System.out.println("Initializing Timeserver");
   }
   public static void main(String arg[]) {
      System.setSecurityManager(new RMISecurityManager());
      try {
         //create an instance of the server
         TimeServerImpl TSI = new TimeServerImpl();
         //bind the server with the name "TimeServer"
         Naming.rebind("TimeServer", TSI);
            System.out.println("Registered with registry");
      } catch (RemoteException e) {
         System.out.println("Error: " + e);
      } catch (java.net.MalformedURLException e) {
         System.out.println("URL Error: " + e);
      }
   }
}
```

# Implementing the TimeServer Client

Essentially, the hard part of writing a network distributed application is over. All of the network protocol handling has been simply taken care of with the few method calls that you implemented in the previous code examples. There are still a couple of loose ends to talk about, such as compiling the class files and then generating the skeleton and stub files—but I'll get to that shortly. First, let's take a look at the client application.

The client must first bootstrap with a registry server to get a handle on the TimeServer object, and then the client will have access to the getTime() method through this handle on the registry. Once the client has this handle, the registry is no longer necessary. The registry is being used only as a phone book that allows a client to look up the phone number of the remote object it is interested in. All of this is done with the java.rmi.Naming class. Just as the server used the Naming class to register itself, a client will use the Naming class to query a registry and get access to the object being exported.

In order to consider a simple example with an emphasis on "how-to," you will write a simple client that will simply look up the server object, call its getTime()

method, and print the `String` that results. This base structure could be used in a number of larger applications that require time synchronization with a central authority. So first, you'll declare the package name and import the `java.rmi` package. The client does not need to extend `UnicastRemoteObject` or implement any of the remote interfaces unless it will also be exporting some of its objects. Also, as this is a stand-alone application, you must define a `main()` method. So in this case, the start of the class definition is very simple:

```
package rmibook.timeserver;
import java.rmi.*;

public class Time {
public static void main(String arg[]) {
```

Next, create a `String` variable called `time` to store the result string in. Just to prevent certain Java compilers from complaining about uninitialized variables, you will explicitly initialize the `String` with `null`:

```
String time = null;
```

Now comes the bootstrapping part. Use the `Naming.lookup()` method to get a handle on the remote object. This method takes a URL to a registry as its argument and returns a `Remote` object. In this case, you want to cast the `Remote` object as the same type that you declared in your `TimeServer` remote interface. This will give us access to the method defined in the interface, namely `getTime()`. The `Naming.lookup()` method will throw a `RemoteException` if any errors occur, so the entire lookup must be in a try/catch phrase that catches the `RemoteException`. If the problem is explicitly the lack of a match between the name supplied in the URL and any names that are currently bound in the registry, a `NotBoundException` will be thrown, and because you are passing a string to be parsed as a URL, a `MalformedURLException` may be thrown. A number of exceptions can be generated, so the following try statement will be matched with a catch clause a little later in the code:

```
try {
   TimeServer TS =(TimeServer)
            Naming.lookup("rmi://foo.com/TimeServer");
```

Notice that the URL includes the machine name of the machine on which you will be running the server and the registry. The term following the machine name is the name that the server was bound with. Because you used the name "TimeServer" when you registered the server with a call to `rebind()`, this is the name that you will look up the service with. After this statement, `TS` will contain a reference to an object implementing the `TimeServer` interface that was exported by the server, or a `RemoteException` will have been thrown if there was a problem finding the server or matching the name with the registry's list of registrants. This reference is technically an instance of a stub class that handles the client side RMI marshaling and arbitration, but effectively, you can think of it as being a reference to the actual object running on the remote server. Once you have this reference, you can use it to call the getTime() method. Because getTime() may also throw a RemoteException, you will keep it within the same try/catch phrase and then catch the RemoteException if it gets thrown. If you do in fact catch an exception, you will simply print a diagnostic error message and exit the application:

```
  time = TS.getTime();
} catch (NotBoundException e) {
  System.out.println("TimeServer was not found in registry");
  System.exit(0);
} catch (RemoteException e) {
    System.out.println("Time error: " + e);
    System.exit(0);
} catch (java.net.MalformedURLException e) {
    System.out.println("URL error: " + e);
    System.exit(0);
}
```

Finally, let's just check to make sure the time variable isn't a null reference, and if it isn't, print the string to standard out:

```
if(time!=null)
    System.out.println("The Time is: " + time);
```

Listing 4-3 is a complete listing of the client application.

**Listing 4-3. The Time Server client application (Time.java)**

```
package rmibook.timeserver;
import java.rmi.*;

public class Time {
    public static void main(String arg[]) {
        String time = null;
        try {
          TimeServer TS =(TimeServer)
                Naming.lookup("rmi://foo.com/TimeServer");
         time = TS.getTime();
        } catch (NotBoundException e) {
         System.out.println
             ("TimeServer was not found in registry");
         System.exit(0);
        } catch (RemoteException e) {
           System.out.println("Time error: " + e);
           System.exit(0);
        } catch (java.net.MalformedURLException e) {
           System.out.println("URL error: " + e);
           System.exit(0);
```

```
        }
        if(time!=null)
            System.out.println("The Time is: " + time);
    }
}
```

The next step is to compile the three files that you just created. Compiling on different platforms is going to be different, so the examples given here will assume that you are using the Java Developer Kit (JDK) from Sunsoft, and that all of your .class files are in a directory called /home/MyClasses. So, using a command similar to the following (all on one line), compile your source code:

```
javac -d /home/MyClasses TimeServer.java TimeServerImpl.java
  Time.java
```

This will create the `rmibook.timeserver.XXX` class files in your /home/MyClasses directory.

# Using RMIC

Once the class files have been created, the stub and skeleton classes must be generated. The stub is the client-side proxy to the remote method, and the skeleton is the server-side proxy. All marshaling of data and method access is done through these two objects. Unlike with RPC, there is no need to write strange header files or generator files in a special language. The stub and skeleton files can be generated directly from the `rmibook.timeserver.TimeServer` class file that you created with JAVAC. Essentially, the RMI stub compiler (rmic) does this for us.

## RMIC for Windows

In general, RMIC is launched from a Windows NT or Windows 95 command prompt in the following form:

```
c:> rmic [options] classFile
```

The *classFile* may be a single file or list that is the qualified class name for the classes that export remote objects and therefore require stub classes. For example, you would create a stub for the `rmibook.timeserver.TimeServerImpl` class, but not for the interface or client. Also, the .class suffix is omitted as it is when using the Java interpreter. The option flags are listed in Table 4-1.

## TABLE 4-1  OPTION FLAGS FOR THE RMIC STUB/SKELETON COMPILER

| Option | Description | Example |
|---|---|---|
| –classpath path | Specify a CLASSPATH rather than using the environment variable. This overrides the CLASSPATH environment variable. (Normally, the CLASSPATH environment variable will be used.) | `-classpath c:\home\ MyClasses;.` |
| –d directory | Specify the base directory for your compiled class files. All class files compiled will end up relative to this directory. | `-d c:\home\ MyClasses` |
| –depend | Cause the compiler to check and recompile files that the current file depends on. Normally, only missing class files or out-of-date files will be recompiled. | `-depend` |
| –g | Generate debugging tables for use with Java debugging tools. These tables will contain information about local variables and line numbers that correspond to the line numbers in the source files. | `-g` |
| –keepgenerated | When the stub and skeleton classes are created, a *xxx*.java source file is generated first. Normally, this file is temporary and is not saved. The -keepgenerated flag will cause the *xxx*.java files to be saved in the same directory that the *xxx*.class files are saved in. | `-keepgenerated` |
| –nowarn | Suppress compiler generated warning messages. | `-nowarn` |
| –O | Optimize the compiled class files. The -O flag will inline static, private, and final methods and suppress line numbers from being included in the object code. It is important to note that the optimization is geared for speed, and not size. So an optimized class file may be larger in size than a standard one. | `-O` |
| –show | Cause a pop-up window to appear that will list the class names of the files that you may want to compile. Essentially, this is the GUI interface for RMIC. | `-show` |

*continued*

TABLE 4-1  OPTION FLAGS FOR THE RMIC STUB/SKELETON COMPILER *(Continued)*

| Option | Description | Example |
|---|---|---|
| –verbose | Cause the files to be compiled in verbose mode. Compiler and linker messages will be displayed that may otherwise have been suppressed. | -verbose |

# RMIC for UNIX

Essentially, the UNIX RMI stub compiler works the same as the Windows version. The only differences are the obvious changes in path delimiters and directory delimiters. Table 4-1 is exactly the same for UNIX except for the following two changes:

◆ The path delimiters used with the -classpath flag are changed from semicolons to colons—for example: `-classpath /home/MyClasses:`

◆ The directory delimiter is a forward slash (/) instead of a backslash (\)—for example: `-d /home/MyClasses`.

Typically, RMIC will be run from the command line as:

```
$ rmic -d /home/MyClasses MyPackage.MyRemoteImpl
```

# Building the Stub and Skeleton for TimeServer

The next order of business is to build the stub and skeleton classes for the `rmi-book.timeserver.TimeServerImpl` class that you compiled earlier in this chapter. Obviously, you need to have access to the `TimeServerImpl.class` file, so this must be in the current working directory or in your CLASSPATH (either the environment variable or explicitly declared using a -classpath flag). In general these classes will be put in the same class directory as the class files with which they are associated. So from the command line, type the following command:

```
rmic -d /home/MyClasses rmibook.timeserver.TimeServerImpl
```

Notice that you used the fully qualified class name for `TimeServerImpl` including the package name. Once this has completed, you should have TimeServerImpl_Skel.class and a TimeServerImpl_Stub.class files in the /home/MyClasses/rmibook/timeserver directory (or similar directory depending on your base class directory, platform, and package names if you are not using the `rmibook.timeserver` package name).

# Starting the Registry

You now have everything you need to employ your TimeServer application. All that is left to do is start the registry, start the TimeServerImpl application, and test it with the Time client application.

It is important that the registry be able to find the stub and skeleton classes while it is running. So either the CLASSPATH has to be set with the appropriate entry before the registry is started or the application must be started with a flag that explicitly sets an RMI property that tells the registry where to find these files. For now, let's assume that the CLASSPATH environment variable includes an entry for the directory that contains your class files.

Generally, it is desirable to run the registry as a background process, so start it up with the following command. It will not give you any feedback if it launches successfully, so if there are no error messages, assume that it has started and is running normally:

```
rmiregistry &
```

# Starting TimeServer

Now, assuming that your registry is running normally, you will start your TimeServerImpl application. Note that you specifically added diagnostic `println()`s in your code, so you should get some feedback when the server starts. It is also desirable to run the server as a background process, so you will start it with the following command in UNIX:

```
java rmibook.timeserver.TimeServerImpl &
```

Upon successful launching, the TimeServerImpl application will start as a background process and print the messages "Initializing Timeserver" and "Registered with Registry" on the command console. An alternative way to launch the application, if the registry wasn't started with the appropriate CLASSPATH set, is the following (all on one line):

```
java -Djava.rmi.server.codebase=<ClassURL>
  rmibook.timeserver.TimeServerImpl&
```

Here, the *<ClassURL>* is any valid URL type that can be used to access the class files for the TimeServerImpl stub and skeleton classes. This includes `http:` and `file:` URLs. For more information on the registry properties, see Chapter 3.

Now, if all went as planned, you have a registry running that is listening for `Naming.lookup()` calls, and a single object registered, namely your

TimeServerImpl object, with the associated name "TimeServerImpl." To test your application, simply run your Time client application. From the command line, type the following:

```
java rmibook.timeserver.Time
```

The result should be two lines of this form:

```
Got Connection, Sending data...
The Time is: Thu Feb 13 16:02:15 EST 1997
```

# A Punch Clock Server

Now that you have the basics down, let's try something a little more complex. Here you will create a punch clock server. The server will track a set of employees. An employee will supply his or her employee ID and a password, and the server will keep track of when employees punch in and when they punch out. All of this will be written to a log file for later perusal. In order to make this easily accessible, the client application will be written as an applet.

## The Remote Interface

Just as in the last example, you must create an interface that subclasses the Remote interface to declare those methods that you want to make available to remote clients. In this interface, you will declare a single method, punch(), that will take an ID String and a password String as parameters and return a String with the status of the transaction. All of the code for this example will be in the rmibook.timeclock package:

```
package rmibook.timeclock;
import java.rmi.*;

public interface TimeClock extends Remote {
        public String punch(String id, String passwd)
                        throws RemoteException;
}
```

This application will use two external files, loosely referred to as the database. The first file will contain a list of employee IDs and passwords of this form:

```
id1 passwd1
id2 passwd2
Troy MyPasswd
. . .
```

This file will be called authFile for the purposes of this example. The second file will contain the transaction logs. The logFile will contain a single entry for every time that a user punches out. The form of the data will be a single line for each entry, consisting of the employee ID followed by two date strings, the punch-in date, and the punch-out date. For example:

```
ID1 Fri Feb 07 12:22:26 EST 1997 Fri Feb 07 12:22:37 EST 1997
```

# The Server Implementation

Now that you have an understanding of what the application will do and what the remote interface is, let's create the server implementation. As in the previous example, this class will extend `UnicastRemoteObject` in order to be exported by its constructor. It must also implement the `TimeClock` interface that you defined in the previous section. The server will maintain a `Vector()` of employees. When a particular employee "punches the clock," the server will check to see if there is an entry for that employee in the `Vector`. If not, an object representing the employee will be added to the `Vector`. If there is already an employee record in the `Vector`, then the server will assume that that employee is "punching off the clock," and the appropriate log entry will be made. There is also a `Vector` that contains a list of valid employee IDs and passwords. This `Vector` is read from the authFile when the server first starts up.

Here are the first few lines of the source file:

```
package rmibook.timeclock;

import java.rmi.*;
import java.rmi.server.*;
import java.io.*;
import java.util.*;

public class TimeClockServer
        extends UnicastRemoteObject
        implements TimeClock {

        Vector employees = new Vector();
        Vector passwd = null;
        RandomAccessFile logFile = null;
```

Next comes your constructor. The constructor will open the logFile, seek to the end of the file so that it is ready to append records, and call a function that reads in the password file to populate the passwd `Vector`:

```
public TimeClockServer() throws RemoteException {
    try {
        logFile = new RandomAccessFile("logFile","rw");
        logFile.seek(logFile.length());
```

```
    } catch (IOException e) {
      System.out.println("logfile: " + e);
    }
    System.out.println("TimeClockServer starting at " +
                            new Date().toString());
    readPasswords();
  }
```

Before you write the readPasswords() method, let's take a look at your implementation for the punch() method that you declared in the TimeClock interface. This method takes an employee ID and password as its arguments. It first checks to see if the ID and password are valid by calling an isValidID() method with the values. The isValidID() method compares the values presented with the ones that you loaded into the password Vector at start time. Once authentication is verified, this method checks to see if the employee is already on the clock. If so, the employee record is removed from the employees Vector, a log entry is made, and a message is returned to the client stating that the employee has been punched off the clock. If the employee was not already on the clock, the current system time is added to the employee record and it is added to the employees Vector until a subsequent call is made with this same ID and password:

```
public String punch( String empID, String passwd ) {
    if(isValidID(new passWord(empID,passwd))){
        if(onTheClock(empID))
            return removeEmployee(empID);
        else
            return addEmployee(empID);
    }
    return "Sorry, Invalid employee or passwd";
}
```

The functionality of removeEmployee(), addEmployee(), and isValidID() should be self-evident. Here are the bodies for these methods:

```
private String addEmployee(String empID){
    //adds an employee to the cache of employees
    //that are "on the clock"
    empRecord emp; //defined in empRecord.java
    employees.addElement(emp = new empRecord(empID));
    return "Employee# " + empID + " punched in at: " +
            emp.timeOn.toString();
}
```

The removeEmployee() method is a little more complicated, because it must deal with the log file, handling the possibility that it was called using an ID that is no longer in the Vector:

```
private String removeEmployee(String empID) {
    //punch out employees and update the log
```

```
    empRecord emp;
    for(int i = 0; i < employees.size(); i++) {
        emp = (empRecord)employees.elementAt(i);
        if(emp.id.equals(empID)) {
          emp.timeOff = new Date();
          employees.removeElementAt(i);
          try {
          logFile.writeChars(emp.id + " " +
                           emp.timeOn.toString() +" "+
                           emp.timeOff.toString() + "\n");
          } catch (IOException e) {
            System.out.println(e);
          }

          return "Employee# " + emp.id +
                 "\nPunched in at: " +
                 emp.timeOn.toString() +
                 "\npunched out at: " +
                 emp.timeOff.toString();
        }
    }
    return "Employee not found";
}
```

The isValidID() method simply checks the ID that is passed to it against the IDs that were read in from the authFile at start time:

```
private boolean isValidID(PassWord pw) {
    PassWord pass;
    for(int i = 0; i < passwd.size(); i++) {
        pass = (PassWord)passwd.elementAt(i);
        if(pass.isEqual(pw))
            return true;
    }
    return false;
}
```

In the punch() method, onTheClock() was called to determine whether an employee was already punched in. This checks the Vector of employees against the ID that is passed to it and returns a Boolean:

```
private boolean onTheClock(String empID) {
    for(int i = 0; i < employees.size(); i++)
        if(((EmpRecord)
             employees.elementAt(i)).id.equals(empID))
           return true;
    return false;
}
```

Now take a look at the main() method. As in the previous example, this method must install a security manager, create an instance of the object that is being exported, and call the `Naming` class to register the object with a registry. You must put the `Naming.rebind()` method and the instantiation of the remote object in a try/catch phrase, because both of these could throw exceptions (`RemoteException` and `MalformedURLException`). Because you will treat any of these exceptions similarly, you will put a single `catch()` statement that catches `Exception`, the base class of any exception thrown:

```
public static void main(String arg[]) {
    System.setSecurityManager(new RMISecurityManager());
    try {
        TimeClockServer TCS = new TimeClockServer();
        Naming.rebind
            ("//scooby/TimeClock",TCS);
        System.out.println("Server Ready");
        } catch (Exception e) {
        System.out.println("TimeClock error: " + e);
        }
}
```

You still have a few loose ends to tie up here. The final method to declare in this file is the `readPasswords()` method. This was called in the class constructor; it essentially populates the password `Vector` with the contents of the authFile:

```
void readPasswords() {
    String s;
    passwd = new Vector();
    BufferedReader authFile = null;

    try {
        authFile = new BufferedReader(new
                        FileReader("authFile"));
        while(true) {
            if((s = authFile.readLine())==null){
                authFile=null;
                return;
            }
            passwd.addElement(new
                passWord(s.substring(0,s.indexOf(' ')),
                s.substring(s.indexOf(' ')+1)));
        }
    } catch (FileNotFoundException e) {
            System.out.println("authfile not found: " + e);
    } catch (IOException e) {
            authFile = null;
    }
}
```

Listing 4-4 is a complete code listing.

**Listing 4-4. The Punch Clock application (TimeClockServer.java)**

```java
package rmibook.timeclock;

import java.rmi.*;
import java.rmi.server.*;
import java.io.*;
import java.util.*;

public class TimeClockServer
        extends UnicastRemoteObject
        implements TimeClock {

        Vector employees = new Vector();
        Vector passwd = null;
        RandomAccessFile logFile = null;
public TimeClockServer() throws RemoteException {
    try {
        logFile = new RandomAccessFile("logFile","rw");
      logFile.seek(logFile.length());
    } catch (IOException e) {
      System.out.println("logfile: " + e);
    }
    System.out.println("TimeClockServer starting at " +
                          new Date().toString());
    readPasswords();
}
public String punch( String empID, String passwd ) {
    if(isValidID(new passWord(empID,passwd))){
        if(onTheClock(empID))
           return removeEmployee(empID);
        else
           return addEmployee(empID);
    }
    return "Sorry, Invalid employee or passwd";
}

private String addEmployee(String empID){
    //adds an employee to the cache of employees
    //that are "on the clock"
    empRecord emp; //defined in empRecord.java
    employees.addElement(emp = new empRecord(empID));
    return "Employee# " + empID + " punched in at: " +
            emp.timeOn.toString();
}

private String removeEmployee(String empID) {
    //punch out employees and update the log
    empRecord emp;
    for(int i = 0; i < employees.size(); i++) {
       emp = (empRecord)employees.elementAt(i);
       if(emp.id.equals(empID)) {
         emp.timeOff = new Date();
```

```
            employees.removeElementAt(i);
            try {
            logFile.writeChars(emp.id + " " +
                            emp.timeOn.toString() +" "+
                            emp.timeOff.toString() + "\n");
            } catch (IOException e) {
              System.out.println(e);
            }

            return "Employee# " + emp.id +
                    "\nPunched in at: " +
                 emp.timeOn.toString() +
                 "\npunched out at: " +
                 emp.timeOff.toString();
        }
      }
      return "Employee not found";
   }

   private boolean isValidID(passWord pw) {
       passWord pass;
       for(int i = 0; i < passwd.size(); i++) {
          pass = (passWord)passwd.elementAt(i);
          if(pass.isEqual(pw))
             return true;
       }
       return false;
   }

   private boolean onTheClock(String empID) {
       for(int i = 0; i < employees.size(); i++)
          if(((empRecord)
              employees.elementAt(i)).id.equals(empID))
             return true;
     return false;
   }

   public static void main(String arg[]) {
       System.setSecurityManager(new RMISecurityManager());
       try {
           TimeClockServer TCS = new TimeClockServer();
           Naming.rebind
               ("//scooby/TimeClock",TCS);
           System.out.println("Server Ready");
           } catch (Exception e) {
           System.out.println("TimeClock error: " + e);
           }
   }

   void readPasswords() {
       String s;
       passwd = new Vector();
       BufferedReader authFile = null;
```

```
    try {
        authFile = new BufferedReader(new
                        FileReader("authFile"));
        while(true) {
            if((s = authFile.readLine())==null){
                authFile=null;
                return;
            }
            passwd.addElement(new
                passWord(s.substring(0,s.indexOf(' ')),
                s.substring(s.indexOf(' ')+1)));
        }
    } catch (FileNotFoundException e) {
        System.out.println("authfile not found: " + e);
    } catch (IOException e) {
        authFile = null;
    }
}
```

The TimeClockServer uses two additional classes. One is a structure to hold the employee data when it is added to the employees `Vector` (shown in Listing 4-5), and the other holds the password data when it is added to the password `Vector` (shown in Listing 4-6). They are both simple and straightforward.

**Listing 4-5. The Employee Record object (empRecord.java)**

```
package rmibook.timeclock;
import java.util.*;

class empRecord {

        String id;
        Date timeOn;
        Date timeOff;

        empRecord(String id){
            this.id = id;
            timeOn = new Date();
        }
}
```

**Listing 4-6. The Password object (passWord.java)**

```
package rmibook.timeclock;

class passWord {
    String id;
    String passwd;

    passWord(String id, String passwd) {
        this.id = id;
```

```
            this.passwd = passwd;
      }

   public boolean isEqual(passWord pw) {
         if(pw.id.equals(this.id)&&
           pw.passwd.equals(this.passwd))
            return true;
         else
            return false;
      }
}
```

Now you have the complete server part of the code. Compile these with JAVAC, and then generate the stub and skeleton file with RMIC:

```
javac -d /home/MyClasses TimeClock.java \
TimeClockServer.java empRecord.java passWord.java

rmic -c rmibook.timeclock.TimeClockServer
```

## The Punch Clock Applet

This is a pretty simple client applet (see Figure 4-2). In its init() method, it creates TextField instances for the employee ID and password, a TextArea for displaying messages, and a Button used to submit the data. An applet can only connect to a registry that exists on the same machine that the applet was loaded from. So instead of hard-coding the server name in a URL when you call the Naming.lookup() method, you will construct a URL from the codebase of the applet. As before, you put the lookup() call in a try/catch phrase in case a RemoteException or MalformedURLException is thrown:

```
package rmibook.timeclock;

import java.rmi.*;
import java.applet.*;
import java.awt.*;

public class TimeClockApplet extends Applet {

   private TextField id;
   private TextField passwd;
   private TextArea status;
   TimeClock TC;

   public void init() {
      add(id = new TextField(20));
      add(passwd = new TextField(20));
      add(status = new TextArea(5,20));
      add(new Button("Punch"));
```

```
        status.setEditable(false);
        try {
            TimeClock TC = (TimeClock)
                        Naming.lookup("rmi://" +
                        getCodeBase().getHost() +
                        "/TimeClockServer");
        } catch (Exception e) {
            System.out.println("Error: " + e.toString());
            status.setText(e.toString());
        }
    }
```

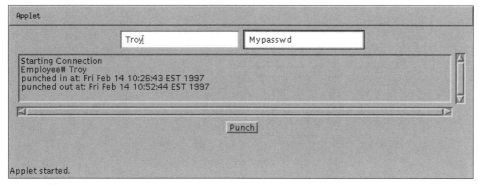

Figure 4–2. The Punch Clock applet

The only thing left to do is handle the event when the Punch button is pressed. When the button is pressed, the values from the ID and password TextFields will be read and passed as parameters to the punch() method of the remote object referenced by TC. The return value will be displayed in the status TextArea. All of this is handled by the following simple event handler:

```
public boolean handleEvent(Event e) {
    if(e.target instanceof Button) {
        try {
            status.setText(TC.punch(id.getText(),
                            passwd.getText()));
            return true;
        } catch (RemoteException ex) {
            status.setText(ex.toString());
        }
    }
    return false;
}
```

That's it. Pretty simple. Listing 4-7 is a complete listing of the applet source.

**Listing 4-7. The Punch Clock applet (TimeClockApplet.java)**

```
package rmibook.timeclock;

import java.rmi.*;
import java.applet.*;
import java.awt.*;

public class TimeClockApplet extends Applet {

    private TextField id;
    private TextField passwd;
    private TextArea status;
    TimeClock TC;

    public void init() {
        add(id = new TextField(20));
        add(passwd = new TextField(20));
        add(status = new TextArea(5,20));
        add(new Button("Punch"));

        status.setEditable(false);
        try {
            TimeClock TC = (TimeClock)
                          Naming.lookup("rmi://" +
                          getCodeBase().getHost() +
                          "/TimeClock");
        } catch (Exception e) {
            System.out.println("Error: " + e.toString());
            status.setText(e.toString());
        }
    }
    public boolean handleEvent(Event e) {
        if(e.target instanceof Button) {
            try {
                status.setText(TC.punch(id.getText(),
                              passwd.getText()));
                return true;
            } catch (RemoteException ex) {
                status.setText(ex.toString());
            }
        }
         return false;
    }
}
```

To recap, this applet checks the registry on the machine that it was served from for an object registered under the name "TimeClock." The applet then waits for user input. Once a Button event is caught, the values of two textFields are sent to the TimeClockServer through its punch() method. The applet then checks authentication and adds the employee to its "on the clock" vector. A second call would take the employee off the clock and add an entry to the logFile. All results are printed in the status TextArea in the applet. This applet needs to be compiled, but because it doesn't export any objects, there is no need to generate a stub or skeleton class:

```
javac -c /home/MyClasses TimeClockApplet.java
```

# Embedding the Applet in a Little HTML

An applet is only an applet if it is embedded in an HTML document. Listing 4-8 shows a simple HTML document that embeds the TimeClockApplet that you just created. Let's assume that your machine is named www.foo.com, and that all of the class files that you have created can be found on this server with the URL http://www.foo.com/home/MyClasses.

Listing 4-8. The Punch Clock applet document (TimeClockApplet.html)

```
<HTML>
<HEAD>
<TITLE>TimeClockApplet</TITLE>
</HEAD>
<BODY>
<H1>Please type in your Employee id and passwd to puch in or
 out</H1>
<APPLET   code="rmibook.timeclock.TimeClockApplet.class"
          codebase="/home/MyClasses/"
          width=400
          height=300 >
</APPLET>
</BODY>
</HTML>
```

# Starting the Applet

Now that all the pieces are together, let's start it up. If rmiregistry is not already running, start it as you did in the previous example. Now, before starting the TimeClockServer, you must first create an authFile. The authFile can be created with a text editor and placed in the same directory as the TimeClockServer class file. Alternatively, in the TimeClockServer.java source file, you could give an absolute path to the file in the local file system. In either case, the contents of the file are ID/password pairs separated by linefeeds as follows:

```
Troy foo
Bob bar
mary mypass
id2 otherpass
. . .
```

Once this file is in place, start the server with the following command:

```
java -d /home/MyClasses rmibook.timeclock.TimeClockServer &
```

To test the server, use appletviewer or an HTML browser that supports JDK 1.1 applets and load the HTML file you created over the network. If you are using appletviewer, the following command will take care of this:

```
appletviewer http://www.foo.com/TimeClockApplet.html
```

# Summary

You have created your first RMI-based clients and servers. As you can see, this can be a very simple process. The steps include defining a remote method interface, implementing the interface, registering with an RMI registry server, building a client that locates the object using a URL to the same registry, and then calling the methods as you would any other local methods. The examples you have used were relatively simple.

The following chapter deals with more complex examples and leads into complex parameters and return types.

# Chapter 5

# Passing and Returning Parameters on a Network

IN THIS CHAPTER

- ◆ Sending data the old-fashioned way
- ◆ Serializing data
- ◆ Implementing serialization protocols
- ◆ Sending data with RMI

RMI IS HEAVILY DEPENDENT on the ability to send objects to and from methods on remote machines. I will start out by taking a look at handling data structures by hand, and then conclude with the RMI model for representing objects in a form that can be easily passed to remote methods over the network.

One of the outstanding differences between remote method invocations and remote procedure calls is the underlying structure of the programs and the "procedures" being invoked. RPC is a procedurally based client-server architecture. It assumes that procedures on a machine will be called from a remote client, that parameters will be network representations for simple data types, and that it doesn't allow remote memory references to be passed around among peers. RMI in its most refined form gives us the same basic functionality, but, and this is the important part, it assumes an object-oriented architecture. RMI was designed with objects in mind.

When a client wants to invoke a method on a remote machine, it doesn't simply ask for the address of the method, it requests a handle to the actual object that implements the method. This object may contain other methods that can also be invoked once the object handle has been obtained. On the other hand, an application that was written in an object-oriented system takes more than simple data types as arguments, and returns more than simple data types as return values. In many cases, methods are used to create new objects, requiring objects to be passed as parameters when they are invoked. You might think that this is the same as passing the addresses of structures when writing programs in C, but once the method or procedure migrates to another machine, the reference no longer means anything, as a pointer is nothing more than a memory location on a particular machine.

Requirements change drastically once an application is distributed between two or more machines. Data that would normally be passed by reference must now be passed by value. In other words, the original variable stays intact because you are passing the address of the variable rather than just a value. But in certain circumstances, you really do want to pass a reference to data that resides physically somewhere else. This opens up an entirely new set of problems, requiring that objects be accessed via proxies or some other communication mechanisms so a remote client can remotely affect data that resides elsewhere.

In the RMI model, both of these problems are addressed. The basic model is that any object that is sent to a remote procedure as a parameter or returned by a remote procedure as a return value is passed by value. This means that a copy of the object is passed, and not the original or a reference to the original. The exception to this rule is an object that has been exported as a remote object—in other words, an object that implements remote methods. In this case, a client-side proxy or "stub" is passed to the client. This stub represents an object that resides on the host, or server machine. Any interactions with the stub are forwarded to the original, which takes care of actually performing any of the operations that were requested of the stub.

In this chapter, you are going to take a look at the needs for handling nontrivial parameter passing, or passing of parameters that are not simple data types. This should demonstrate the pros and cons of low-level data transfer verses the use of high-level interfaces for data transfer.

# Moving Data the Old-Fashioned Way

When sending data structures from one machine to another, you must put the data into a form that can be sent across the network. This normally involves implementing a transmission protocol, including some sort of markers for delimiting the fields and records being sent over the line. Network connections are, for the most part, serial, and the data must be "flattened" before it can be transmitted over these serial connections.

When working with a heterogeneous set of machines, you must also worry about varied representations of simple data types due to differences in sizes and byte order. For example, one machine may assume that an integer is a two-byte quantity with the bytes in big-endian order, and a second machine may assume that an integer is a four-byte quantity in little-endian order. Under these circumstances, a standard "network order" is usually assumed, and any particular platform knows how to convert integers, floats, and other data types from network order to local representation.

In the RMI model, one can assume a homogeneous platform, namely the Java platform, as RMI is a Java-specific implementation of a distributed object system, similar to an ORB in the CORBA model. But even assuming a homogeneous environment, at some level, a protocol must be developed to handle the disassembly, transmission, and reconstruction of data. Take a look at how you

## Big Endian/Little Endian

When designing computer chips, the chip designer must decide how to store data. In essence, the byte order of multibyte quantities varies among different types of hardware. Big-endian order refers to the most significant byte (MSB) preceding the least significant byte (LSB). In little-endian order, the bytes are swapped to LSB/MSB. The name is a reference to characters in *Gulliver's Travels*, by Jonathan Swift, who thought it was better to crack an egg from the big end rather than the small end. Thus, the big-endians versus the little-endians.

could transmit an object over a socket connection in Java and rebuild an object on the receiving side. You will use the standard `java.net.*` class libraries to create a socket and transmit data over that socket.

First, create a class that contains the data that you wish to transmit. This is a simple class that essentially is equivalent to a struct in a C program:

```
class MyData {
  int x;
  int y;
  String[] s;
  MyData(int x, int y, String[] s) {
    this.x=x;
    this.y=y;
    this.s = s;
  }
}
```

If you were using only numeric types, this would be a simple set of data to send. Because the size of simple types is well-defined in a homogeneous environment, you could write all of the data to a socket stream, and the data could be read right back into the appropriate variable types. In other words, the receiver would know that an `int` is always 32 bits, so it could just read 32 bits from a socket stream and store that directly into an integer variable. In this class, you also have an array of strings. An array of strings can be of arbitrary size, so you must handle either delimiting the strings or tagging the array with an integer that represents the number of strings that it contains. This way the receiver can read a simple type—an integer—and from the value of that integer determine how many strings must be read in order to read the entire array. In this case, not only will the data be sent over the connection, but so will information about one of its fields, namely the s field.

With this in mind, assume that you will send the data in order and insert an integer before the s field that represents the number of strings that are contained in the array. In this case the actual data for this object will appear in the stream as a contiguous string of bytes that look like the representation in Figure 5-1.

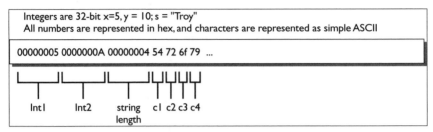

Figure 5-1. A stream representation of a data structure

## Serializing the Data

Serializing the data is the process of breaking down the components into a serial stream of bytes. Before you serialize the data, you must establish a socket to another machine and get the stream associated with that socket. Once you have this, you can create a `DataOutputStream` and write your data directly to that stream. The following code fragment creates a socket and gets a `DataOutputStream` from the socket once created. This stream will be used when writing your data (to make the code simple, I omitted exception handling from it):

```
Socket s = new Socket("host", port);
   //assume host is a real machine name, and port is an
   //integer port number on that machine
DataOutputStream dops = new
DataOutputStream(s.getOutputStream());
```

Once you have the `DataOutputStream`, you can create an instance of your object, and start serializing its data:

```
String[] sa = {"Troy", "Downing"};
MyData md = new MyData(5,6, sa);
dops.writeInt(md.x);
dops.writeInt(md.y);
dops.writeInt(md.s.length); //write the array length
for(int c = 0; c < sa.length; c++)
   dos.writeUTF(sa[c]);
```

Notice that you write the array length before iterating through your `string` array. The receiver must then read the length before reading the appropriate number of `strings` necessary for recreating the data structure. The following code creates a server socket, waits for a connection, gets a `DataInputStream` from the connection, and reads your data structure from that connection:

```
//establish the server
ServerSocket ss = new ServerSocket(port);
//wait for a connection and then return a Socket
```

```
Socket cs = ss.accept();
//get an input stream from the client socket
DataInputStream dis = new DataInputStream(cs.getInputStream());
//Start reading the data
int x = dis.readInt(); //read the first int
int y = dis.readInt(); //read the second int
int len = dis.readInt(); //read the length of the array
String[] s = new String[len]; //create a temp array
for(int c = 0; c < len; c++)  //populate the temp array
    s[c] = dis.readUTF();
MyData md = new MyData(x,y,s); //create the object from
                               //the data
```

That wasn't too painful for the simple example that you just covered. But you made some assumptions about the application that may not be valid. First off, you made the assumption that the server would only read data for `MyData` objects. This may not be the case. In a more realistic application, there may be several types of data that get serialized and rebuilt. In this case, you would want the data to be preceded by another tag, or header, that specified the object that follows. This way, the receiver can decide how to read and interpret the data coming over the line by first reading this header and using the appropriate algorithms for decoding the data and rebuilding the object.

Another consideration is handling more complex data types within your object, `HashTables`, for example. You would have to dissect these complex types and turn them into reasonably simple elements that could then be tagged, sent, and reconstructed. At some level, this must happen regardless. All data must be converted to a representation that is appropriate for sending it through a stream.

## Using a Simple Server to Test Protocols

When developing network applications, it's nice to verify that the data you think is being sent, is in fact that data being sent. This is actually a very simple task when dealing with text-based protocols, such as HTTP. When I want to test a server application, I often use a simple terminal emulator, such as Telnet, and just connect to the port number that the service is running on. Once connected, I can type commands to the server, and any results are displayed back to my terminal. If you've never done this, give it a try.

Connect to port 80 on a Web server using Telnet:

`$ telnet www.foo.com 80`

Once connected, you won't get a response from the server, so just type an HTTP request into the terminal window. The following request will ask for the default homepage on the server:

*continued*

## Using a Simple Server to Test Protocols *(Continued)*

```
GET / HTTP/1.0
```

Be sure to follow the command with two carriage returns (HTTP requires an extra blank line follow the request header). You should now see the source code for the HTML document scrolling down your terminal window. This is a very simple trick for testing servers that use text protocols, but sometimes you want to be able to test the client as well. In this case, you will normally want a server that allows connections to be made and then simply echoes data that is sent over a connection to standard out. This allows you to see what is actually coming over the pipe.

The following code will do exactly that: It will wait for a client to connect and then read the client socket until the connection is closed, printing any data that is read to the standard output stream. Once the connection is closed by the client, the server then waits for another connection and does the same thing over again.

Most of your network applications will use protocols that are not entirely text-based. In this case, you can subclass an application and override the readData() and getConnection() methods to deal with the particular protocol you are testing. Just to get started, run this program on a free port, and then connect to it with a Web browser. The URL will simply be the machine name that the server is running on followed by a colon and the port number that you started it on. For example: http://foo.com:6060. Listing 5-1 shows the server.

**Listing 5-1. The Server Testing Code (ServerTest.java)**

```java
package rmibook.util;

import java.net.*;
import java.io.*;

//Simple server that listens to a port and prints out
//any data that comes in over the socket.

public class ServerTest {

    private static final int DEFAULT_PORT = 6000;

    private static int port; //the port to listen to
    private static Socket client;//the client socket
    private static ServerSocket server;//the Server socket
    private static BufferedReader stream;//the stream used
                                        //for reading data

    public static void main (String arg[]) {
        //determine the port to listen to
        if(arg.length == 1)
            port = Integer.parseInt(arg[0]);
        else
```

```
            port = DEFAULT_PORT;
        //set up the server socket.
        try {
            server = new ServerSocket(port);
            System.out.println("Server started on port# " +
                port);
        } catch (IOException e) {
            System.out.println(e.toString());
            System.exit(0);
        }

        //loop waiting for socket
        //connections and reading from them
        while(true){
            getConnection();
            readData();
        }
    }

    static void readData(){
    //read data from the stream buffer. You may want to
    //override this for applications with specific protocol
    //requirements.

        try {
            while(true)
                System.out.println(stream.readLine());
        } catch (IOException e) {
            System.out.println("Connection closed.");
        }
    }

    static void getConnection(){
    // wait for a client connection, then create a
    // buffered reader from the connection. In apps that
    // don't use text protocols, you may want to override
    // this and use a DataInputStream, or other type of
    // stream interface

        System.out.println(" Waiting for connection...");
        try {
            client = server.accept();
            System.out.println("Got Connection");
            stream = new BufferedReader(new
                InputStreamReader(client.getInputStream())); }
catch (IOException e) {
            System.out.println(e.toString());
            System.exit(0);
        }
    }
}
```

# Implementing a Communications Protocol

In the previous example, you dealt with the representation of data in a stream, but not with the communication between the client and the server. In your example, you assumed that a server would wait for a connection and then immediately read data that represented a MyData object. This is a pretty simple model for most applications. In many cases, you will also implement a client/server communications protocol that allows one or the other to send or request data as needed. For example, your server may want to be able to send data back to the client rather than just accept what the client has offered. The client may also want to request data from the server or, at the very least, acknowledgment that the data was received and makes sense.

A simple protocol for doing this would be to set some rules that any data or request is preceded with an opcode that represents the type of operation. This could be easily represented as unique integers that are read when available and interpreted to mean something specific within the protocol. Let's assume you have the following opcodes defined:

```
int REQUESTOBJECT = 1;
int HELLO = 2;
int OBJECTFOLLOWS = 3;
int OBJECTRECEIVED = 4;
int ERROR = 5;
int RESEND = 6;
```

With this very simple set of opcodes, you could establish a communication protocol such as the following, as illustrated in Figure 5-2:

1. The server waits for a connection from a client.

2. A client connects.

3. The client notifies the server that it has connected by sending a HELLO to the server.

4. The server returns a HELLO, so both client and server can be reasonably sure that they are speaking with the same protocol.

    If either client or server fail to transmit a HELLO opcode, an error is produced.

5. The client requests an object by sending a REQUESTOBJECT opcode.

6. The server responds with an OBJECTFOLLOWS opcode followed by the serialized object.

7. The client reads the object, and if all is well, it sends an OBJECTRECEIVED opcode. Otherwise, an ERROR opcode is sent.

    The client has the option of re-requesting the object by sending a RESEND opcode, in which case the transaction is repeated.

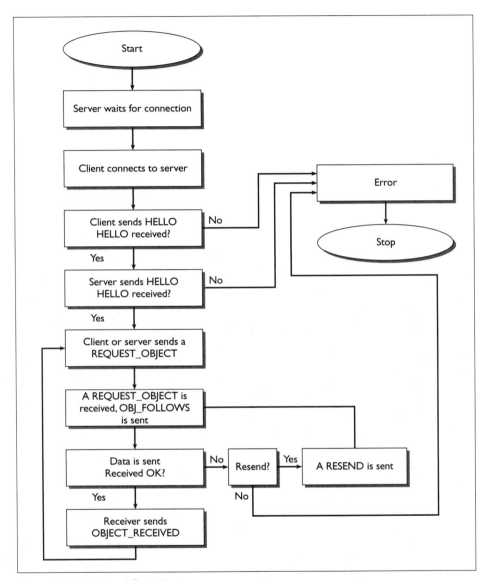

Figure 5-2. A protocol flow chart

In this model, either client or server will read integers from its input stream and take action based on those integers. Either party has the option of sending an object by preceding the object with an OBJECTFOLLOWS opcode or requesting an object with a REQUESTOBJECT opcode. The serialized objects can then define a header tag that identifies the object type, and the receiver can reconstruct the appropriate type based on that header.

In any nontrivial network application, it is necessary to have some sort of protocol for doing all of the transaction processing and data brokerage.

## Advantages of a Simple Serialization Protocol

One of the advantages of serializing data in the manner just described is that every code/decode algorithm can be written in a very efficient manner. For example, an object that contains only simple types such as a fixed number of integers, floats, and Booleans has a fixed and well-defined size. A receiving application knows exactly how many bytes to read at the beginning and can buffer the entire object from the input stream before rebuilding it locally. Or if a fixed number of objects are expected that are also of a fixed size, the receiving application can read a large number of objects at once and then rebuild them from the buffer, making the communication part of the application much more efficient than in more general-purpose solutions. For example, a protocol that allows arbitrary data of varying size often requires the inefficient method of searching the input stream for stop characters and/or length tags. This can result in smaller blocks of data being read at a time and thereby affect performance.

## Disadvantages of a Simple Serialization Protocol

One of the biggest disadvantages of this type of low-level handling of the transfer of data structures is the time and attention that must be given to writing handlers for every structure you create. In the previous example, you had to define a transfer mechanism for every field of your structure. This problem compounds once you start including other objects other than simple types as field values. Ideally, you would want to create a method for each structure that knows how to handle the transfer for that particular structure. If you defined an interface that all of your objects implemented, you could use a convention whereby every object implemented a writeMe method that handled the transfer of its field values. Assuming that any objects that are also field values in this first object also implemented such an interface, you could structure an object graph and traverse the graph calling every field's writeMe method until the entire object was transferred. Of course, the reconstruction of the objects would also be complicated, and the objects would have to know how to reconstruct themselves on the other side as well. (See Figure 5-3.)

It should be obvious that the level of detail required to program such a system creates a heavy burden on the programmer. Using this model, you can spend more time writing the serialization and transfer protocols than working on the main areas of your program. What you really want is a very simple interface to a system that handles this for us. This way, you can assume that any object you create will know how to write and read itself to a stream, and all you have to worry about as programmers is the structure of your main program, not the details of sending data.

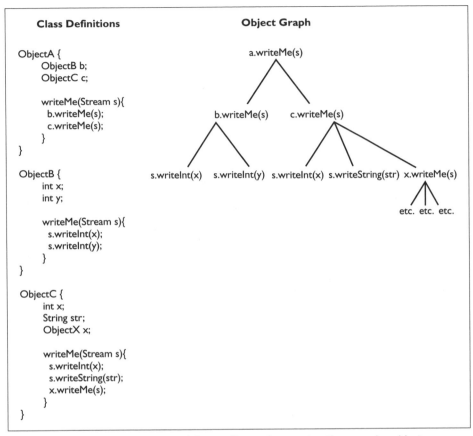

**Class Definitions**

ObjectA {
    ObjectB b;
    ObjectC c;

    writeMe(Stream s){
        b.writeMe(s);
        c.writeMe(s);
    }
}

ObjectB {
    int x;
    int y;

    writeMe(Stream s){
        s.writeInt(x);
        s.writeInt(y);
    }
}

ObjectC {
    int x;
    String str;
    ObjectX x;

    writeMe(Stream s){
        s.writeInt(x);
        s.writeString(str);
        x.writeMe(s);
    }
}

**Object Graph**

a.writeMe(s)

b.writeMe(s)        c.writeMe(s)

s.writeInt(x)  s.writeInt(y)  s.writeInt(x) s.writeString(str)  x.writeMe(s)

etc. etc. etc.

Figure 5–3. An object graph traversal for sending and reconstructing complex objects

By assuming a high-level interface to such a mechanism, it enables us to write applications, quickly, without concern for the gory details (but a general-purpose solution may not always be as efficient as a low-level algorithm). For the most part, however, it is better to be able to quickly prototype and implement your programs than to worry about the absolute fastest algorithms for transferring your data.

Sometimes the general-purpose solution is not good enough. You also need a means to override the general and implement the specific. You can assume that the general solution will look at the structure of your classes that you want to send over the line, construct an object graph for the class, and traverse the graph, sending the field data for all of the fields to be read and reconstructed on the receiver's side. Well, in some instances, you may not want *all* of the field values to be sent. Perhaps you want them to be reset to default values on the receiver's side. Or you may want to calculate new field values when the class is reconstructed. In other words, you need some means for overriding the general-purpose solutions so that you can impose such policies on the transfer of your data.

# Passing Parameters the Newfangled Way

Now that you have a pretty good idea of the issues surrounding sending nontrivial data over a stream, I'll put them into perspective with the RMI architecture.

RMI requires a simple mechanism for sending objects on a data stream. One of the major reasons for using RMI in the first place is that it provides a simple interface for writing code that calls methods on remote machines. So it only makes sense that a simple mechanism should also exist for sending the data associated with these remote calls.

On the most basic level, RMI is based on the fact that a remote client must interact with the methods implemented in a class file on another machine. In order to interact with a remote object, the client must be able to obtain that object. Well, actually, the client will obtain a stub, or proxy, to the remote object, but nonetheless, an object must be returned. In this case, the object is, for all practical purposes, just a reference to an object that exists elsewhere. The stub acts as a local instance of the object, but in fact, all computation is happening on the remote host machine and not on the client machine.

The second issue is that you would have a pretty useless mechanism if remote procedure calls could take only simple data types as parameters. As a system developer, you want to be able to create rich, clever objects for solving your problems and not have to worry about how they will be passed and returned as parameters.

RMI was constructed in a way that allows us to easily pass most of the standard Java object types as parameters. Pretty much everything in the `java.lang.*` and `java.util.*` packages can be passed as parameters and returned as return values from remote method calls. This is due to the fact that most of the core classes in the Java API implement the `java.io.Serializable` interface. This interface tags these objects as appropriate for sending over a data stream. In general, any of the nonstatic and nontransient fields in the classes will be restored on the receiving end.

When you want to start crafting complex classes that can be sent to remote methods or returned from them, you must also implement this interface. The majority of your classes can literally just implement this interface. This is the general-purpose solution that you were discussing earlier. But the serialization facilities in Java also enable us to specify the means to serialize and reconstruct your classes. With these mechanisms in place, they allow us to quickly create complex types that can be sent to remote methods, while providing us the flexibility to specify serialization policies when the need arises.

# Summary

I have demonstrated the various issues involved in sending nontrivial data across a network, and the pros and cons associated with high-level interfaces and low-level protocol implementations for handling these data transfers.

At the core of the RMI model is the need to send objects over the network. You need to send a proxy to a local object, as well as send copies of an object for remote reconstruction. The `java.io.*` package defines a serializable interface that is used to tag objects, which can be serialized and sent over a stream. This package also defines methods for sending objects over various input and output streams. The basic architecture enables us to create objects that can take advantage of these methods quickly and easily. It also gives us the ability to customize these transactions.

All of this is based on the object serialization facilities that were introduced with the core libraries of the JDK version 1.1.

In Chapter 6 you will take a look at the object serialization architecture, including customized transmission of objects and the underlying mechanisms that make this work. You will also learn about object security issues and the various implementation issues that surround serializing and externalizing objects.

# Chapter 6

# Crafting Serializable Objects

## IN THIS CHAPTER

♦ Object serialization architecture

♦ Read/write routines

♦ Transient and static fields

♦ Externalized objects

♦ Object streams and their formats

AS MENTIONED IN CHAPTER 5, the RMI architecture would be impossible to implement without some method for sending objects over network connections. Without this facility, parameters and return values would be limited to simple data types, thereby rendering the system useful for only the most trivial of applications. But even if that were the case, there would still be the need to send the data for stub objects to do the remote objects' bidding on the remote client's system.

In this chapter, I discuss *object serialization*–the methods used to duplicate an object by writing its field values to a stream and recreating a copy of the object from these field values. This chapter focuses on the high-level usage of object serialization. I also discuss lower-level details, but I don't cover the byte-level representation of serialized objects in detail. For detailed information on the actual byte-level representation of a traversed object graph, consult the online documentation at www.javasoft.com.

It is important to note that the recreation of the object is a copy and not the original object. Serialized objects are always copies of an original. When it is desirable to send a reference to an object, rather than a copy (to pass by reference instead of pass by value), simply use a Remote object, or in other words, an object that is exported either implicitly by extending java.rmi.server.UnicastRemoteObject or explicitly by passing the object to UnicastRemoteObject.exportObject(Remote) and in either case, implementing a Remote interface. For a list of serializable classes in the standard Java class libraries, see Table 6-1. (Any classes in the core libraries that extend the classes in Table 6-1 are also serializable.)

TABLE 6-1 Serializable Classes

| Package | Class(es) |
|---------|-----------|
| java.lang | Character, Boolean, String, Throwable, Number, StringBuffer |
| java.util | HashTable, Random, Vector, Date, BitSet, |
| java.io | File |
| java.net | InetAddress |
| java.awt | BorderLayout, Color, Component, Dimension, Event, Font, Polygon, CardLayout, FontMetrics, Image, Window, FlowLayout, GridLayout, Point, Rectangle, MenuComponant, Insets, CheckboxGroup, MediaTracker, GridBagLayout, GridBagConstraints, Cursor, SystemColor |

# Object Serialization Architecture

Essentially all of the classes in the core Java class libraries that it makes sense to serialize are *serializable*. Most of the classes in the `java.*`, for instance, are serializable. In general, a class that contains *only* static and/or transient fields isn't serializable. Also, classes that are used to represent objects or resources that are specific to a local Virtual Machine are not serializable. In these cases, it really doesn't make sense to be able to send the object down a stream, and it also may be a security risk to send these objects.

In general, any object that is serializable must implement the `Serializable` interface, implement a subclass of the `Serializable` interface, or extend an object that already implements the `Serializable` interface. This interface does not define any fields or methods but is used simply as a marker to tag objects that should be permitted serialization. I could oversimplify object serialization by saying "any object can be serialized by implementing the `java.io.Serializable` interface." This, in a simple sense, is true. The problem is that it doesn't always make sense to serialize objects, or to pass on values in objects that may not make sense out of context. You need a method to protect certain values from being sent with an object and to manually rebuild objects with special needs.

When using the default serialization of an object, note that any fields marked transient or static will not be serialized with the object. When the object is reconstructed from the stream that it was sent to, the default values for transient and static fields are set. Essentially, these field values are set to the values they would have if the object had just been instanced from scratch. This provides you with a mechanism for making data secure, and for preventing data from being sent that doesn't really make sense outside of the context that it was created in. For many applications, default serialization is all you need for serializing and reconstructing data.

## The Bytecode of Serialized Objects

Object serialization is not magic. An object stream, or a subclass of a stream that is capable of carrying objects, does not transmit the bytecode for an object. In other words, the compiled class file is not transmitted (a common misunderstanding), but rather a representation of its structure and related data. An object stream contains some header information that is used to rebuild objects that it contains, along with the data for these objects. In order to transmit an object over an object stream, the sending system writes the type of that object and the values of each of its fields to the stream. To rebuild an object, the receiver first reads the type of the object from the stream, then constructs a new object of that type, and then reads the values of the fields for the object from the stream. This means that the receiver of the object must know what type of object it is reading. So how does this work?

When an object is being read from an object stream, the run-time environment on the receiving side must have access to the bytecode for the class of the object. The .class file for the object being recreated must be accessible either via the local classpath or via standard class loader mechanisms (such as the codebase in a URL).

When the object is being recreated, the bytecode is loaded from the local system, if it's available. If it can't be found locally, the AppletClassLoader or the RMIClassLoader (whichever is being used by the current run-time system) attempts to load the .class file. If the bytecode is inaccessible via either of these mechanisms, a ClassNotFoundException is thrown and deserialization fails.

When you are using RMI, this all happens automatically. If a sender passes an instance of a class to a remote system and the remote system doesn't know the class type of the instance, the class is loaded dynamically—possibly by downloading it from the sender. For more information, consult an online document such as

```
http://java.sun.com/products/jdk/1.1/docs/guide/rmi/spec/rmi-
arch.doc.html#280
```

where this behavior is discussed in detail.

# Defining Your Own Read/Write Routines

Take a look at a simple object and how it is sent down an object stream:

```
class MyObject implements java.io.Serializable {
  int x;
  int y;
  MyObject(int x, int y){
    this.x = x;
    this.y = y;
  }
}
```

This is a pretty simple object that could be used to describe a point in 2-space. Because it implements the Serializable interface, this object could be sent to an object stream with the following code:

```
MyObject point = new MyObject(10,20);
ObjectOutputStream oos = new ObjectOutputStream(SomeOutputStream);
oos.writeObject(point);
```

With some minor exception handling, the previous code example creates a new MyObject, creates an ObjectOutputStream (assuming that SomeOutputStream is a valid OutputStream object), and writes the MyObject data to that stream.

Using the default serialization methods, the system figures out (through reflection mechanisms) the composition of the object and sends the values of x and y to the stream along with header and version information that is used to identify the class type. The receiver can then rebuild the object, assuming there is local access to the MyObject bytecode, with the following code:

```
MyObject point;
ObjectInputStream ois = new
   ObjectInputStream(SomeInputStream);
point = (MyObject)ois.readObject();
```

Notice that you had to cast the object being read to the appropriate type. The readObject() method returns a java.lang.Object, so the standard rules for casting in Java are in effect.

Now that you've seen how to read and write an object using the default serialization mechanisms, look at how to create custom serialization methods. First off, how do you manually deconstruct/construct an object? Essentially, there are three rules for creating custom serialization:

1. The object must implement java.io.Serializable.

2. The object must define a no-argument constructor.

3. The object must define its own readObject() and writeObject() methods.

In the case of default serialization, only rule 1 applies. The class only needs to implement the Serializable interface or subclass a class that does this already.

So what does this mean? Well, when an object is being serialized, the system checks to see whether the object defines a readObject() and writeObject() method. Then it checks for a no-argument constructor. If it finds these, the system calls the writeObject() method for the object and passes it an ObjectStream so that the object can essentially serialize itself. Then, on the receiving side, the object is instanced using its no-argument constructor. The readObject() method is then called and passed an ObjectInputStream object that is used to reconstruct the object data.

Take another look at your MyObject class. This time, create your own serialization routines for writing and reconstructing the object. In this example, I won't do anything fancy but just demonstrate how the process works:

```
Class MyObject implements java.io.Serializable {
    int x;
    int y;
    public MyObject() {
     //no-arg constructor
    }

    public MyObject(int x, int y){
     this.x=x;
     this.y=y;
    }

    void writeObject(ObjectOutputStream s)
        throws java.io.IOException {
      s.writeInt(x);
      s.writeInt(y);
    }

    void readObject(ObjectInputStream s)
        throws java.io.IOException {
      x = s.readInt();
      y = s.readInt();
    }
}
```

In this trivial example, the reconstructed object is no different than if you had used the default serialization, but the readObject and writeObject methods can be used to calculate new field values or handle special processing of data.

Some objects contain other objects. An array object, for example, can contain many other objects. When serializing an object that contains other objects, you must make sure that all of these are serializable. Accordingly, if you serialize a more complex object, such as one that has fields that are not simple types, you must take care that all of the references contained in the object that are not marked transient or static are serializable. For example, a Vector is serializable, but what happens if the Vector contains objects that are not serializable? Well, just what you'd think: An exception is thrown and serialization fails.

When the object is being serialized, a graph representing the object and the object references that it contains is constructed. When the object is being written to an object stream, this graph is traversed and the data for all of the objects in the graph are serialized in the same manner.

# Transient and Static Fields

As I mentioned earlier, by default serialization does not send the data for transient or static fields. So assume that you want to prevent certain fields from being serialized. Simply marking them as static or transient takes care of this for you. You should note, however, that changing a variable from an instance variable to a static variable changes the semantics of this field and affects how the whole class works. So if you simply want to hide a field, without otherwise changing the behavior of the class, mark the field as transient rather than static. For example, using your previous example, make the two fields transient:

```
class MyObject implements java.io.Serializable {
  transient int x;
  transient int y;

  public MyObject(int x, int y) {
    this.x=x;
    this.y=y;
  }
}
```

In this example, it really makes no sense to serialize the object, since the values for x and y are both set to the default value, 0, upon reconstitution. This behavior can be overridden if you design custom readObject() and writeObject() methods.

Sometimes, it is desirable to set the values of static fields from a serialized object. Because the static fields won't be serialized using default serialization, you must write the values and restore them with readObject() and writeObject() methods. This is similar to the example that you saw in the beginning of this section.

# Object Streams

Serialization is built upon stream objects that have been extended to take care of all of the dirty work involved with deconstructing and reconstructing Objects.

These stream objects implement either the `ObjectInput` or `ObjectOutput` interfaces (which in turn extend either the `DataInput` or `DataOutput` interfaces).

The `ObjectInput` interface declares a set of methods used to read simple data and objects and to perform basic stream operations such as closing and flushing. Likewise, the `ObjectOutput` interface declares a set of methods used to write simple data and objects as well as perform basic stream operations.

## The ObjectInputStream Class

The `ObjectInputStream` class is used to access objects that have been written to an `ObjectOutputStream` stream. An object is reconstituted by calling the `readObject()` method of the `ObjectInputStream` object. The syntax is as follows:

```
Object o = MyObjectInputStream.readObject();
```

The object is reconstituted in the following manner. First, a header is read from the stream identifying the object. The `ByteCode` for the object is accessed via a local classpath or through standard `ClassLoader` mechanisms. An instance of the object is created using its no-argument constructor. The `ObjectInputStream` then sets the object's field values through calls to its `readObject()` method. If a `readObject()` method was not defined, the `defaultReadObject()` method is called on the object; this method performs a default reinitialization of the object by reading the values for its nontransient and nonvolatile fields from the `ObjectInputStream`.

## The ObjectOutputStream Class

The `ObjectOutputStream` class is used to store serialized objects. The objects that are written to the `ObjectOutputStream` can be read from the receiving side of the stream by an `ObjectInputStream` object.

The `ObjectOutputStream` implements the `ObjectOutput` interface and extends the `OutputStream` class, so any of the methods used to manipulate the stream or write data using an `OutputStream` can also be used with an `ObjectOutputStream`. When an object is written to the stream using the `ObjectOutputStream`, the object is evaluated to see if it extends the `Serializable` interface (through standard Java type checking mechanisms), and then the object is written to the stream by calling the object's `writeObject()` method if it exists. If a `writeObject()` method is not found, default serialization occurs. Essentially, a header is written to the stream identifying the object, and then all of the nonstatic and nontransient field values are written to the stream.

# Externalized Objects

When serializing objects, the system handles most of the dirty work. For example, all class dependencies are handled automatically, so an object that extends another object doesn't need to worry about the parent object, which is automatically serialized and reconstituted if necessary. In other words, a class that uses default serialization is serialized from the ground up. Each superclass is serialized, and the readObject and writeObject methods only concern themselves with the class(es) to which they belong. After a parent class is serialized, the subclasses are then serialized in the same manner. The readObject and writeObject methods only bother reading and writing fields declared in their class; they don't bother with fields in any superclasses. Sometimes it is desirable to take control of the entire process and handle the serialization of the entire object graph. In this case, your serializable object must extend the Externalizable interface instead of the Serializable one. (Actually, Externalizable extends Serializable, so you are still dealing with Serializable objects.)

One major difference between Externalizable and Serializable objects is that an Externalizable object must define read and write methods. There is no default serialization for an Externalizable object. In the case of a Serializable object, you had the option to define readObject() and writeObject() methods to deconstruct and reconstruct your objects. Now, using the Externalizable interface, you are required to define readExternal() and writeExternal() methods to handle not only the serialization of the object fields but also the traversal of the object graph and the serialization of any base classes that were extended to create your external object.

As an example, an externalizable class may call methods in its superclass to cause the superclass to be written to an object stream. The following code is a base class that stores an instance of a derived class and explicitly calls its readExternal and writeExternal methods:

```
class ExternBase implements Externalizable {
   ExternSub es;//store subclass when it calls super()
   ExternBase(ExternSub es){
      this.es=es;
   }
   public void readExternal(ObjectInput oi) throws IOException {
      //read data for this class
      eb.readExternal(oi);
   }
   public void writeExternal(ObjecOutput oo) throws IOException {
      //write data for this class
      eb.writeExternal(oo);
   }
}
```

# Securing Sensitive Data

I've already discussed preventing fields from being serialized automatically by flagging them as either static or transient. This prevents the fields from being written to a stream that is calling the `defaultWriteObject()` method. In order to enforce this protection, a field can also be marked as private, thereby preventing any access to the field from outside of the class.

Classes with particularly sensitive data should not be serialized at all, but in most cases, simply marking the fields as private and transient should prevent any unwanted access.

To further protect fields that are reconstituted using the `readObject()` and `writeObject()` class methods, you may sometimes find it desirable to allow the reading/writing of sensitive data given certain criteria are met. In this case, the `readObject()` and `writeObject()` methods can simply throw a `NotSerializableException` if access to these fields is not permitted. This prevents any further attempts to serialize or deserialize the object.

# Versioning Serializable Classes

In order to facilitate class evolution, serializable classes define a version ID that is used to determine which version of a class is being serialized, and which version is expected when reconstituting. The version ID number is stored in the serializable class as a long integer. The version is stored in the field:

```
static final long Seria lVersionUID = nnnnn;
```

The version number of any class can be determined with a utility that is supplied with the JDK called "serialver." The serialver application takes a class, determines its `SerialVersionUID`, and prints out a string that can be pasted directly into an evolved class.

A `SerialVersionUID` is derived from the class and can be cut and pasted into all compatible classes based on an original. If the ID is not set, then a hash is generated for the class and is used for versioning purposes.

# Object Stream Formats

Data in an object stream is written in blocks with record tags. As Backus-Naur Form (BNF) is the standard technique for defining the syntax of a language, Table 6-2 shows a BNF-style representation of the basic grammar used to represent an object in an `ObjectStream`. Each term is followed by a set of rules that can be located somewhere else in the list. The *stream:* rule is the base representation. It can be described by the three terms that follow it—which are themselves described later on in the list using the same conventions. Table 6-3 represents some of the constants that are used in Table 6-2.

**TABLE 6-2 Rules for Representing a Serialized Object in an ObjectStream**

**Term: Rule1 Rule2 ...**

stream: magicnumber version contents

contents: data contents data

data: object blockdata

object: newObject newClass newArray newString newClassDesc prevObject nullReference exception

newClass: TC_CLASS classDesc newHandle

classDesc: newClassDesc nullReference (ClassDesc)prevObject

superClassDesc: classDesc

newClassDesc: TC_CLASSDESC className serialVersionUID newHandle classDescInfo

classDescInfo: classDescFlags fields classAnnotation superClassDesc

className: (UTF format String)

serialVersionUID: *long integer*

classDescFlags: *byte*

fields: (short) <count>fieldDesc[count]

fieldDesc: primitiveDesc objectDesc

primitiveDesc: prim_typecode fieldName modifiers

objectDesc: obj_typecode fieldName modifiers className

fieldName: (UTF format String)

modifiers: *short integer*

className: (String)object

classAnnotation: endBlockData contents endBlockData

prim_typecode: B | C | D | F | I | J | S | Z

obj_typecode: [ | L

*continued*

**Term: Rule1 Rule2 ...**

newArray: TC_ARRAY classDesc newHandle (int)<size> values[size]

newObject: TC_OBJECT classDesc newHandle classdata[]

classdata: nowrclass // SC_WRRD_METHOD &!classDescFlags wrclass objectAnnotation //SC_WRRD_METHOD & classDescFlags

nowrclass: values

wrclass: nowrclass

objectAnnotation: endBlockData contents endBlockData

blockdata: TC_BLOCKDATA (byte)<size>(byte)[size]

blockdatalong: TCBLOCKDATALONG (int)<size>(byte)[size]

endBlockData: TC_ENDBLOCKDATA

newString: TC_STRING newHandle (UTF format String)

prevObject: TC_REFERENCE (int) handle

nullReference: TC_NULL

exception: TC_EXCEPTION (Throwable)object

resetContext: TC_RESET

magicnumber: STREAM_MAGIC

version: STREAM_VERSION

values: *described by* classDesc

newHandle: *number in sequence assigned to object being serialized*

TABLE 6-3 **Serialized Object Representation Constants**

| Type | Name | Value |
| --- | --- | --- |
| short | STREAM_MAGIC | 0xaced |
| short | STREAM_VERSION | 5 |

*continued*

TABLE 6-3  Serialized Object Representation Constants  *(Continued)*

| Type | Name | Value |
|---|---|---|
| byte | TC_NULL | 0x70 |
| byte | TC_REFERENCE | 0x71 |
| byte | TC_CLASSDESC | 0x72 |
| byte | TC_OBJECT | 0x73 |
| byte | TC_STRING | 0x74 |
| byte | TC_ARRAY | 0x75 |
| byte | TC_CLASS | 0x76 |
| byte | TC_BLOCKDATA | 0x77 |
| byte | TC_ENDBLOCKDATA | 0x78 |
| byte | TC_RESET | 0x79 |
| byte | TC_BLOCKDATALONG | 0x7A |
| byte | TC_EXCEPTION | 0x7B |
| byte | SC_WRRD_METHODS | 0x01 |
| byte | SC_SERIALIZABLE | 0x02 |
| byte | SC_EXTERNALIZABLE | 0x04 |

A class that is serialized is represented in an `ObjectStream` using rules outlined in the preceding table. This format enables the system to easily read and identify the component parts of the serialized class and reconstruct it. For further reading, look for the online documentation on object serialization at `www.javasoft.com`.

# Summary

Object serialization involves a pretty straightforward and simple mechanism. In most cases, simply implementing the `Serializable` interface is all you need to do to create a serializable object. You should be aware of certain design issues when doing this, however, such as the performance hits you will suffer as an object graph grows more complex. Essentially, any object that extends another and contains many fields that point to other objects has the overhead of serializing not only its own base classes but also all of the classes to which its nonstatic and nontransient fields point (plus their base classes).

As far as rapid deployment is concerned, if you need to pass an object as a parameter or return value to a remote method invocation, all you need do is implement `Serializable` when you code your parameter object.

In Chapter 7, you will start to put some of this to work and look at designing applications that both use RMI and pass serializable objects as parameters.

# Part III

## Real-World Applications of Java RMI

# Chapter 7

# Building a Distributed Communication Server

IN THIS CHAPTER

- ◆ Basic server architecture
- ◆ Defining and implementing server and client interfaces
- ◆ Server threads
- ◆ Encapsulating messages

SOME OF THE MORE popular and intriguing applications popping up on the Internet involve personal communications. These may be text-only "chat" rooms, or graphical multiuser domains (MUDs). In either case, these applications involve arbitrating communication among many participants through a central server. The server is responsible for receiving and sending messages from and to the participants as well as maintaining lists of active participants.

In this chapter, you are going to write the server side of a distributed chat server. The server enables clients to register themselves and maintains a table of active participants. When a participant wishes to send a message to other participants that are currently logged on, a message is sent to the server application and is then distributed to the other participants. In Chapter 8, you will write a client that connects to this server and sends text messages and line drawings to other participants on the server (see Figure 7-1).

## Basic Server Architecture

The design of this server is relatively simple. The server starts a registry service and registers itself with that registry. It exports a method to enable clients to register themselves, query the server for a list of current participants, and post messages to the current group of participants (see Figure 7-2).

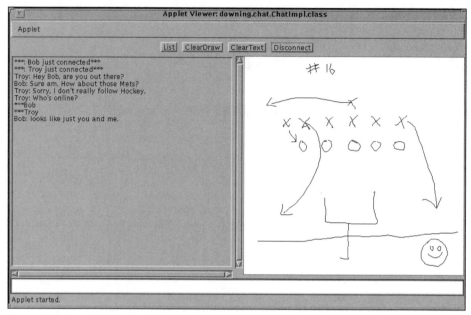

Figure 7-1. The Chat application interface

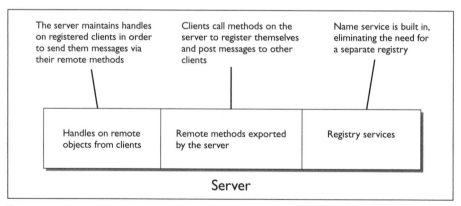

Figure 7-2. The server architecture

When a client registers itself, it passes a reference to itself that the server uses to send messages back to the client. This way, the client can remain idle until messages are received, and it doesn't have to do any server polling. In this application, accordingly, a client makes initial contact with the server via a registry, but it then passes a reference to one of its own remote objects via a remote method that is invoked on the server.

The server uses a simple Message object that can contain text messages or line drawings. This object could be easily extended to support more complex graphic elements, or other multimedia data types.

In order to maintain reasonable performance among clients, a thread is created to handle the sending of data to each individual client that is receiving data. This way, a client with a particularly slow connection does not cause the other clients to wait for it to catch up. This model introduces a minor problem in that some platforms have a limit to the number of threads that can be started, which effectively limits the number of connections that this server could maintain, but it is not unreasonable to consider linking multiple servers together to balance the load, or to group clients together sharing threads. The "thread group" solution is not ideal as it still may cause performance problems within a thread group if one of the peers goes down or performs poorly (see Figure 7-3).

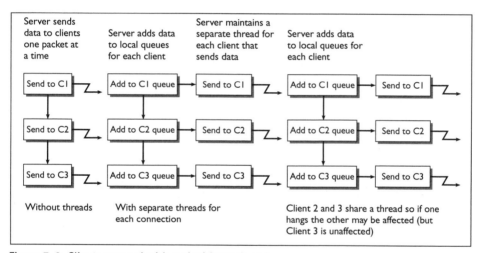

Figure 7-3. Clients grouped with and without threads

Because this chapter covers a full implementation of a server, I've included a lot of source code to help you. Sample sections of code are introduced and explained, but complete listings of particular source files are listed only after the code for a single source has been fully explained. All source code in this example is grouped in the rmibook.chat.* package. This way it matches the file structure on the CD. The source files that you create in this chapter are listed in Table 7-1.

TABLE 7-1 Source Code Components of the Chat Server

| Filename | Description |
| --- | --- |
| ChatServer.java | The interface that describes the remote methods that are exported by this server. This includes methods to register, post messages, and get participant lists. |
| ChatServerImpl.java | The implementation of the server. This implements the methods described in the `ChatServer` interface. |
| Line.java | A simple object that represents a line segment. This is used by the `Message` class for including line drawings in messages. |
| Message.java | This describes a simple message. It may contain a line, a text message, or both. This is the atomic form of messages sent from client to server to clients. |
| Talker.java | An extension of the `Thread` class that is used to send messages to individual clients. A new Talker is created for each client that connects to the server. |
| Chat.java | The interface that must be implemented by a client that connects to this server. |

# Defining the Server Interface

The first order of business is to describe the interface for the methods that you allow to be invoked remotely. The interface must be a subclass of the `java.rmi.Remote` interface and describe methods for registering a client, posting a message on the server, and retrieving a list of clients that are currently connected.

All of the source files for this server application are part of the `rmibook.chat.*` package. Accordingly, the file starts out with the following code:

```
package rmibook.chat;
import java.rmi.*;

public interface ChatServer extends Remote {
```

The first method that I describe is the `register()` method. This method takes a `Chat` object and a `String` as parameters. The `Chat` object is described in Chapter 8; it is essentially an interface that enables the server to perform callback methods on the client. This way, a client can be notified when data are available without querying or "polling" the server, which can be expensive.

The name string that is passed as the second parameter is simply an identification String that the server uses when queried about current participants:

```
public void register(Chat c, String name)
    throws RemoteException;
```

The next method in this interface, postMessage(), is used by the client to post messages to the server. When a message is posted, the server adds the message to the queue of every Talker thread that is currently associated with a participant. (As mentioned earlier, every client that connects to the server gets its own thread to handle communication to the particular client.) Once the message has been added to the queues of each of the participants, their individual Talkers forward the messages when they are able.

The postMessage() method takes a single argument, a Message object. This object contains the name of the client that sent it and either a text message to be broadcast, a line segment to be drawn, or both:

```
public void postMessage(Message m)
    throws RemoteException;
```

The final method of this interface, listChatters(), is used to query the server for a list of current participants. An array of Strings is returned, with each String corresponding to a participant's name that was passed when the participant registered with the server:

```
public String[] listChatters()
    throws RemoteException;
```

Listing 7-1 shows the complete interface. Three methods are described for registering, sending messages, and requesting user lists from a server.

**Listing 7-1. Chat server interface (ChatServer.java)**

```
package rmibook.chat;
import java.rmi.*;

public interface ChatServer extends Remote {

    //register a chatter with the server. Pass a reference
    //to the Chat client, and a name that it will be used
    //to identify the user
    public void register(Chat c,String name)
        throws RemoteException;

    //This is used to post broadcast messages
    //to the server
    public void postMessage(Message m)
        throws RemoteException;
```

```
//This will return a list of all of the chatters that
//are currently logged onto this server
public String[] listChatters()
    throws RemoteException;
}
```

# Implementing the Server Interface

This next section describes the bulk of this application. The `ChatServerImpl` class describes a `main()` method that sets a security manager, creates an instance of itself to be exported, creates a registry so that clients can locate it using simple URL addresses and the `java.rmi.Naming` class, and maintains a list of the clients that register themselves.

This class extends the `java.rmi.server.UnicastRemoteObject` class, which exports the remote object upon instantiation. This file uses objects from many of the Java packages, so there are a number of `import` statements at the beginning of the file that starts with these lines:

```
package rmibook.chat;

import java.rmi.*;
import java.rmi.server.*;
import java.rmi.registry.*;
import java.util.*;

public class ChatServerImpl
    extends UnicastRemoteObject
    implements ChatServer {
```

The next order of business is to create storage space for the clients that register themselves. Here you use a `Vector` to store the individual connections. Actually, when a user connects, a `Talker` object is created for it and added to this `Vector`. This way, when a message is broadcast to the participants, the application simply traverses the `Vector` and adds the message to each client's `Talker` object:

```
private Vector chatters = new Vector();
```

Now for your class constructor. The constructor takes no arguments but simply calls the constructor of the super class (`UnicastRemoteObject`). This would be done implicitly if omitted, but the `super()` method call is included here just to remind you that the `UnicastRemoteObject` constructor is being called and is exporting your remote object so that its methods can be invoked remotely. After calling the super constructor, you print a message explaining that the server is coming up:

```
public ChatServerImpl() throws RemoteException {
   super();
   System.out.println("Initializing Server.");
}
```

In the `main()` method, you first declare a variable for storing a registry that is used to access your server. Then set the security manager to be an instance of the RMI security manager. This is necessary because if a security manager is not explicitly set, stub classes will be allowed to load only from the local file system and not over the network. This behavior was described in Chapter 2.

Once your security manager is set, create an instance of a `ChatServerImpl` object that is bound in the registry under the name "ChatServerImpl." Then create a registry using the `LocateRegistry.createRegistry()` method and run it on port 5050. (This is an arbitrary port number that must be known by any client that connects to this server.) Once the registry is created, bind your `ChatServerImpl` object and print an informative message stating that the server is ready. In this example, you are creating a registry at run time instead of binding to another registry that is already running, such as the RMI registry application that I discussed in Chapter 3.

Instantiation of the `ChatServerImpl` object can produce a `RemoteException` if the system is unable to export this object. Also, the `Registry.bind()` method can produce an `AlreadyBoundException` if the name you chose is already bound in this registry (which is extremely unlikely, considering you created the registry within this application). In the case of either exception, print an informative message and exit the application.

Here is the `main()` method:

```
public static void main(String args[]){
   Registry reg;

   //A security manager must be set to allow stub
   //loading over the network
   System.setSecurityManager(new RMISecurityManager());
   try {
      //create an instance of the ChatServerImpl object
      //to export
      ChatServerImpl cs = new ChatServerImpl();

      //create a new registry running on port 5050
      reg = LocateRegistry.createRegistry(5050);

      //bind our cs object to this registry
      reg.bind("ChatServerImpl", cs);
      System.out.println("Server Ready");
   } catch (AlreadyBoundException e) {
      System.out.println("Name is already bound: " + e);
      System.exit(0);
   } catch (RemoteException e) {
      System.out.println("General Server Error: " + e);
      System.exit(0);
```

```
    }
}
```

Now implement the methods that were described in the `ChatServer` interface. The first one, `register()`, is simple. It simply takes a `Chat` object and a name as parameters, creates a `Talker` object with these parameters so that they have their own private thread for receiving messages, and then adds the `Talker` object to the `chatters` `Vector`. As you may recall, this `Vector` maintains a list of all of the registered chat clients:

```
synchronized public void register(Chat c, String name) {
    chatters.addElement(new Talker(c,name));
}
```

The next method is only slightly more complicated. The `listChatters()` method returns a list of all of the currently registered participants. It first creates an array of `Strings` that has the same number of elements as the `chatters` `Vector`. It then loops through the `Vector` and extracts the `Talker` objects in it. Each `Talker` keeps a reference to the name of its client. The names are extracted from the `Talker` objects and added to the array of `Strings`. Once the entire `Vector` has been traversed, the `String` array is returned:

```
public String[] listChatters() {
    String list[] = new String[chatters.size()];
    Talker c;

    for(int i=0; i< list.length; i++){
        c=(Talker)chatters.elementAt(i);
        list[i] = c.getChatterName();
    }
    return list;
}
```

The final remote method is the `postMessage()` method. This method is used by clients to post a message to the server. The server then distributes the message to each of the clients that are registered. As this method is called by many clients, take the precaution of declaring it synchronized. This prevents the possibility of messages getting out of order because one client called this method while it was still processing the previous invocation.

The messages are posted to registrants via their `Talker` objects. The `addMessage()` method is called on each `Talker` in the `chatters` `Vector`. The `addMessage()` method returns `true` if the message was added and is expected to be sent. If a value of `false` is returned, the client has either logged off or crashed. So if a `false` is returned, the `Talker` at the current index in the `chatters` `Vector` is removed and will no longer be a participant unless the client re-registers with the server:

```
synchronized public void postMessage(Message m){
```

```
        Talker t;
        for(int i=0; i < chatters.size() ; i++){
            t = (Talker)chatters.elementAt(i);
            if(!t.addMessage(m))
                chatters.removeElementAt(i--);
        }
    }
}
```

That was it for the `ChatServerImpl` implementation of your `ChatServer` interface. Listing 7-2 shows a complete listing of this source file.

**Listing 7-2. Implementation of the ChatServer interface (ChatServerImpl.java)**

```
package rmibook.chat;

import java.rmi.*;
import java.rmi.server.*;
import java.rmi.registry.*;
import java.util.*;

public class ChatServerImpl
    extends UnicastRemoteObject
    implements ChatServer {

    private Vector chatters = new Vector();

    public ChatServerImpl() throws RemoteException {
        super();
        System.out.println("Initializing Server.");
    }

    public static void main(String args[]){
        Registry reg;

        //A security manager must be set to allow stub
        //loading over the network
        System.setSecurityManager(new
            RMISecurityManager());
        try {
            //create an instance of the ChatServerImpl object
            //to export
            ChatServerImpl cs = new ChatServerImpl();

            //create a new registry running on port 5050
            reg = LocateRegistry.createRegistry(5050);

            //bind our cs object to this registry
            reg.bind("ChatServerImpl", cs);
            System.out.println("Server Ready");
        } catch (AlreadyBoundException e) {
            System.out.println("Name is already bound: " + e);
            System.exit(0);
```

```
        } catch (RemoteException e) {
          System.out.println("General Server Error: " + e);
          System.exit(0);
        }
    }

    synchronized public void register(Chat c,String name)
    {
        chatters.addElement(new Talker(c,name));
    }
    public String[] listChatters() {
        String list[] = new String[chatters.size()];
        Talker c;

        for(int i=0; i< list.length; i++){
            c=(Talker)chatters.elementAt(i);
            list[i] = c.getChatterName();
        }
        return list;
    }

    synchronized public void postMessage(Message m){
        Talker t;
        for(int i=0; i < chatters.size() ; i++){
            t = (Talker)chatters.elementAt(i);
            if(!t.addMessage(m))
                chatters.removeElementAt(i);
        }
    }
}
```

# Adding Threads to the Server

I discussed the Talker class a lot in the previous sections, so let's take a look at what that is. The Talker creates a separate execution thread for each client connected to the server. This approach enables the server to add messages to a client's queue without having to wait around for the client to receive the message. It also enables clients to receive messages at their own speed without slowing down the rest of the participants, and it further prevents a client that has crashed from hanging the system. Only a single thread is affected (see Figure 7-4).

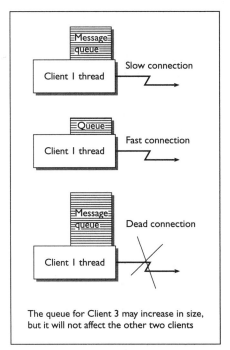

The queue for Client 3 may increase in size,
but it will not affect the other two clients

Figure 7-4. Partial failure on a threaded system

Threads are an integral part of many server applications because of the natural mapping of client communication to execution threads. In your server application, the `Talker` checks for messages in its queue. As long as there are messages, it attempts to send them to the client. As soon as the message queue is empty, the thread puts itself to sleep until more messages are added to its queue. Let's take a look at the `Talker` class.

You start out with the usual package and import statements, and then you declare your `Talker` class to extend the `Thread` class:

```
package rmibook.chat;
import java.util.*;
import java.rmi.*;

public class Talker extends Thread {
```

Now get the instance variables out of the way. First create your message queue. In this case, the messages are stored in a `Vector` called `messages`. Then declare a `Chat` variable that stores a reference to the client that this object will be sending its messages to. Create an `isActive` variable to note whether this is an active connection or not, and finally create a `String` in which to store the name of the `Chat` client:

```
private Vector messages = new Vector();
private Chat c;
boolean isActive = true;
private String name;
```

In your constructor, take a Chat object and a String as parameters. The Chat object is the client you are communicating with, and the String contains the name that the client is referred by. Set your instance variables with the values of these parameters, then call the start() method. This causes the thread to start executing, essentially looping through its run() method, which I will declare a bit later:

```
public Talker(Chat c, String name) {
    this.c = c;
    this.name=name;
    this.start();
}
```

Our Talker continues attempting to send messages as long as there are messages in the messages Vector. When a message is sent, it is removed from this Vector. Once the Vector is emptied, the thread puts itself in a sleep state. When a new message is added, the thread is then awakened and continues attempting to send messages until the queue is again emptied. The addMessage() method is used to add messages to the queue. This method first verifies that the connection is still alive by checking the isActive variable. (This variable will be set to false if a RemoteException is thrown while attempting to send a message.)

If the connection is still active, the thread is awakened with a call to the resume() method. Then, the message is added to the messages Vector to be sent along when the Talker is able. This method returns a Boolean value that is used to determine whether it should be dealt with in the future. In general when your server calls the addMessage() method, it checks the return value. If the value returned is false, the server assumes that there is a dead connection and removes this Talker from its client list. Here's the code:

```
public boolean addMessage(Message e){
    if(!isActive)
        return false;

    messages.addElement(e);
    resume();
return true;
}
```

In the main execution loop of your thread, check to make sure that there is at least one element in your messages Vector. If so, take the zeroth element in the Vector and send it to your client using the chatNotify() method described in the Chat interface. Once the message is sent, remove that element from the Vector and repeat until there are no more elements. At this point, put the thread to sleep with a call to the `suspend()` method. The thread will then be resumed the next time a message is added using the `addMessage()` method.

If a `RemoteException` is thrown, assume that the client connection has been lost, set your `isActive` variable to `false`, and shut down by stopping the thread.

As with any thread, the execution body is described by the `run()` method with an infinite loop declared inside:

```
public void run() {
    while(true){
        try {
            if(messages.isEmpty())//check our message queue
                suspend();
            c.chatNotify((Message)messages.elementAt(0));
            messages.removeElementAt(0);
        } catch (RemoteException e) {
            //our connection went down, kill the thread
            System.out.println("Removing "+name);
            isActive=false;
            this.stop();
        }
        yield(); //just to be polite to other threads
                 //competing for resources
    }
}
```

The only method left in this class is used to get the name of the `Chat` client that is registered with this `Talker`:

```
public String getChatterName() {
    return name;
}
```

That's it for the server-side threading. This little bit of code will save you a lot of time and frustration when your clients start misbehaving or connecting from behind slow connections. Listing 7-3 shows a complete listing of the `Talker` class.

**Listing 7-3. Server thread handling (Talker.java)**

```
package rmibook.chat;
import java.util.*;
import java.rmi.*;

public class Talker extends Thread {
    private Vector messages = new Vector();
    private Chat c;
    boolean isActive = true;
    private String name;
    public Talker(Chat c, String name) {
        this.c = c;
        this.name=name;
```

```
        this.start();
    }

    public boolean addMessage(Message e){
        if(!isActive)
            return false;
        resume();
        messages.addElement(e);
        return true;
    }

    public void run() {
        while(true){
            try {
                if(messages.isEmpty())
                    //check our message queue
                    suspend();
                c.chatNotify((Message)messages.elementAt(0));
                messages.removeElementAt(0);
            } catch (RemoteException e) {
                //our connection went down, kill the thread
                System.out.println("Removing "+name);
                isActive=false;
                this.stop();
            }
            yield(); //just to be polite to other threads
                    //competing for resources
        }
    }

    public String getChatterName() {
        return name;
    }
}
```

# Describing the Client Interface

Because both your server and your client act as client and server, there are some dependencies on the remote interfaces needed for both applications. This may sound a little confusing at first, but in this application, both your client and your server are exporting remote objects. The server exports objects used to send messages between other clients, and the clients export objects that are used to notify them that there is data to be read (or more explicitly, these methods are used to send data to the client). The server is a client in the sense that it calls the chatNotify() method on Chat clients that connect to it. The client exports this method in the same way that your server exports its remote methods. With this in mind, it becomes obvious that the server cannot be built without knowledge of the remote interfaces of the client with which it will interact.

The Chat interface declares two methods, a chatNotify() method that is used to send messages to a Chat client, and a getName() method that can be used to query the client for its name. This interface won't be implemented until Chapter 8, but is shown in Listing 7-4 because of the dependency of the server on the interface's definition.

Listing 7-4. The Chat interface (Chat.java)

```
package rmibook.chat;
import java.rmi.*;

public interface Chat extends Remote {

    public void chatNotify(Message m)
        throws RemoteException;
    public String getName() throws RemoteException;
}
```

# Encapsulating Messages

The Message class in this application is pretty simple. It encapsulates a text message, a possible Line object, and the name of the client that originated the message. This is a pretty simple model, but there is a lot of room to expand. An application could extend the message class to contain geometry for rendering more complex images, or to contain sound bytes to be played when received, or perhaps to include URLs to other arbitrary objects or Web documents.

In this implementation, stick to the basics. But even this basic structure must have more than a placeholder for the message String, the name String, and the Line object. Because the Message object gets passed around to remote machines, it must be serializable. In other words, it must be of a type that can be converted to and from a stream.

In Chapter 6, I talked about the java.io.* support for serializing objects. This included the use of special methods for sending and reconstructing an object over a stream. Luckily, this object doesn't have any special needs for reconstruction and doesn't contain any transient or static fields that you have to worry about. Simply stated, it's a simple object that can be made serializable by just implementing the java.io.Serializable interface.

The Message class contains holders for a message String, a name String, and a Line object. These holders are initialized when the object is created. Define two constructors so that the object can be created as a Line Message or a text Message. Here's how it starts:

```
package rmibook.chat;
import java.io.*;
```

```
public class Message implements Serializable {

    private String sender = null;
    private String message = null;
    private Line l = null;
```

With that out of the way, take a look at the constructors. The first one creates the object with a text message; the second creates the object with a Line message:

```
public Message(String sender, String message){
    this.sender = sender;
    this.message = message;
}
public Message(String sender, Line l){
    this.sender = sender;
    this.l = l;
}
```

All access to the data is made through access methods. These methods give access to the name, message, or Line object in a Message object:

```
public String getSender(){
    return sender;
}
public String getMessage(){
    return message;
}
public Line getLine(){
    return l;
}
```

That's it. Listing 7-5 shows the code.

**Listing 7-5. Encapsulating a message (Message.java)**

```
package rmibook.chat;
import java.io.*;

public class Message implements Serializable {

    private String sender = null;
    private String message = null;
    private Line l = null;
    public Message(String sender, String message){
        this.sender = sender;
        this.message = message;
    }
    public Message(String sender, Line l){
        this.sender = sender;
        this.l = l;
    }
```

```
public String getSender(){
    return sender;
}
public String getMessage(){
    return message;
}
public Line getLine(){
    return l;
}
}
```

The final code segment necessary to build the server is a trivial representation of a line segment. This is used by the Chat client to share line drawings, as in Figure 7-5. This object must also implement the java.io.Serializable interface, as it is passed around along with the Message object. Listing 7-6 shows the code for Line.java.

**Listing 7-6. The Line Object (Line.java)**

```
package rmibook.chat;

class Line implements java.io.Serializable {
    public int x,y,dx,dy;
    public Line(int x, int y, int dx, int dy){
        this.x=x;
        this.y=y;
        this.dx=dx;
        this.dy=dy;
    }
}
```

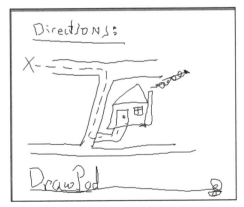

Figure 7-5. Representing a line for the drawing routines (Line.java)

# Putting It All Together

In this chapter you have built a multithreaded communication server that can deal with text messages and drawings but can easily be extended to handle more complex types. The only thing left to do is to build it and start it. If you are following the file and package structure on the CD-ROM, then you can build the applications by changing your working directory to the rmibook\chat directory and typing the following command all on one line (assuming MYCLASSES is where you want the class files to end up):

```
javac -d MYCLASSES ChatServer.java ChatServerImpl.java Chat.java
  Message.java Line.java Talker.java
```

Now you need to build the stub and skeleton classes. Assuming you maintained the packages structure, the following command should build the stub and skeleton classes:

```
rmic -c MYCLASSES rmibook.chat.ChatServerImpl
```

Finally, to start the application, you can use the following command:

```
java rmibook.chat.ChatServerImpl &
```

---

## A Separate Registry

It is not necessary to start the RMI registry before running this application. In the `ChatServerImpl` class, you created your own registry running on port 5050 and bound your remote object to that registry. Any client can connect to this server by using a URL that points to this machine and to port 5050.

---

# Summary

Here you have created a Chat server that can handle a shared whiteboard application. It's a multithreaded server with many possibilities for customization. The Server is, of course, only half of the application, and the utility of this server greatly depends on the applications that are built for it.

In Chapter 8, you will build a Chat application that registers with the server you just built and displays a message window for sending text messages to the server for distribution, and a drawing window so that a user can scribble drawings that are shared among clients connected to this server.

# Chapter 8

# Building a Distributed Communication Client

## IN THIS CHAPTER

◆ Basic client architecture

◆ Implementing the Chat interface

◆ Client threads

◆ Defining a virtual whiteboard and Name dialog box

In Chapter 7, you created a server for distributing messages among clients. The server is reasonably general purpose and can handle a number of participants that each get their own thread for server-to-client communication. The server expects any client that connects to it to implement the `Chat` interface that was also described in Chapter 7. This interface provides a callback mechanism allowing the server to notify the clients when new data have arrived (as well as send the data to the client). In essence, the clients in this model are also acting as servers. They are exporting an object that is used to remotely invoke the `chatNotify()` method that is defined in the `Chat` interface.

The server also exports a remote object that the clients use to post messages to other clients, register themselves so that the server has a handle on their callback mechanism, and query the server for a list of participants.

In this chapter, you will take a look at a client that implements the `Chat` interface and uses the server from Chapter 7 to distribute messages and drawings among other participants. The application uses a text field that monitors the client-to-client communications, and a virtual whiteboard that is used to collaboratively draw images that appear on all of the participants' screens (see Figure 8-1).

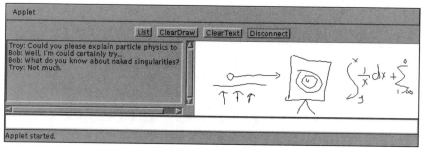

Figure 8-1. The ChatImpl applet

# Basic Client Architecture

This implementation is written as an applet. Because Java doesn't support multiple inheritance (so that a class may have only one superclass), you must export the remote interfaces manually, rather than implicitly through subclassing the UnicastRemoteObject class as you did in the server. Upon invocation, this applet first queries the user for a name to be used when communicating. Essentially, any sent messages include the sender name that is supplied by the user at this step.

Once the name has been assigned, the applet attempts to locate a registry that corresponds to the server application described in Chapter 7. Upon success, the applet keeps a handle on the server's remote object and registers itself with the server. Finally, the applet builds its user interface that consists of a Button panel, a TextArea that lists messages sent among participants, a TextField used to type in messages that are sent to other participants, and a Canvas used as a virtual shared whiteboard.

## Find Out More About It

For further reading on GUI programming or—more specifically—the Abstract Windowing Toolkit, take a look at *Java AWT Reference* by John Zukowski, or a similar reference on the AWT.

The applet is then free to remain idle until either an event is created from user interaction or the chatNotify() method is invoked by the server that the applet registered with. If a message is entered into the TextField, or if something is drawn to the Canvas, the applet adds the associated data to a ServerTalker thread that keeps a queue of outgoing messages and sends them along to the server as it's able. This is written as a thread to allow the drawing tool and basic user interaction to happen as quickly as possible without waiting for remote method calls to return.

When a message is returned to the applet via the `chatNotify()` method, any message data is appended to the `TextArea` object, any `Line` objects are added to an offscreen buffer, and the applet is redrawn. An offscreen buffer is used to avoid unnecessary flicker between redraws. Once the `ServerTalker` has emptied its message queue, and all redraw requests that were results of calls to `chatNotify()` are executed, the applet then goes idle again waiting for the next GUI event or `chatNotify()` invocation.

The applet defines a simple set of interface widgets for interaction. Essentially a panel of buttons is created and added to the applet that allow the user to disconnect from the server, query the server for a list of current participants, and clear the `TextArea` or the `Canvas` of any text or drawings that have accumulated. The clear operations work only on the local client and do not clear the whiteboard or `TextAreas` on other clients that are participating in the conversation. This means that the drawings and text lists may be out of sync among participants. Essentially anything drawn to the screen is sent as an addition to whatever was already on other participants' screens. Thus if you are annotating an image on your screen, the annotation appears on the other participants' screens, but they may have removed the image that you are referring to. I felt that it wasn't wise to permit a user to clear the screens of other participants, so I adopted this model. In a more complex version, it may suit the needs of some installations to create a number of virtual whiteboards and enable participants to pick and choose among them when sending images and annotating them.

Now take a look at this applet. The applet depends on the source files listed in Table 8-1. A few of these were described in Chapter 7, and the rest will be explained as you progress through this chapter. The table lists the names and functions of the various source files that you need to build your applet. Files that are followed by an asterisk were described in Chapter 7.

## TABLE 8-1 Components of the Chat Client

| Filename | Description |
| --- | --- |
| Chat.java* | This is the interface that describes the remote methods that are exported by the client application. This interface declares the `chatNotify()` method that is used to notify a client of new data. |
| ChatApplet.java | This is an interface that is used to identify the client as a `ChatApplet`. This is used by your drawing routine to add line segments to the message queue as the user draws on the virtual whiteboard. |

*continued*

TABLE 8-1  Components of the Chat Client *(Continued)*

| Filename | Description |
|---|---|
| ChatImpl.java | This is the actual implementation of your applet. This defines the methods in the `Chat` and `ChatApplet` interfaces. |
| ChatServer.java* | This is the interface that declares the remote methods available on the server application. The applet you are creating here needs this to create a handle to the server application and access its remote methods. |
| DrawPad.java | This is your whiteboard application. It captures mouse events and translates them into line drawings. It also renders drawings that have been received from other participants in the conversation. |
| Line.java* | An abstraction for a line segment. |
| Message.java* | An abstraction for a `Message`. This may contain a line, a text message, or both as well as the name of the originator of the message. |
| ServerTalker.java | This is a `Thread` extension used to send messages to the server. By using a thread, you can quickly add messages to a queue that will be sent to the server via a separate `Thread` without slowing down the responsiveness of the user interface. |
| NameDialog.java | This is a simple dialog box that requests the name that a user wants to be known as during this chat session. |

With the exception of the `NameDialog` class, all of these files describe classes in the rmibook.chat package. The `NameDialog` class is a member of the rmibook.util package.

# Implementing the Chat Interface

The `Chat` interface was described in Chapter 7 but is shown here in Listing 8-1 as a reminder; you will actually implement its methods in this section. The interface contains a method used to send messages to a client application, and a method used to retrieve the user name of the participant from the client.

Listing 8-1. Code of the Chat interface (Chat.java)

```
package rmibook.chat;
import java.rmi.*;
```

```
public interface Chat extends Remote {

    public void chatNotify(Message m)
        throws RemoteException;
    public String getName()
        throws RemoteException;
}
```

# Extending the Applet Class

Our implementation is an applet (a subclass of the Applet class), so it cannot extend the UnicastRemoteObject class directly. Instead, export your remote object explicitly when you initialize the applet. First off, get the class declaration and package information out of the way. Extend Applet and implement Chat and ChatApplet. The ChatApplet interface is described later; it is used by the whiteboard to notify the applets of line drawings:

```
package rmibook.chat;
import java.rmi.*;
import java.rmi.server.*;
import java.net.*;
import java.awt.*;
import java.util.*;
import java.applet.*;
import rmibook.util.*;

public class ChatImpl
    extends Applet
    implements Chat, ChatApplet {
```

Now take a look at the instance variables. Here you maintain variables for your various GUI components, your user name, and your message Thread. You also define your class constructor, which simply prints a start-up message to standard out:

```
private TextArea ta;        //the main text window
private TextField tf;       //used to input messages
private ChatServer cs;      //a reference to the server
private String name = null;//The user's name
private DrawPad dp;         //our Whiteboard app
private NameDialog nd;      //pop-up to request user name
private ServerTalker st;    //Thread for handling message
                            //sending
public ChatImpl() throws RemoteException {
    System.out.println("Starting up Chatter");
}
```

# Defining the GUI

When the applet is first loaded by a browser, or appletviewer, the init() method is called. In your init() method, you create your GUI components, add them to the Applet panel, query the user for a user name, and then call a routine to register your applet with the server. First, set a layout manager for the applet and create a Panel that contains the user interface buttons used to control this applet. Here you create instances of Button objects and add them to this:

```
public void init(){
    //set the Applets layout manager
    this.setLayout(new BorderLayout());

    //create a Panel to add our button
    //interface to
    Panel p = new Panel();
    p.setLayout(new FlowLayout());
    //add our interface buttons to the Panel
    p.add(new Button("List"));    //list users
    p.add(new Button("ClearDraw")); //clear drawing screen
    p.add(new Button("ClearText")); //clear text screen
    Button b = new Button("Disconnect"); //disconnect from
                                          //server
    b.setBackground(Color.pink); //for dramatic effect
    p.add(b);
```

The next thing to do in your init() method is to create your text widgets and an instance of your whiteboard application. The DrawPad object expects a ChatApplet object to be passed in the constructor. This is used to get ahold of a method that the DrawPad object uses to send lines to the applet and then to other clients. Because the applet implements the ChatApplet interface, you just pass a reference to this:

```
//create our text widgets and drawing window
ta = new TextArea(4,40); //message window
ta.setEditable(false);    //read-only window
tf = new TextField(40);   //text entry field
dp = new DrawPad(this);   //whiteboard
dp.setSize(400,400);
```

Finally, add all of your widgets to the applet to be placed by the layout manager that you set earlier. Once all of the widgets have been added, create a dialog box to request a user name and then call the registerChatter() method to handle registering this applet with the server. This completes the init() method:

```
//add all of our widgets to the Applet
add(dp,"East");   //add the whiteboard
add(ta,"Center"); //add the message board
add(tf,"South");  //add the text entry field
```

```
add(p,"North");    //add the button controlpanel

//create a dialog box to ask for the user name
nd = new
   NameDialog(new Frame("Enter Name"),"Enter your name",
   false);
registerChatter(); //register the Applet with the server
}
```

Once the GUI initialization is complete, take care of the network initialization. Using the name supplied with the NameDialog object, you can attempt to register this applet with the server (after getting rid of the NameDialog, of course).

Before you register the applet, export it as a remote object. Because the applet isn't a subclass of the UnicastRemoteObject class, you have to do this explicitly. Call the UnicastRemoteObject.exportObject() method, which expects a Remote object as a parameter. Because you implement the Chat interface, which extends the Remote interface, you can simply pass it a reference to this, and the methods declared in the Chat interface will be made available to remote clients (or servers in this case).

Once the applet has been exported, get a handle to your server using the Naming class. Because an applet can only create network connections to the same machine that it was served from, use the CodeBase from the applet to create the RMI URL used to look up the server's remote object. You must also remember to add the port number that the server is using, because you set it to be a nonstandard one. Once you have registered with the server, create a ServerTalker thread with a handle to the server's remote methods. This thread maintains a queue of messages and sends them to the server by invoking its remote methods.

The following code gets the user name from the NameDialog, closes the NameDialog, exports the applet using the class, looks up the server using the Naming class, registers your applet with the server, starts a ServerTalker thread, and checks for error conditions:

```
public void registerChatter(){
   name = nd.getName(); //get name from NameDialog
   nd.setVisible(false);//get rid of NameDialog
   nd = null;

   try {
      //export our remote methods
      UnicastRemoteObject.exportObject(this);

      //lookup the server's remote object
      cs = (ChatServer)Naming.lookup("rmi://" +
                  getCodeBase().getHost() +
                  ":5050/ChatServerImpl");

      //register our Applet with the server
      cs.register(this,name);
```

```
      //start a communication thread
      st = new ServerTalker(cs,name);
   } catch (RemoteException e) {
      System.out.println("Couldn't locate Registry ");
      System.exit(0);
   } catch (MalformedURLException e) {
      System.out.println("Bad binding URL: ");
      System.exit(0);
   } catch(NotBoundException e) {
      System.out.println("Service not bound." );
      System.exit(0);
   }
}
```

To handle basic user interaction, define an event handler. The event handler looks for action events that are instances either of your TextField or of Buttons. If the TextField is the target of an ACTION event, you can assume that the user typed a message into the field and hit the Enter key. Grab the text from the field and create a new Message object with the data. The Message is then added to your ServerTalker's message queue and you are returned from your event handler. If the ServerTalker's addMessage() method returns a value of false, the ServerTalker has lost contact with the server and you can assume that the connection is no longer valid. The TextArea then sends an error message to notify the user of a problem. Here is the first part of your handler, which looks for TextField ACTION events:

```
public boolean handleEvent(Event e){
   if(e.target == tf&&e.id==Event.ACTION_EVENT) {
      if(!st.addMessage(new
          Message(name,tf.getText().trim())))
         ta.append("***Server Error***\n");
      tf.setText("");
      return true;
   }
}
```

If a Button event is captured, you can check the Label of the Button and perform an action based on that. You can either clear the text screen, clear the drawing screen, query the server for participants, or disconnect from the server. Here is the rest of the event handler:

```
if(e.target instanceof Button){
   if(e.arg == "ClearText") {
      ta.setText("");
   } else if(e.arg == "ClearDraw") {
      dp.clearScreen();
   } else if(e.arg == "Disconnect") {
      st.addMessage(new
         Message("***"+name,"Logged off. Bye"));
      cs = null;
      System.exit(0);
```

```
      return true;
    } else if(e.arg == "List") {
      getUserList();
    }
  }
}
```

Now you implement the sendMessage() method that was declared in the ChatApplet interface. This method is used by the whiteboard application to send lines to the applet, which turns them into Messages and adds them to the ServerTalker thread:

```
public void sendMessage(Line l) {
    //System.out.println("Sending line");
    if(!st.addMessage(new Message(name,l)))
      ta.append("***Server Error***\n");
}
```

When a user clicks on the List button in the applet, the event handler calls the getUserList() method. This method calls the listChatters() method on the server, which returns an array of Strings that represents all of the clients that are currently registered with the server. The array is then traversed, and each String is appended to the TextArea. If there is an error, a new String array is created with a single element containing an error message:

```
public void getUserList(){
    String users[] = null;
    try {
      users = cs.listChatters();
    } catch (RemoteException e) {
      System.out.println(e);
      users = new String[1];
      users[0] = "***Error";
    }

    //add the user names to the TextArea
    for(int i = 0; i < users.length; i++)
      ta.append("***"+users[i]+"\n");
}
```

# Implementing the Remote Methods

Finally, you need to implement the methods declared in the Chat interface. The getName() method is simple. It simply returns the String referenced by the name variable. The chatNotify() method is a little more complicated, but not much. It must declare that it throws a RemoteException, and you can declare it synchronized for this application to avoid confusion if two servers happen to have handles to this method. The chatNotify() method then checks to see whether there is either a message string or a Line object in the message. In the case of a string, the String and the name of the sender is appended to the `TextArea`; in the case of a `Line`, the line is added to your whiteboard application's `Vector` of `Line` objects to be rendered. As a modest optimization, the sender field is checked for line items and is not re-rendered if they show the same name under which you are currently registered:

```
public synchronized void chatNotify(Message m)
   throws RemoteException {
   if(m.getMessage()!=null)
      ta.append(m.getSender() + ": " +
         m.getMessage()+"\n");

   if(m.getLine()!=null&&!m.getSender().equals(name))
      dp.addLine(m.getLine());
}

public String getName(){
   return name;
}
```

This concludes your `Applet` implementation of the `Chat` interface. Listing 8-2 shows the complete applet.

**Listing 8-2. The complete applet (ChatImpl.java)**

```
package rmibook.chat;
import java.rmi.*;
import java.rmi.server.*;
import java.net.*;
import java.awt.*;
import java.util.*;
import java.applet.*;
import rmibook.util.*;

public class ChatImpl
   extends Applet
   implements Chat, ChatApplet {
   private TextArea ta;          //the main text window
   private TextField tf;         //used to input messages
   private ChatServer cs;        //a reference to the server
   private String name = null;   //The user's name
   private DrawPad dp;           //our Whiteboard app
   private NameDialog nd;        //pop-up to request user name
   private ServerTalker st;      //Thread for handling message
                                 //sending
public ChatImpl() throws RemoteException {
   System.out.println("Starting up Chatter");
}
public void init(){
   //set the Applet's layout manager
   this.setLayout(new BorderLayout());

   //create a Panel to add our button
```

```
    //interface to
    Panel p = new Panel();
    p.setLayout(new FlowLayout());
    //add our interface buttons to the Panel
    p.add(new Button("List"));    //list users
    p.add(new Button("ClearDraw")); //clear drawing screen
    p.add(new Button("ClearText")); //clear text screen
    Button b = new Button("Disconnect"); //disconnect from
                                         //server
    b.setBackground(Color.pink); //for dramatic effect
    p.add(b);
    //create our text widgets and drawing window
    ta = new TextArea(4,40); //message window
    ta.setEditable(false);    //read-only window
    tf = new TextField(40);   //text entry field
    dp = new DrawPad(this);   //whiteboard
    dp.setSize(400,400);
    //add all of our widgets to the Applet
    add(dp,"East");   //add the whiteboard
    add(ta,"Center"); //add the message board
    add(tf,"South");  //add the text entry field
    add(p,"North");   //add the button controlpanel

    //create a dialog box to ask for the user name
    nd = new
        NameDialog(new Frame("Enter Name"),
            "Enter yourname", false);
    registerChatter(); //register the Applet with the server
}

public void registerChatter(){
    name = nd.getName(); //get name from NameDialog
    nd.setVisible(false);//get rid of NameDialog
    nd = null;

    try {
        //export our remote methods
        UnicastRemoteObject.exportObject(this);

        //lookup the server's remote object
        cs = (ChatServer)Naming.lookup("rmi://" +
                    getCodeBase().getHost() +
                    ":5050/ChatServerImpl");

        //register our Applet with the server
        cs.register(this,name);
        //start a communication thread
        st = new ServerTalker(cs,name);
    } catch (RemoteException e) {
        System.out.println("Couldn't locate Registry ");
        System.exit(0);
    } catch (MalformedURLException e) {
        System.out.println("Bad binding URL: ");
        System.exit(0);
```

```
        } catch(NotBoundException e) {
          System.out.println("Service not bound." );
          System.exit(0);
        }
    }

    public boolean handleEvent(Event e){
        if(e.target == tf&&e.id==Event.ACTION_EVENT) {
          if(!st.addMessage(new
              Message(name,tf.getText().trim())))
            ta.append("***Server Error***\n");
            tf.setText("");
            return true;
          }
        }

    if(e.target instanceof Button){
        if(e.arg == "ClearText") {
          ta.setText("");
        } else if(e.arg == "ClearDraw") {
          dp.clearScreen();
        } else if(e.arg == "Disconnect") {
          st.addMessage(new
              Message("***"+name,"Logged off. Bye"));
          cs = null;
          System.exit(0);
          return true;
        } else if(e.arg == "List") {
          getUserList();
        }
    }
    }
    public void sendMessage(Line l) {
        //System.out.println("Sending line");
        if(!st.addMessage(new Message(name,l)))
          ta.append("***Server Error***\n");
    }

    public void getUserList(){
        String users[] = null;
        try {
          users = cs.listChatters();
        } catch (RemoteException e) {
          System.out.println(e);
          users = new String[1];
          users[0] = "***Error";
        }

        //add the user names to the TextArea
        for(int i = 0; i < users.length; i++)
          ta.append("***"+users[i]+"\n");
    }

    public synchronized void chatNotify(Message m)
```

```
   throws RemoteException {
   if(m.getMessage()!=null)
      ta.append(m.getSender() + ": " +
         m.getMessage()+"\n");

   if(m.getLine()!=null&&!m.getSender().equals(name))
      dp.addLine(m.getLine());
}

public String getName(){
   return name;
}
}
```

# Adding Threads to the Client

If the client had to wait for a remote method invocation on the server to complete before continuing, user interface performance could noticeably degrade with large numbers of invocations. In order to avoid these problems, you can use a `Thread` queue much like the one you used for the server in Chapter 7.

The `ServerTalker` class extends the `Thread` class and maintains a `Vector` of messages to be sent to the server. If the queue is empty, the `Thread` is put to sleep and wakes up when something new is added to the queue. This allows you to add new messages independent of how backed up the server communication gets. This could also introduce synchronicity problems, as the queue could be filled with messages that haven't been sent and that will get lost if the server connection goes down before completion. The user may assume that the messages have been distributed, when in fact they never made it off of the queue.

To start off, you can extend the `Thread` class and create variables for your message queue, along with a reference to the server that you will be sending the messages to:

```
package rmibook.chat;
import java.util.*;
import java.rmi.*;

class ServerTalker extends Thread {

        private Vector messages = new Vector();
        private ChatServer cs;
```

In your class constructor, you should pass two arguments—a reference to the server that this `Thread` should be sending messages to and the name by which the user is logged on. The constructor assigns the server reference to a class variable, sends a connection message to the server, and then calls the `start()` method of the `Thread` to begin its execution:

```
public ServerTalker(ChatServer cs, String name) {
   this.cs = cs;
   //Send a welcome message
   messages.addElement(new
      Message("***", name + " just connected***"));
   this.start();
}
```

To add messages to the queue, the addMessage() method is called. This method adds the Message passed along with it to the message Vector and then calls the resume() method in case the Thread was idle. If the server reference is null, false is returned, notifying the caller that the server connection has gone down:

```
public boolean addMessage(Message e){
   if(cs==null) {
      System.out.println("Server reference is null");
      return false;
   }
   resume();
   messages.addElement(e);
   return true;
}
```

Finally, the main execution loop of the thread checks the first element of the message Vector. The element is sent to the server and removed from the Vector until no more elements exist. Once the Vector is emptied, the thread is put to sleep until the addMessage() method is called again, at which time the Thread is resumed:

```
public void run() {
   while(true){
      try {
         if(messages.isEmpty())
            suspend();
         cs.postMessage((Message)
            messages.elementAt(0));
         messages.removeElementAt(0);
      } catch (RemoteException e) {
         System.out.println("Error: Server down?");
         cs = null;
         this.stop();
      }
      yield();
   }
}
```

Listing 8-3 shows the complete code listing.

**Listing 8-3. The communication thread (ServerTalker.java)**

```
package rmibook.chat;
import java.util.*;
```

```
import java.rmi.*;

class ServerTalker extends Thread {

      private Vector messages = new Vector();
      private ChatServer cs;
public ServerTalker(ChatServer cs, String name) {
     this.cs = cs;
     //Send a welcome message
     messages.addElement(new
        Message("***", name + " just connected***"));
     this.start();
   }

public boolean addMessage(Message e){
     if(cs==null) {
        System.out.println("Server reference is null");
        return false;
     }
     resume();
     messages.addElement(e);
     return true;
   }

public void run() {
     while(true){
        try {
           if(messages.isEmpty())
              suspend();
           cs.postMessage((Message)
              messages.elementAt(0));
           messages.removeElementAt(0);
        } catch (RemoteException e) {
           System.out.println("Error: Server down?");
           cs = null;
           this.stop();
        }
        yield();
     }
   }
}
```

# Defining a Virtual Whiteboard

One of the central elements of this applet is a shared, virtual *whiteboard*—an application that enables users to collaboratively draw images or diagrams (see Figure 8-2). This version is relatively simple and only enables users to draw black lines, but it could easily be extended to handle more complex drawing tools that include images, geometry, and perhaps different types of pens.

Figure 8-2. The DrawPad screen

This application extends the `Canvas` class and captures mouse events. When the user drags the mouse across the surface, lines are added to an internal buffer for rendering and sent to the applet that was used to create the canvas so that the lines can be distributed to other clients and rendered on their whiteboards as well.

The `DrawPad` class keeps track of the last time the mouse button was clicked, or the last time a `mouseDrag` event was processed. When a `mouseDrag` or `mouseUp` event is captured, the new *x* and *y* coordinates of the mouse are used along with the previous values to create a `Line` object. This `Line` object is added to a local rendering queue and sent to the `ChatApplet` that created the `DrawPad` in order to have the `Line` forwarded to other clients.

All rendering is done from a rendering queue, to an off-screen image. The image is then used to double-buffer the `Canvas` display, thus eliminating much of the flicker that would occur otherwise.

The application extends `Canvas` and takes a `ChatApplet` as a parameter to its constructor. This `ChatApplet` reference is stored in order to notify the `ChatApplet` when new `Line` objects need to be distributed:

```
package rmibook.chat;

import java.awt.*;
import java.util.*;

class DrawPad extends Canvas {

    int lastx, lasty;
    int lastIndex = 0; //used to mark our drawing vector
    Vector lines = new Vector();
    ChatApplet c;  //the client that created the DrawPanel
```

```
Image i; //for double buffering
Graphics db; //used to access the offscreen buffer

public DrawPad(ChatImpl c) {
    super();
    this.c=c;
}
```

You can override the `Canvas`'s `paint()` method with one that simply performs a check to make sure that your off-screen buffer exists and either draws the buffer at its origin or prints a message stating that the image is still being initialized:

```
public void paint(Graphics g) {
    if(i!=null)
        g.drawImage(i,0,0,this);
    else{
        g.drawString("Initializing...", 5,30);
        render();
    }
}
```

Normally, whenever a request is made to repaint a `Canvas`, the screen is cleared with the background color first. In order to prevent this behavior, which could cause the screen to flash, you should override the `update()` method. Instead of first clearing the screen and then calling `paint()`, you just call `paint()`:

```
public void update(Graphics g) {
    paint(g);
}
```

Your renderer first checks to make sure that your offscreen buffer exists and then, if necessary, create it. Once the buffer has been created, the renderer traverses the `Vector` that you've stored your `Line` objects in and draws them as lines to the offscreen buffer. Once all of the lines have been drawn, `repaint()` is called to cause the system to request the `paint()` method—thereby drawing your offscreen buffer. Be sure to keep track of where you are in your `Vector` so that lines don't unnecessarily get redrawn to the buffer:

```
public void render() {
    Line l;

    if(i==null) {
        i = this.createImage(400,400);
        db = i.getGraphics();
        db.setColor(Color.white);
        db.fillRect(0,0,400,400);
        db.setColor(Color.red);
        db.drawRect(0,0,400-1,400-1);
        db.setColor(Color.black);
```

```
    }
    for(int i = lastIndex; i < lines.size(); i++){
        l = (Line)lines.elementAt(i);
        db.drawLine(l.x, l.y, l.dx, l.dy);
    }
    lastIndex = lines.size();
    repaint();
}
```

Occasionally, the user may want to clear the screen, so you should define a method
that resets the values of the offscreen buffer, as well as the Line Vector. This causes
the render method to create a new off-screen buffer and start again from scratch:

```
public void clearScreen(){
    i = null;
    lines = new Vector();
    lastIndex=0;
    render();
}
```

Now for the event handlers: This drawing application is driven by mouse events.
When a mouseDown is captured, the lastx and lasty variables are updated to
remember your starting point. Then when either a mouseUp or mouseDrag event is
captured, a Line object is created that starts at the coordinates (lastx, lasty) and
extends to the coordinates (x, y). A simple check is first made to confirm that the
line is at least one pixel long; if this is so, the Line is added to the local rendering
queue and sent off to the ChatApplet to be distributed to other clients. The three
mouse event handlers and the drawLine() method follow:

```
public boolean mouseDown(Event e, int x, int y) {
    lastx=x;
    lasty=y;
    return true;
}

public boolean mouseDrag(Event e, int x, int y){
    getGraphics().drawLine(lastx,lasty,x,y);
    drawLine(x,y);
    return true;
}

public boolean mouseUp(Event e, int x, int y){
    getGraphics().drawLine(lastx,lasty,x,y);
    drawLine(x,y);
    return true;
}
void drawLine(int x, int y) {
    if((Math.abs(lastx-x)>1)||(Math.abs(lasty-y)>1)){
        Line l = new Line(x,y,lastx,lasty);
        addLine(l);
```

```
            c.sendMessage(l);
            lastx=x;
            lasty=y;
        }
    }
```

Finally, a method is defined that enables the `ChatApplet` to add lines to the renderer queue that it receives from the server:

```
public void addLine(Line l) {
    lines.addElement(l);
    render();
}
```

That's it, we're almost finished with your applet. Listing 8-4 shows a complete listing of the `DrawPad` source.

**Listing 8-4. The whiteboard (DrawPad.java)**

```
package rmibook.chat;

import java.awt.*;
import java.util.*;

class DrawPad extends Canvas {

    int lastx, lasty;
    int lastIndex = 0; //used to mark our drawing vector
    Vector lines = new Vector();
    ChatApplet c; //the client that created the DrawPanel
    Image i; //for double buffering
    Graphics db; //used to access the offscreen buffer

    public DrawPad(ChatImpl c) {
        super();
        this.c=c;
    }

public void paint(Graphics g) {
        if(i!=null)
           g.drawImage(i,0,0,this);
        else{
           g.drawString("Initializing...", 5,30);
           render();
        }
    }

public void update(Graphics g) {
        paint(g);
    }
public void render() {
        Line l;
```

```
            if(i==null) {
                i = this.createImage(400,400);
                db = i.getGraphics();
                db.setColor(Color.white);
                db.fillRect(0,0,400,400);
                db.setColor(Color.red);
                db.drawRect(0,0,400-1,400-1);
                db.setColor(Color.black);
            }
            for(int i = lastIndex; i < lines.size(); i++){
                l = (Line)lines.elementAt(i);
                db.drawLine(l.x, l.y, l.dx, l.dy);
            }
            lastIndex = lines.size();
            repaint();
        }

    public void clearScreen(){
            i = null;
            lines = new Vector();
            lastIndex=0;
            render();
        }

    public boolean mouseDown(Event e, int x, int y) {
            lastx=x;
            lasty=y;
            return true;
        }

        public boolean mouseDrag(Event e, int x, int y){
            getGraphics().drawLine(lastx,lasty,x,y);
            drawLine(x,y);
            return true;
        }

        public boolean mouseUp(Event e, int x, int y){
            getGraphics().drawLine(lastx,lasty,x,y);
            drawLine(x,y);
            return true;
        }
        void drawLine(int x, int y) {
            if((Math.abs(lastx-x)>1)||(Math.abs(lasty-y)>1)){
                Line l = new Line(x,y,lastx,lasty);
                addLine(l);
                c.sendMessage(l);
                lastx=x;
                lasty=y;
            }
        }

        public void addLine(Line l) {
```

```
            lines.addElement(l);
            render();
    }
}
```

# Defining the Name Dialog Box

When the applet first starts, it needs to query the user for a user name:

Basically, all messages sent to the server contain the name provided. A very simple dialog box is created to ask the user to supply a name; it is destroyed once the name has been retrieved. This is the one file that is not in the rmibook.chat package but rather the rmibook.util package because it will come in handy for some other applications that I will discuss. Because this is a general utility, the code is just shown in Listing 8-5 and not dissected as the other source files have been.

Listing 8-5. A GUI dialog box (NameDialog.java)

```
package rmibook.util;
import java.awt.*;

public class NameDialog extends Dialog {

    private TextField tf = new TextField(20);
    private String value = null;
    private boolean set = false;

    public NameDialog(Frame p, String t, boolean modal){
        super(p,t,modal);
        setLayout(new FlowLayout());
        this.add(new Label("Enter your name:"));
        this.add(tf);
        this.add(new Button("OK"));
        this.pack();
        this.show();
    }

    public boolean handleEvent(Event e){
        if(e.target instanceof Button){
            if(tf.getText().length()>1){
                value = tf.getText().trim();
                set = true;
            }
```

```
            return true;
        }

        return false;
    }

    public String getName() {
        while(value==null) ;
        return value;
    }
}
```

# Putting It All Together

Because this client is run as an applet, you must define the HTML code that embeds the applet in an HTML document. The following `ChatApplet.html` code sample has reasonable values depending on your local configuration:

```
. . .
<APPLET code="ChatImpl.class"
        codebase="/MyClasses/"
        width=800
        height=400 >
</APPLET>
. . .
```

The only thing left for you to do is compile your source files and compile the stub and skeleton classes for the `ChatImpl` class (because it is exporting its own remote object). Make sure you have a server running, and finally test the applet with a Web browser or applet viewer.

Compile the source files that are listed in Table 8-1 with your favorite Java compiler. Be sure to set the destination directory to a location that is accessible to your Web server, as this applet will be accessed over the network. On my system, I would change to my source directory and type the following command:

```
javac -d /usr/MyClasses/ *.java
```

Next, use the RMIC compiler to generate your stub file. Be sure to use the complete package name to the `ChatImpl` class:

```
rmic -d /usr/MyClasses rmibook.chat.ChatImpl
```

Start your server as described in Chapter 7:

```
java rmibook.chat.ChatServerImpl &
```

Now access the HTML document you created with a browser or applet viewer:

```
appletviewer http://www.foo.com/ChatApplet.html
```

Try a couple of instances of appletviewer to make sure that the messages are getting passed around. If all went well, you should have a mini chat session going.

# Summary

The server you created in Chapter 7 and the client you just created in Chapter 8 give you the basis for a communication system. The server could easily be extended to link to other servers as well as clients for distributing the load and increasing the number of potential participants. The client could also be extended to expand tools used for the whiteboard application and create methods for requesting the Chat remote object from individual clients for direct peer-to-peer communication.

Coming up in Chapter 9, you will look at an RMI-based distributed database. This database uses abstraction tools such as the Java Database Connectivity classes to interact with arbitrary SQL or ODBC databases. All client/server communication is handled through RMI mechanisms.

# Chapter 9

# Writing an RMI Database Server

## IN THIS CHAPTER

◆ The bootstrap server interface and implementation

◆ The `ClientHandler` interface and implementation

◆ The `Database` object

◆ The `ResultCopier` interface and implementation

Now that you've taken a look at a few RMI applications such as the chat server and your time clock application, you may have noticed that the actual RMI specific sections of the code are relatively small compared with the rest of the application. RMI provides simple mechanisms for distributing an application without your having to do a disproportionate amount of coding that is not specific to the goal of your application.

In these last two chapters, I show you a few more applications that use RMI for database applications. This chapter features an application that uses the Java Database Connectivity libraries (JDBC) and RMI to create a server that accesses a computer price list database and uses RMI callback mechanisms to forward the results. This section is heavy on code, but I have attempted to mark the interesting sections both as source code comments and in the chapter text. When all is said and done, you'll have a simple RMI server application that can connect to standard, real-world database implementations. The source code in this section is based on an RMI database application developed by Zia Khan at Xenosys Corporation. The components of this application are listed in Table 9-1.

---

### TABLE 9-1. SERVER COMPONENTS

| Class/Interface | Description |
| --- | --- |
| `CompPriceInterface.java` | Server Remote interface |
| `CompPrice.java` | Implementation of the `Remote` interface |

147

*continued*

---

TABLE 9-1. SERVER COMPONENTS *(Continued)*

| Class/Interface | Description |
| --- | --- |
| `ClientHandlerInterface.java` | Interface for handling the RMI client |
| `ClientHandler.java` | `ClientHandler` implementation |
| `Database.java` | Database abstraction class |
| `ResultCopierInterface.java` | Interface for moving database data |
| `ResultCopier.java` | Implementation of the `ResultCopierInterface` |
| `ResultSetCopy.java` | Copy of the SQL result set |

# The Bootstrap Server Interface

The bootstrap server interface is the interface that defines your remote methods. This is used by the `CompPrice` class that exports a remote method. It is also used for the initial connection of a client to the database server. The client must register, or "bootstrap," with the server before database transactions can begin. Listing 9-1 shows this code.

Listing 9-1. The Remote interface (CompPriceInterface.java)

```
package rmibook.database;
public interface CompPriceInterface extends java.rmi.Remote
{
   String handshake(String message)
      throwsjava.rmi.RemoteException;
   ClientHandlerInterface getClientHandler()
      throws java.rmi.RemoteException;
}
```

This code simply defines two methods for remote access. The first is used by a client to send a message when first connecting, and the second is used to get a handle on a `ClientHandler` object that is used for interacting with the database.

# The Bootstrap Server Implementation

The first part of the application you will look at is the bootstrap server. This class extends the `UnicastRemoteObject` class and provides the registry call for registering the application with a registry server. This is where you implement the remote interfaces that I've described in connection with the `CompPriceInterface` class. Listing 9-2 shows this code.

### Listing 9-2. Remote object implementation (CompPrice.java)

```
package rmibook.database;
import java.rmi.RemoteException;
import java.rmi.Naming;
import java.rmi.server.UnicastRemoteObject;
import java.rmi.server.StubSecurityManager;

public class CompPrice extends UnicastRemoteObject
                        implements CompPriceInterface
{
    //We Define the Database class a little later,
    //This encapsulates the JDBC calls for interacting
    //with the database
    Database Pricebase;

    //Our constructor calls the super() to explicitly
    //export our remote object through the
    //UnicastRemoteObject constructor that we are
    //deriving from. Then, we create a new database
    //object passing it the parameters referring to
    //a jdbc/odbc database
    public CompPrice() throws RemoteException
    {
        super();
        Pricebase = new Database("jdbc:odbc:microage");
    }

    //The handshake method just prints out a message that
    //is sent by the client. Just a little feedback
    //telling us that a connection has been established.
    //It also returns a string identifying the server
    //to the client that is connected.
    public String handshake(String message)
            throws RemoteException
    {
        System.out.println("New Client message:" +
                            message);
        return "Xenosys Computer Price Server" ;

    }

    //This is the main access point to the database.
    //A ClientHandler object is returned that was
    //created with the database object that we instanced
    //earlier.
    public ClientHandlerInterface getClientHandler()
            throws RemoteException
    {
```

```
        return new ClientHandler(Pricebase);
    }

    //In the main() method, we create the necessary
    //security manager, create a new instance of the
    //CompPrice class, and bind it with a Registry that
    //is presumed running on the same machine.
    public static void main(String args[])
    {
        try
        {
            //Install security manager
            System.setSecurityManager(new
                    StubSecurityManager());

            System.out.println("Initializing Server");
            CompPrice price = new CompPrice();
            System.out.println("binding PriceServer");
            //bind CompPrice object to a registry under
            //the name "PriceServer"
            Naming.rebind("PriceServer", price);
        }
        catch(Exception e)
        {
            System.out.println("Exception occurred: "
                        + e.getMessage());
            e.printStackTrace();
        }
        System.out.println("Server Ready");
    }
```

# The ClientHandler Interface

The client interacts with the database through a ClientHandler object. There is a new ClientHandler object created for each new client connection as described previously for the getClientHandler() method. The ClientHandler (see Listing 9-3) is also a Remote object and therefore must also implement a Remote interface. This interface declares two methods, one for accessing the database and another for testing purposes. (A lot of the code in this section is specific to JDBC and SQL. For further reading on these packages, take a look at *Database Programming with JDBC* by George Reese.)

**Listing 9-3. Remote interface for the client handler (ClientHandlerInterface.java)**

```
package rmibook.database;
import java.sql.*;

public interface ClientHandlerInterface extends
```

```
                        java.rmi.Remote
{
   //This is the main access method for interacting
   //with the database
   public ResultCopierInterface matchDesc(String
                   PartialDescription,
                   int chunkSize,
                   ServerHandlerInterface Client)
                   throws java.rmi.RemoteException,
                       SQLException;

   public String testMessage() throws
                java.rmi.RemoteException;
}
```

# The ClientHandler Implementation

The ClientHandler (see Listing 9-4) is instanced for each client connection that the server handles. When a client requests a connection, the server creates a new ClientHandler object with the database that it is serving and returns the ClientHandler for remote access.

**Listing 9-4. Implementation of the client handler (ClientHandler.java)**

```
package rmibook.database;

import java.sql.*;
import java.rmi.RemoteException;
import java.rmi.server.UnicastRemoteObject;

//This object is an RMI object, so it extends
//UnicastRemoteObject and implements the Remote interface
//ClientHandlerInterface
public class ClientHandler extends UnicastRemoteObject
implements ClientHandlerInterface
{
   //create pointers for the database
   Database PriceBase;
   Database CustomerBase;

   //The constructor is called with a reference to
   // a database that it stores locally in PriceBase
   public ClientHandler(Database PriceBase)
                      throws RemoteException
   {
      super();
      this.PriceBase = PriceBase;
   }
```

```
//Here is where the database lookups happen, and
//a ResultCopier is returned for grabbing the search
//results. Essentially, we are making the
// Database queries and returning an object
// that is used to transport the results
public ResultCopierInterface matchDesc(String
        PartialDescription, int chunkSize,
        ServerHandlerInterface Client)
        throws RemoteException, SQLException
{
    //Here we are checking for a string match and
    //storing the result set.
    ResultSet data =
        PriceBase.comparePartialString("*", "rmibook.database",
                                    "Description",
                                    PartialDescription);
    ResultCopierInterface RCopier = new
                ResultCopier(data, chunkSize, Client);
    return (ResultCopierInterface) RCopier;

}   public String testMessage() throws RemoteException
{
    return "This is the Client Handler" ;
}
```

# The Database Object

The database object is used to implement the JDBC components of the application. Basically, this is the database abstraction layer that your application uses. This object can be configured to use arbitrary ODBC databases. See Listing 9-5.

**Listing 9-5. Abstraction of the database (database.java)**

```
package rmibook.database;

import java.net.URL;
import java.sql.*;

class Database
{
    Connection con;
    DatabaseMetaData dma;

 //The constructor is called with a string that is used
 //to create a connection with a particular database.
 //the constructor attempts to load the JdbcOdbcDriver
 //and prints out diagnostic messages.

    public Database(String url)
```

```
{
   try {  //initialize the JDBC driver
      Class.forName ("jdbc.odbc.JdbcOdbcDriver");
      con = DriverManager.getConnection(url);
      checkForWarning(con.getWarnings());
      dma = con.getMetaData ();
      System.out.println("\nConnected to " +
                          dma.getURL());
      System.out.println("Driver        " +
                          dma.getDriverName());
      System.out.println("Version       " +
                          dma.getDriverVersion());
   }catch (SQLException ex){
      System.out.println ("\n*** SQLException ***\n");

      //loop through the exceptions and print
      //diagnostics
      while (ex != null)
      {
         System.out.println ("SQLState: " +
                                ex.getSQLState ());
         System.out.println ("Message:  " +
                                ex.getMessage ());
         System.out.println ("Vendor:   " +
                                ex.getErrorCode ());
         ex = ex.getNextException ();
         System.out.println ("");

      }
   }
   catch (java.lang.Exception ex)
   {
      ex.printStackTrace();
   }

}

//This second constructor is used for implementations
//that require authentication. This constructor is
//not used in our applet for this section, but is
//in place to show one way to authenticate database
//transactions.
public Database(String url, String userID,
                String password)
{
   try
   {
      Class.forName ("jdbc.odbc.JdbcOdbcDriver");
      con = DriverManager.getConnection(url, userID,
                                         password);
      checkForWarning(con.getWarnings());
      dma = con.getMetaData ();
      System.out.println("\nConnected to " +
```

```
                                           dma.getURL());
              System.out.println("Driver        " +
                                  dma.getDriverName());
              System.out.println("Version       " +
                                  dma.getDriverVersion());

         }
         catch (SQLException ex)
         {
              System.out.println ("\n*** SQLException ***\n");
              while (ex != null)
              {
                   System.out.println ("SQLState: " +
                                        ex.getSQLState ());
                   System.out.println ("Message:  " +
                                        ex.getMessage ());
                   System.out.println ("Vendor:    " +
                                        ex.getErrorCode ());
                   ex = ex.getNextException ();
                   System.out.println ("");
              }
         }
         catch (java.lang.Exception ex)
         {
              ex.printStackTrace ();
         }
    }

    //This method makes a query in the database and
    //returns a result set.
    public ResultSet selectQuery(String query)
         throws SQLException
    {
         Statement stmt;
         ResultSet rs;

         try
         {
              stmt = con.createStatement();
              rs = stmt.executeQuery(query);
              return rs;
         }
         catch (SQLException ex)
         {
              System.out.println("\n***Query Exception***\n");
                   throw ex;
         }
    }

//This method allows database modification.
//The modification string is an SQL statement for
//modifying the database
   public int databaseModification(String modification)
```

```
                throws SQLException
{

    Statement stmt;
    int rowsUpdated;
    try
    {
       stmt = con.createStatement();
       rowsUpdated = stmt.executeUpdate(modification);
       return rowsUpdated;
    }
    catch (SQLException ex)
    {
       System.out.println ("\n*** SQLException caught" +
                       "in databaseModification ***\n");

       //loop through the exceptions…
       while (ex != null)
       {
          System.out.println ("SQLState: " +
                              ex.getSQLState ());
          System.out.println ("Message:   " +
                              ex.getMessage ());
          System.out.println ("Vendor:    " +
                              ex.getErrorCode ());
          ex = ex.getNextException ();
       }
       throw ex;
    }
}

//return a result set based on a partial string
//comparison
public ResultSet comparePartialString(String columns,
        String tables, String compareColumn, String
        matchString) throws SQLException
{
    return selectQuery("Select " + columns + " FROM " +
                       tables + " WHERE " +
                       compareColumn + " LIKE " + "'%"
                       + matchString + "%'");
}

//close the database connection
public void close()
{
    try
    {
       con.close();
    }
    catch (SQLException ex)
    {
       System.out.println ("\n*** SQLException caught" +
```

```
                                          "when closing ***\n");

            //loop through exceptions
            while (ex != null)
            {
                System.out.println ("SQLState: " +
                                        ex.getSQLState ());
                System.out.println ("Message:  " +
                                        ex.getMessage ());
                System.out.println ("Vendor:   " +
                                        ex.getErrorCode ());
                ex = ex.getNextException ();
                System.out.println ("");
            }
        }
    }

    //check for sql warnings
    public static boolean checkForWarning(SQLWarning warn)
                        throws SQLException
    {
        boolean rc = false;
        if (warn != null)
        {
            System.out.println ("\n *** Warning ***\n");
            rc = true;

            //loop through and print warnings.
            while (warn != null)
            {
                System.out.println ("SQLState: " +
                                        warn.getSQLState ());
                System.out.println ("Message:  " +
                                        warn.getMessage ());
                System.out.println ("Vendor:   " +
                                        warn.getErrorCode ());
                System.out.println ("");
                warn = warn.getNextWarning ();
            }
        }
        return rc;
    }

    //This will print a set of results. This can
    //be used to generate the data result tables
    //on the console. This is useful for debugging
    //and non-GUI implementations.
    public static void dispResultSet(ResultSet rs)
    {
        try
        {
            int i;
            ResultSetMetaData rsmd = rs.getMetaData();
```

```
       int numCols = rsmd.getColumnCount();
       for (i=1; i<=numCols; i++)
       {
          if (i > 1) System.out.print(",");
          System.out.print(rsmd.getColumnLabel(i));
       }
       System.out.println("");
       boolean more = rs.next();
       while(more)
       {
          for (i=1; i<=numCols; i++)
          {
             if (i > 1) System.out.print(",");
             System.out.print(rs.getString(i));
          }
          System.out.println("");
          more = rs.next ();
       }
    }
    catch (SQLException ex)
    {
       System.out.println ("\n*** SQLException caught" +
                             "in dispResultSet ***\n");

       while (ex != null)
       {
          System.out.println ("SQLState: " +
                                ex.getSQLState ());
          System.out.println ("Message:  " +
                                ex.getMessage ());
          System.out.println ("Vendor:   " +
                                ex.getErrorCode ());
          ex = ex.getNextException ();
          System.out.println ("");
       }
    }
 }
}
```

# The ResultCopier Interface

This interface (see Listing 9-6) is implemented by the ResultCopier class. It is used to usher data to the client as they become available. Essentially, this uses call-back routines to send data results as they are returned from the database.

**Listing 9-6. The** ResultCopier **remote interface (ResultCopierInterface.java)**

```
package rmibook.database;

import java.sql.*;
```

```
import java.rmi.server.UnicastRemoteObject;
import java.rmi.RemoteException;

public interface ResultCopierInterface
    extends java.rmi.Remote
{
    public ResultSetCopy columnLabel()
          throws RemoteException;

    public ResultSetCopy nextChunk()
          throws RemoteException;

    public int getNumOfRows() throws RemoteException;

    public ResultSetCopy getChunkNumber(int number)
          throws RemoteException;

    public int getNumOfChunks() throws RemoteException;

    public boolean processingDone()
          throws RemoteException;

    public boolean nextChunkAvailable()
          throws RemoteException;

    public boolean columnLabelAvailable()
          throws RemoteException;
```

# The ResultCopier Implementation

Here is the implementation of the `ResultCopierInterface` (see Listing 9-7).
Essentially, this handles the transfer of data between client and server. It explicitly
sends the data in "chunks" so that it can be tweaked for performance issues.
Alternatively, the data could be sent as one large object and the RMI system would
take care of getting the data across the connection.

Listing 9-7. Implementation of the `ResultCopier` (**ResultCopier.java**)

```
package rmibook.database;

import java.sql.*;
import java.util.*;
import java.rmi.server.UnicastRemoteObject;
import java.rmi.RemoteException;

public class ResultCopier extends UnicastRemoteObject
                        implements
                        ResultCopierInterface, Runnable
{
```

```
ResultSet rs; //the results of the query
int numCols; //the number of columns of data
ResultSetMetaData rsmd; //Metadata related to results
Vector ResultDataCopies; //Used to contain data
ResultSetCopy ResultColumnCopy;
Thread ResultCopierThread; //the Main execution thread
boolean ColumnFlag; //mark columns
boolean ProcessingDoneFlag; //set when processing
                            //is complete
int chunkSize; //the size of the data chunks to
               //transfer
int index;
int numOfRows; //rows for data table
ServerHandlerInterface  Client; //client's
                                //Remote object
public ResultCopier (ResultSet RSet, int chunk,
ServerHandlerInterface client) throws RemoteException, SQLException
    {
        super();
        try
        {
            rs = RSet;
            chunkSize = chunk;
            ColumnFlag = false;
            ProcessingDoneFlag = false;
            index = 0;
            numOfRows = 0;
            Client = client;
            ResultDataCopies = new Vector(10, 10);
            rsmd = rs.getMetaData();
            numCols = rsmd.getColumnCount();
            ResultColumnCopy = new ResultSetCopy(numCols);
            ResultCopierThread = new Thread (this);
            ResultCopierThread.start();
        }
        catch (SQLException ex)
        {
            System.out.println ("\n*** SQLException caught" +
                    "in ResultCopier:ColumnLabel ***\n");

            throw ex;
        }
    }

    //Thread body
    public void run ()
    {
        int i;
        Object[] row;
        boolean more;
        int j;

        // get the column label from result set and put it
```

```
//in ResultColumnCopy

try
{
    System.out.println("ResultCopier::run -" +
                        "preparing column copy");
    String[] names = new String[numCols];
    for (i=1; i<=numCols; i++)
    {
        names[i-1] = rsmd.getColumnLabel(i);
    }

    synchronized (this)
    {
        ResultColumnCopy.setNames(names);
        ColumnFlag = true;
    }
}
catch (SQLException ex)
{
    System.out.println ("\n*** SQLException caught" +
                "in ResultCopier:ColumnLabel ***\n");
}

// Now get the chunks of data from result set and keep
//adding them in ResultDataCopies

try
{
    System.out.println("ResultCopier::run -" +
                        "processing data chunks");

    do
    {
        ResultSetCopy rsCopy = new
                ResultSetCopy(numCols);
        more = rs.next();
        j = 1;
        while((more) && (j <= chunkSize))
        {
            row = new Object[numCols];
            for (i=1; i<=numCols; i++)
            {
                row[i-1] = rs.getObject(i);
            }
            rsCopy.setRow(row);
            synchronized (this)
            {
                numOfRows++;
            }
            more = rs.next();
            j++;
        }
```

```java
        synchronized (ResultDataCopies)
        {
           ResultDataCopies.addElement(rsCopy);
        }

        if (ResultDataCopies.size() == 1)
        {
           try
           {
              Client.callBackFirstChunk(rsCopy);
              index++;
           }
           catch (Exception e)
           {
              System.out.println("\n***Exception" +
                          "caught while invoking" +
                          "callBackFirstChunk***");
           }
        }
        else
        {
           try
           {
              Client.callBackNextChunkAvailable();
           }
           catch (Exception e)
           {
              System.out.println("\n***Exception" +
                          "caught while invoking" +
                       callBackNextChunkAvailable***");
           }
        }
     } while (more);
     synchronized (this)
     {
        ProcessingDoneFlag = true;
        //tell the world I am done processing
     }
     try
     {
        Client.callBackStatus(numOfRows,
              ResultDataCopies.size());
     }
     catch (Exception e)
     {
        System.out.println("\n***Exception caught" +
              "while invoking callBackStatus***");
     }
  }
catch (SQLException ex)
{
   System.out.println ("\n*** SQLException caught" +
```

```
                              "in ResultCopier:NextChunk ***\n");
    }
}
// get the data table column label.
public ResultSetCopy columnLabel() throws RemoteException
{
    System.out.println("ResultCopier::columnLabel");
    if (ColumnFlag)
        return (ResultSetCopy) ResultColumnCopy;
    else
        return (ResultSetCopy) null;
}

public synchronized ResultSetCopy nextChunk()
        throws RemoteException
{
    System.out.println("ResultCopier::nextChunk,size ="
        +ResultDataCopies.size() +" index = " +index);
    if (ResultDataCopies.size() > index)
        return (ResultSetCopy)
                ResultDataCopies.elementAt(index++);
    else
        return (ResultSetCopy) null;
}

public synchronized ResultSetCopy
        getChunkNumber(int number)
        throws RemoteException
{
    System.out.println("ResultCopier::getChunkNumber");
    if (ResultDataCopies.size() > number)
        return (ResultSetCopy)
                ResultDataCopies.elementAt(number);
    else
        return (ResultSetCopy) null;
}

public synchronized int getNumOfRows()
        throws RemoteException
{
    System.out.println("ResultCopier::getNumOfRows");
    return numOfRows;
}

public synchronized int getNumOfChunks() throws RemoteException
{
    System.out.println("ResultCopier::getNumOfChunks");
    return ResultDataCopies.size();
}

public synchronized boolean processingDone()
        throws RemoteException
{
```

```
                System.out.println("ResultCopier::processingDone");
                return ProcessingDoneFlag;
        }

    public synchronized boolean nextChunkAvailable()
            throws RemoteException
    {
System.out.println("ResultCopier::nextChunkAvailable");
        if (ResultDataCopies.size() > index)
            return true;
        else
            return false;
    }
public synchronized boolean columnLabelAvailable() throws
RemoteException
    {
System.out.println("ResultCopier::ColumnLabelAvailable");
        return ColumnFlag;
    }
```

# The ResultSetCopy Class

Finally you have a class that encapsulates the data chunks that are extracted from the database (see Listing 9-8). This class is not a remote object, so it is serialized and passed by copy rather than by reference. In other words, it is serialized and copied rather than having a reference to it sent across the network. Copy by reference is restricted to objects that implement the Remote interface, such as those I defined earlier.

Listing 9-8. Result set encapsulation (ResultSetCopy.java)

```
package rmibook.database;
import java.util.*;
import java.io
//encapsulate a result set data chunk
public class ResultSetCopy implements Serializable
{
    int numCols;
    String[] namesCols;
    Vector result;
    int cursor = 0;
    Object[] row;

    public ResultSetCopy(int numCols)
    {
        this.numCols = numCols;
        result = new Vector(15,15);
    }
```

```java
public void setNames(String[] namesCols)
{
   this.namesCols = namesCols;
}

public void setRow(Object[] row)
{
   result.addElement(row);
}

public void done()
{
   result.trimToSize();
}

public int getSize()
{
   return result.size();
}

public int getColumnCount()
{
   return numCols;
}

public void setCursor(int cursor)
{
   this.cursor = cursor;
}

public boolean next()
{
   if(cursor < result.size())
   {
      cursor = cursor + 1;
      row = (Object[]) result.elementAt(cursor -1);
      return true;
   }
   else return false;
}

public int getInt(int col)
{
   Integer current = (Integer) row[col - 1];
   return current.intValue();
}

public double getDouble(int col)
{
   Double current = (Double) row[col - 1];
   return current.doubleValue();
}
```

```java
public String getString(int col)
{
    return (String) row[col -1];
}

public int getNumeric(int col) getNumeric(int col)
{
    Integer i = (Integer) row[col-1];
    return i.intValue();
}

public java.sql.Date getData(int col)
{
    return (java.sql.Date) row[col-1];
}

public java.sql.Time getTime(int col)
{
    return (java.sql.Time) row[col-1];
}

public java.sql.Timestamp getTimestamp(int col)
{
    return (java.sql.Timestamp) row[col-1];
}

public String toStringLabel()
{
    StringBuffer data = new StringBuffer();
    for(int i = 1; i <= numCols; ++i)
    {
        data.append((String)namesCols[i -1]);
        data.append(", ");
    }
    data.append("\n");
    return data.toString();
}

public String toStringData()
{
    StringBuffer data = new StringBuffer();
    while(next())
    {
        for(int i = 1; i <= numCols; ++i)
        {
            data.append(row[i -1]);
            data.append(", ");
        }
        data.append("\n");
    }
    return data.toString();
}
```

# Putting It Together

Now you have all of the pieces for the server with the exception of the actual database. In order to deploy this, first create an ODBC database in a package such as MS Access, Sybase SQL Everywhere, or MS SQL Server, and modify the database code to point to your particular data. Then compile all of the pieces, run the registry on your server, and start the database server.

Here are the steps:

1. First, compile the code listed previously with your Java compiler (such as javac):

```
javac *.java
```

2. Once the class files have been compiled, compile the stub and skeleton classes using rmic:

```
rmic CompPrice
rmic ClientHandler
rmic ResultCopier
```

3. Finally, launch the application using the Java interpreter:

```
java rmibook.database.CompPrice
```

To do any of this, you must have a database server configured with the JDBC hooks modified to fit the database. Note that the example code in this chapter requires that you have access to a JDBC-enabled database. I have tested the code with Access, so the exact details may differ slightly if you are using a different database. For more information on JDBC, check the Javasoft Web site, www.javasoft.com, or pick up any reference on JDBC.

# Summary

Here you took a look at a database server that uses both the JDBC database library and RMI to provide remote access to a database. The RMI-specific parts of the code are a simple and small part of the entire application, the bulk of which is occupied with database abstraction. In order to use this code, you still need to create an access client. In Chapter 10, you will create an applet that accesses this database and formats it into tables.

# Chapter 10

# Writing an RMI Database Client

## IN THIS CHAPTER

- ◆ The `ServerHandler` class
- ◆ The `Table` object
- ◆ The `Applet` subclass

IN CHAPTER 9 YOU built a database server that uses JDBC to connect to a database and RMI to connect to the server and make queries from the database. In Chapter 10 you are going to look at the client side of this application. The client is built as an applet that uses RMI to connect to the server from Chapter 9. The applet has a handle on the server's exported objects, but the applet also exports an object that is used as a callback mechanism so that the server can send the result back in chunks as it is read from the database.

This chapter contains a lot of code—code that connects with the server that you built in Chapter 9 as well as code for extending the `Applet` class, formatting the results of database queries, and building a basic user interface. The components of this application are listed in Table 10-1.

### TABLE 10-1. CLIENT COMPONENTS

| Class/Interface | Description |
| --- | --- |
| ServerHandlerInterface.java | A `Remote` interface used to interact with a database server. |
| ServerHandler.java | The implementation of the `ServerHandlerInterface`. |
| Table.java | The graphic component used to format the data results. |
| TableObserver.java | An observer object used to update the table generated in `Table.java`. |
| CompApplet.java | An extension of the `Applet` class. This is the main entry point of the client application. Events and main GUI construction are defined in this section. |

# The ServerHandler Class

First of all, take a look at the RMI components of this client. ServerHandler is a Remote object that is used to interact with the server. It is created as a separate object that forwards server calls to the applet so that it can extend UnicastRemoteObject directly instead of using the UnicastRemoteObject.exportObject() method. Thus the applet is not actually a Remote object and does not export any of its methods. Instead, it creates an instance of a ServerHandler that exports its methods and returns results to the applet.

First take a look at the Remote interface that is implemented by the ServerHandler class (see Listing 10-1).

Listing 10-1. The interface to the database server (ServerHandlerInterface.java)

```
package rmibook.database;
import java.rmi.server.UnicastRemoteObject;
import java.rmi.RemoteException;

public interface ServerHandlerInterface
                extends java.rmi.Remote
{
    public void callBackStatus(int rows, int chunks)
            throws RemoteException;
    public void
        callBackFirstChunk(ResultSetCopy firstChunk)
        throws RemoteException;
    public void callBackNextChunkAvailable()
        throws RemoteException;
}
```

Pretty straightforward—three methods for checking the status, getting the first chunk of data, and getting the next chunk available. Now take a look at the implementation (see Listing 10-2).

Listing 10-2. Interacting with the database server (ServerHandler.java)

```
package rmibook.database;
import java.rmi.server.UnicastRemoteObject;
import java.rmi.RemoteException;

public class ServerHandler
        extends UnicastRemoteObject
        implements ServerHandlerInterface
{
    //used to store a reference to the Applet for
    //forwarding results
    CompApplet applet;

    public ServerHandler(CompApplet applet)
```

```
            throws RemoteException
    {
        super();
        this.applet = applet;
    }

    public void callBackStatus(int rows, int chunks)
                            throws RemoteException
    {
        applet.callBackStatus(rows, chunks);
    }

    public void
            callBackFirstChunk(ResultSetCopy firstChunk)
            throws RemoteException
    {
        applet.callBackFirstChunk(firstChunk);
    }

    public synchronized void callBackNextChunkAvailable()
                                throws RemoteException
    {
        applet.callBackNextChunkAvailable();
    }
}
```

# The Table Object

The Table object that you used in the CompApplet class is a GUI component that formats your data into rows and generates an event when a row is selected (see Figure 10-1; the code appears in Listing 10-3). It also generates column headings to make your data user-friendly.

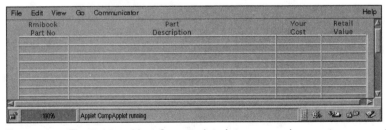

Figure 10-1. The Table object formats data into rows and generates an event when a row is selected.

**Listing 10-3. The graphic table object (Table.java)**

```java
package rmibook.database;
import java.awt.*;

public class Table extends Canvas
{
    //define some variables
    public static final int leftJustify = 1;
    public static final int rightJustify = 2;
    int cellHeight = 15;
    int rows;
    int columns;
    int[] columnWidth;
    String[][] cell;
    String[] LabelLine1;
    String[] LabelLine2;
    int[] justify;
    TableObserver observer;
    boolean selected = false;
    int selectedRow = 0;

    //The constructor expects the number or rows and
    //their widths and an observer object that we
    //define in TableObserver.java
    public Table(int rows, int[] widths,
                 TableObserver observer)
    {
        this.observer = observer;
        this.rows = rows;
        columns = widths.length;
        columnWidth = widths;
        cell = new String[rows][columns];
        LabelLine1 = new String[columns];
        LabelLine2 = new String[columns];
        justify = new int[columns];
        for (int i = 0; i < rows; i++)
        {
            for(int j = 0; j < columns; j++)
            {
                cell[i][j] = new String(" ");
            }
        }

        for(int i = 0; i < columns; i++)
        {
            LabelLine1[i] = new String(" ");
            LabelLine2[i] = new String(" ");
        }

        for(int i = 0; i < columns; i++)
        {
            justify[i] = leftJustify;
```

```java
      }
}

public synchronized void setCell(int row, int column,
                                    String content)
{
   cell[row - 1][column - 1] = content;
}

public synchronized void setColumn(int column,
                        String Line1,String Line2,
                        int justification)
{
   LabelLine1[column - 1] = Line1;
   LabelLine2[column - 1] = Line2;
   justify[column - 1] = justification;
}

public synchronized void setColumn(int column,
                                    String Line1,
                                    String Line2)
{
   LabelLine1[column - 1] = Line1;
   LabelLine2[column - 1] = Line2;
}

public void updateTable()
{
   repaint();
}

public synchronized void paint(Graphics g)
{
   Dimension d = size();
   int cx, cy;
   g.setColor(Color.black);
   for(int i = 0; i <= rows; i++)
   {
      cy = (i+2) * cellHeight;
      g.setColor(getBackground());
      g.draw3DRect(0, cy, d.width, 2, true);
   }
   cx = 0;
   for(int i = 0; i < columns; i++)
   {
      g.setColor(getBackground());
      g.draw3DRect(cx, 2 * cellHeight, 1,
                   d.height, true);
      cx += columnWidth[i];
   }
  cx = d.width - 1;
  g.draw3DRect(cx, 2 * cellHeight, 1, d.height, true);
```

```
if(selected)
{
    g.setColor(Color.white);
    g.fillRect(2, (selectedRow * cellHeight) + 2,
            d.width, cellHeight -2);
}

g.setColor(Color.blue);
FontMetrics fm = g.getFontMetrics();
int LabelCenterAdj;
int columnStart = 0;
int sWidth;

for ( int i = 0; i < columns; ++i)
{
    cy = cellHeight;
    sWidth = fm.stringWidth(LabelLine1[i]);
    LabelCenterAdj = ((columnWidth[i] -
                    sWidth) / 2);
    cx = columnStart + LabelCenterAdj;
    g.drawString(LabelLine1[i], cx , cy - 1);
    cy += cellHeight;
    sWidth = fm.stringWidth(LabelLine2[i]);
    LabelCenterAdj = ((columnWidth[i] -
                    sWidth) / 2);
    cx = columnStart + LabelCenterAdj;
    g.drawString(LabelLine2[i], cx , cy - 1);
    columnStart += columnWidth[i];
}

g.setColor(Color.red);
int cWidth;
for(int i = 0; i < rows; ++i)
{
    cx = 2;
    cy = (i + 3) * cellHeight;

    for(int j = 0; j < columns; ++j)
    {
        if(justify[j] == rightJustify)
        {
            sWidth = fm.stringWidth(cell[i][j]);
            cWidth = columnWidth[j];
            int diff = cWidth - sWidth;
            g.drawString(cell[i][j], cx + diff - 2,
                        cy -1);
        }
        else
        {
            g.drawString(cell[i][j], cx, cy -1);
        }
        cx += columnWidth[j];
    }
```

```
        }
    }
    public synchronized Dimension preferredSize()
    {
        int tableHeight = (cellHeight *  rows) +
                          (cellHeight * 2) + 2;
        int tableWidth = 0;
        for(int i = 0; i < columns; ++i)
        {
            tableWidth += columnWidth[i];
        }
        tableWidth += 3;
        return new Dimension(tableWidth,tableHeight);
    }

    public synchronized Dimension minimumSize()
    {
        int tableHeight = (cellHeight *  rows) +
                          (cellHeight * 2) + 2;
        int tableWidth = 0;
        for(int i = 0; i < columns; ++i)
        {
            tableWidth += columnWidth[i];
        }
        tableWidth += 3;
        return new Dimension(tableWidth,tableHeight);
    }

    public boolean mouseDown(Event evt, int x, int y)
    {
        Double approxRow = new Double(y / cellHeight);
        int currentSelectedRow = approxRow.intValue();
        if (currentSelectedRow < 2)
            return true;
        else
        {
            selected = true;
            selectedRow = currentSelectedRow;
            repaint();
            observer.rowSelection(selectedRow - 1);
            return true;
        }
    }
}
```

Now you will create the observer for this Table (see Listing 10-4). The observer is used to capture events and take the appropriate action. Essentially, it lets an object know when a row selection has been made in the Table.

**Listing 10-4. Watching for row selection events (TableObserver.java)**

```
package rmibook.database;
public interface TableObserver
```

```
{
    public void rowSelection(int row);
}
```

# The Applet Subclass

Now take a look at the `Applet` subclass (see Listing 10-5). The applet (shown in Figure 10-2) is the main part of your application here. It handles rendering the graphic user interface (GUI) and all of the GUI events. This is the class that will be embedded in an HTML document when the application is deployed.

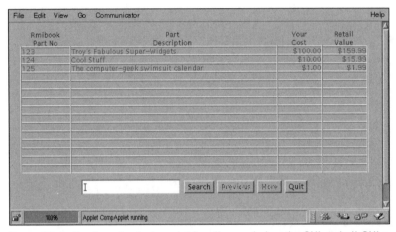

Figure 10-2: The `CompApplet` applet handles rendering the GUI and all GUI events.

Listing 10-5. The main applet (CompApplet.java)

```
package rmibook.database;

import java.io.*;
import java.util.*;
import java.awt.*;
import java.sql.*;
import java.rmi.Naming;

public class CompApplet extends java.applet.Applet
            implements TableObserver
{

    //Let's define our variables first…
    public static final double profitMargin = 1.1;
```

```
private static final int tableLines = 15;
private Table displayList;
private CompPriceInterface server;
private ClientHandlerInterface handler;
private ResultCopierInterface queryHandler;
ResultSetCopy results;
ServerHandler proxy;
ResultSetCopy currentDataChunk = null;
Panel p;
TextField descField;
int totalRows = 0;
int totalChunks = 0;
int shownChunks = 0;
int completedChunks = 0;
int storedVectorSize = 0;
boolean finishedProcessing = false;
Button moreButton;
Button previousButton;
Vector allData;
int currentViewIndex = 0;

//In our init method, we create a ServerHandler
//instance, create a table object, and add GUI
//components to our applet.
public void init()
{
   try
   {
      //ServerHandler is defined in
      //ServerHandler.java
      proxy = new ServerHandler(this);
   }
   catch(Exception e)
   {
      System.out.println("Unable to create Remote" +
                     "Client Class: ServerHandler");
   }

   //Here we start defining our interface and
   //add it to a Panel
   int[] cellWidth = new int[5];
   cellWidth[0] = 90;
   cellWidth[1] = 370;
   cellWidth[2] = 80;
   cellWidth[3] = 80;
   setBackground(Color.lightGray);

   //Table is defined in Table.java
   displayList = new Table(tableLines, cellWidth,
                        this);
   add("Center", displayList);
   displayList.setColumn(1, "rmibook", "Part No");
   displayList.setColumn(2, "Part", "Description");
```

```
            displayList.setColumn(3, "Your", "Cost",
                                Table.rightJustify);
            displayList.setColumn(4, "Retail", "Value",
                                Table.rightJustify);
            p = new Panel();
            p.setLayout(new FlowLayout());
            descField = new TextField("", 20);
            p.add(descField);
            p.add(new Button("Search"));
            previousButton = new Button("Previous");
            p.add(previousButton);
            moreButton = new Button("More");
            p.add(moreButton);
            p.add(new Button("Quit"));
            add("South", p);
            moreButton.disable();
            previousButton.disable();
            allData = new Vector(100, 100);
        }

    //This is called when the applet is loaded
    //and connects to the database server.
    public void start()
    {
        try
        {
            //connect to our database server
            getConnected();
        }
        catch(Exception e)
        {
            System.out.println("Exception: " +
                                e.getMessage());
            e.printStackTrace();
        }
    }

    //return our first result chunk after a query is made    public
  synchronized void
callBackFirstChunk(ResultSetCopy firstChunk)
    {
        storedVectorSize = 0;
        currentViewIndex = 0;
        completedChunks  = 0;

        try
        {
            allData.addElement(firstChunk);
            showNextChunk(firstChunk);
        }
        catch(Exception e)
        {
            System.out.println("Exception: " +
```

```
                        e.getMessage());
        e.printStackTrace();
    }
    storedVectorSize++;
    currentViewIndex++;
    completedChunks++;

    System.out.println("callBackFirstChunk, " +
                        "completedChunks = " +
                        completedChunks);
}

//This is used to retrieve data after the first
//chunk has arrived.
public synchronized void callBackNextChunkAvailable()
{
    completedChunks++;
    System.out.println("callBackNextChunkAvailable, " +
                        "completedChunks =" +
                        completedChunks );
    moreButton.enable();
}

//this establishes a connection with the server
public boolean getConnected()
        throws java.rmi.RemoteException,
                java.net.UnknownHostException,
                java.rmi.NotBoundException,
                java.net.MalformedURLException
{
    server = (CompPriceInterface)

    //Insert the name of your registry server here...
Naming.lookup("rmi://rmibook.database.com/PriceServer");
    //This will send a message to the server and
    //get one back. Basically just to say hello.
    String message = server.handshake("Connected!");

    System.out.println("Received: " + message);
    //Here's were we get our handler
    handler = (ClientHandlerInterface)
                server.getClientHandler();
    return true;
}

//Here is our remote method for returning the
//object that is used for our callbacks.
public ResultCopierInterface
        descQuery(String description)
        throws java.rmi.RemoteException,
                java.sql.SQLException
{
    //create a ResultHandler and return it
```

```
            ResultCopierInterface currentQueryHandler =
                            (ResultCopierInterface)
                            handler.matchDesc
                            (description, tableLines, proxy);
            return currentQueryHandler;
    }

    public void showNextChunk(ResultSetCopy dataChunk)
            throws java.rmi.RemoteException
    {
        if (dataChunk != (ResultSetCopy) null)
        {
            System.out.println("showNextChunk: data not null");
            currentDataChunk = dataChunk;
            String data;
            double value;
            Float dollars;
            int i = 1;
            dataChunk.setCursor(0);
            while(dataChunk.next())
            {
                data = dataChunk.getString(2);
                displayList.setCell(i, 1, data);
                data = dataChunk.getString(4);
                displayList.setCell(i, 2, data);
                value = (dataChunk.getDouble(6) *
                        profitMargin);
                dollars = Float(value);
                displayList.setCell(i, 3,
                        dollars.toString());
                value = dataChunk.getDouble(7);
                dollars = new Float(value);
                displayList.setCell(i, 4,
                        dollars.toString());
                ++i;
            }
            if(i < tableLines)
            {
                while(i <= tableLines)
                {
                    displayList.setCell(i, 1, " ");
                    displayList.setCell(i, 2, " ");
                    displayList.setCell(i, 3, " ");
                    displayList.setCell(i, 4, " ");
                    ++i;
                }
            }
            displayList.updateTable();
        }
        else
        {
            System.out.println("showNextChunk: data null");
        }
```

```
}
//status message when a row is selected
public void rowSelection(int row)
{
    System.out.println("rowSelection: " + row);
}

public void callBackStatus(int rows, int chunks)
{
    totalRows = rows;
    totalChunks = chunks;
    System.out.println("callBackStatus:  Rows: " +
                        rows + "  Chunks: " + chunks);
}

//this is our GUI event handler.
public boolean action(Event evt, Object arg)
{

    ResultSetCopy nextResult;
    ResultSetCopy thisData;
    //if the event was a search.
    if (arg.equals("Search"))
    {
        String textInput = descField.getText();
        synchronized (this)
        {
            storedVectorSize = 0;
            currentViewIndex = 0;
            completedChunks  = 0;
            allData = new Vector(100, 100);
            previousButton.disable();
            moreButton.disable();
        }
        try
        {
            queryHandler = descQuery(textInput);
        }
        catch(Exception e)
        {
            System.out.println("Exception: " +
                                e.getMessage());
            e.printStackTrace();
        }
    }
    else if (arg.equals("Previous"))
    {
        System.out.print("*Prev: Entry* storedVectSize="
                          + storedVectorSize);
        System.out.print(", currViewIndx = " +
                          currentViewIndex);
        System.out.println(", completeChunks = " +
                           completedChunks);
```

```
synchronized (allData)
{
   currentViewIndex-;
   thisData = (ResultSetCopy)
       allData.elementAt(currentViewIndex - 1);
}
try
{
   showNextChunk(thisData);
   showNextChunk(thisData);
}
catch(Exception e)
{
   System.out.println("Exception: " +
                       e.getMessage());
   e.printStackTrace();
}
synchronized (this)
{
   moreButton.enable();
}
if (currentViewIndex > 1)
{
   synchronized (this)
   {
      previousButton.enable();
   }
}
else
{
   synchronized (this)
   {
      previousButton.disable();
   }
}
System.out.print("*Prev: Exit* storedVectSize= "
                 + storedVectorSize);
System.out.print(", currViewIndx = "
                 + currentViewIndex);
System.out.println(", completeChunks = " +
                   completedChunks);
}
else if (arg.equals("More"))
{
   System.out.print("*More Entry* storedVectSize= "
                    + storedVectorSize);
   System.out.print(", currViewIndx = " +
                    currentViewIndex);
   System.out.println(", completeChunks = " +
                      completedChunks);
   if (storedVectorSize == currentViewIndex)
   {
      try
```

```
        {
            nextResult = queryHandler.nextChunk();
            synchronized (this)
            {
                allData.addElement(nextResult);
                storedVectorSize++;
                currentViewIndex++;
            }
            showNextChunk(nextResult);
            synchronized (this)
            {
                previousButton.enable();
                if (completedChunks > storedVectorSize)
                {
                    moreButton.enable();
                }
                else
                {
                    moreButton.disable();
                }
            }
        }
        catch(Exception e)
        {
            System.out.println("Exception: " +
                            e.getMessage());
            e.printStackTrace();
        }
    }
    else if (currentViewIndex < storedVectorSize )
    {
        synchronized (this)
        {
            currentViewIndex++;
            thisData = (ResultSetCopy)
            allData.elementAt(currentViewIndex - 1);
        }
        try
        {
            showNextChunk(thisData);
        }
        catch(Exception e)
        {
            System.out.println("Exception: " +
                            e.getMessage());
            e.printStackTrace();
        }
        synchronized (this)
        {
            previousButton.enable();
        }

        if (storedVectorSize == currentViewIndex)
```

```
            {
                synchronized (this)
                {
                    if (completedChunks > storedVectorSize)
                    {
                        moreButton.enable();
                    }
                    else
                    {
                        moreButton.disable();
                    }
                }
            }
            else
            {
                synchronized (this)
                {
                    moreButton.enable();
                }
            }
        }
        else
        {
            System.out.println("More: Logic Error");
        }

        System.out.print("*More: Exit* storedVectSize= "
                    + storedVectorSize);
        System.out.print(", currViewIndex = " +
                    currentViewIndex);
        System.out.println(", completeChunks = " +
                    completedChunks);
    }
    else if (arg.equals("Quit"))
    {
        System.exit(0);
    }
    else
    {
        return super.action(evt,arg);
    }
    return true;
    }
}
```

# Putting It Together

Now that you have defined all of the classes for your applet, you must compile and
deploy it. The compile part is straightforward, but to deploy it you must first embed

the CompApplet class in an HTML document (see Listing 10-6). Once this has been done, you can open the HTML document in a Web browser, and, providing the server is up and running, you will have access to your database.

**Listing 10-6. HTML document for the** CompApplet **class (CompApplet.html)**

```
<HTML>
<APPLET code=rmibook.database.CompApplet.class
        width=600
        height=400 >
</APPLET>
</HTML>
```

# Summary

You have now constructed a simple RMI-based applet that interacts with a database server that uses both RMI and JDBC. The implementations were pretty simple and straightforward. You should now have a strong understanding of the potential of RMI and of how to implement distributed applications using the RMI facilities.

# Part IV

## Java API Quick Reference

# Reference A

# The java.rmi Package

THE JAVA.RMI PACKAGE CONTAINS a `Remote` interface, a security manager, and a `Registry` lookup and binding class. The interface, `java.rmi.Remote`, must be implemented by any object that is exportable (either directly or through an extension).

## Interface

### Remote

```
public interface Remote {
}
```

The `Remote` interface is used to identify objects that can be referenced remotely. The interface does not define any methods or variables and is usually extended for particular applications. An object that is exported is expected to implement this interface either directly or indirectly through an extension. The only methods that are available to a client using a remote object are declared in an interface that extends `Remote`. The following is a simple example that declares two methods that can be exported and remotely accessed:

```
public interface MyRemote extends java.rmi.Remote {
    public void remoteMeth1() throws RemoteException;
    public void remoteMeth2() throws RemoteException;
}
```

## Classes

### Naming

```
public final class Naming extends Object
```

The `Naming` class is used to interact with a registry. It contains methods that can be used to add objects to a registry and to query a registry for remote objects that have registered with it. Naming gives a high-level, URL-based interface to registry servers. The `Naming` class is final and cannot be subclassed. If you wish to create your own registry services, see the `java.rmi.registry` package.

## CONSTRUCTORS
The `Naming` class contains only static methods and does not define a constructor.

## FIELDS
The `Naming` class does not define any public class variables.

## METHODS

**bind**

```
public static void bind(String url, Remote obj)
    throws AlreadyBoundException,
    MalformedURLException, UnknownHostException,
    RemoteException
```

`Bind` is used to register an object with a specified registry. The `url` String contains a URL to a registry server and the name that the `Remote` object will be referenced by. In its complete form, the URL will resemble "rmi://www.foo.com[:port]/ObjectName." The second parameter, `obj`, is a reference to an object that is being exported. This object must implement a `java.rmi.Remote` interface either directly or through an extension.

`AlreadyBoundException` is thrown if the name supplied by URL is already referencing an object in the registry.

`RemoteException` is thrown if a call to `bind` is unable to locate the registry specified.

**list**

```
public static String[] list(String url) throws RemoteException,
MalformedURLException, UnknownHostException
```

The `list` method is used to query a registry for a list of remote objects that are currently bound. An array of `Strings` will be returned, and each `String` in the array will contain a name that is bound to a remote object on the given registry.

A `String` containing the URL to a registry server is passed as the sole argument.

`RemoteException` is thrown if a call to `list` is unable to locate the registry specified by the URL.

**lookup**

```
public static Remote lookup(String url) throws NotBoundException,
```

```
MalformedURLException, UnknownHostException, RemoteException
```

The `lookup` method is used to get a remote object from a registry server. Lookup is passed a string containing the URL to a remote object reference on a registry server. If the call succeeds, a stub to a remote object is returned. This stub acts as the client-side proxy to the remote object and can be treated by the client as if it were the actual object. Only methods that are declared in an extension of the `Remote` interface and implemented by the object that the stub was generated from can be accessed.

`RemoteException` is thrown if `lookup` is unable to locate the specified registry.

`NotBoundException` is thrown if the name specified in the URL is not bound in the specified registry.

### rebind

```
public static void rebind(String url, Remote obj) throws
RemoteException, MalformedURLException, UnknownHostException
```

The `rebind` method works just like the `bind` method with one difference: `rebind` will replace an object that is already bound with the registry with the new object specified with `obj`. The `String url` contains a URL to a registry server and a name that the `Remote` object, `obj`, will be bound to. The `rebind()` method can be called only from applications that are running on the same physical machine as the registry.

`RemoteException` will be thrown if `rebind` is unable to contact the registry.

### unbind

```
public static void unbind(String url) throws RemoteException,
NotBoundException, MalformedURLException, UnknownHostException
```

The `unbind` method will remove an object reference from a registry. The `url` `String` contains a URL to a named object in a registry. If the name is bound to an object, the reference is removed. This method can be called only by an application that is running on the same registry that is referred to in `url`. The `unbind()` method can be called only from applications that are running on the same physical machine as the registry.

`RemoteException` is thrown if `unbind` is unable to contact the registry.

`NotBoundException` is thrown if the name requested is not bound with the registry.

## RMISecurityManager

```
public class RMISecurityManager extends SecurityManager
```

The `RMISecurityManager` is a subclass of `SecurityManager` with certain security policies in effect that allow RMI to function. If a `SecurityManager` is not explicitly set, an application will not be able to export objects over a network. Under normal circumstances, the `RMISecurityManager` will be used to set the security policies for remote method invocation. By default, Java's virtual machine does not allow an application to dynamically load stub classes over a network from a remote application using RMI unless the application has set up its own `SecurityManager`. This limitation is made to prevent miscreant stub classes from being downloaded into the virtual machine. Typically, applications use the `RMISecurityManager`. This security manager allows stub classes to be downloaded over the network but prevents the downloaded classes from performing any other security-sensitive actions (such as reading local files or opening network connections).

The `RMISecurityManager` is generally instanced and then set to be the current `SecurityManager` with a call to `System.setSecurityManager()`.

With `RMISecurityManager` in place, any code that is loaded as a stub in an application will be allowed class definition and access. An application that does not explicitly set the `RMISecurityManager` will only be able to load stub classes that are accessible through the CLASSPATH environment variable.

The security manager works by throwing an `AccessException` when any of the test methods are called that are not permitted. Accordingly, the system calls certain methods in the `SecurityManager` before allowing certain suspect operations to take place. If an exception is thrown, access is denied. If no exceptions are thrown, the operation is allowed to proceed. With this in mind, note that the Methods section below lists only those operations that are allowed when an `RMISecurityManager` is in place.

## CONSTRUCTOR

```
public RMISecurityManager();
```

Constructs and initializes an instance of `RMISecurityManager`.

## FIELDS
`RMISecurityManager` does not declare any variables.

## METHODS

### checkAccept

```
public synchronized void checkAccept(String host, int port)
```

Does not permit a stub to accept socket connections.

### checkAccess

```
public synchronized void checkAccess(Thread t)
```

Stubs cannot manipulate Threads.

### checkAccess

```
public synchronized void checkAccess(ThreadGroup t)
```

Stubs cannot manipulate Threads.

### checkConnect

```
public synchronized void checkConnect(String host, int port)
```

Stubs are not permitted to make socket connections unless they are loaded locally.

### checkConnect

```
public synchronized void checkConnect(String host, int port, Object
 context)
```

Stubs are not permitted to make socket connections unless they are loaded locally.

### checkConnect

```
public synchronized void checkConnect(String fromHost, String
 toHost)
```

Stubs are not permitted to make socket connections unless they are loaded locally.

### checkCreateClassLoader

```
public syncronized void checkCreateClassLoader()
```

Stubs are not permitted to interact with or create class loaders.

### checkDelete

```
public synchronized void checkDelete(String file)
```

Stubs cannot delete files.

### checkExec

```
public synchronized void checkExec(String command)
```

Stubs cannot execute code or fork processes.

### checkExit

```
public synchronized void checkExit(int StatusCode)
```

Stubs cannot kill the Virtual Machine.

### checkLink

```
public synchronized void checkLink(String Library)
```

Stubs cannot link to dynamic libraries.

### checkListen

```
public synchronized void checkListen(int port)
```

A stub cannot listen to a port.

### checkMemberAccess

```
public synchronized void checkMemberAccess(class c, int which)
```

This method checks for access privileges to class members. It will provide access to all public fields, and it will provide nonstub classes access to fields with default, package, and private privileges.

### checkPackageAccess

```
public synchronized void checkPackageAccess(String package)
```

Checks for package access. This will deny stub access to external packages.

### checkPackageDefinition

```
public synchronized void checkPackageDefinition(String package)
```

A stub cannot define classes in other packages.

### checkPrintJobAccess

```
public synchronized void checkPrintJobAccess()
```

Stubs cannot access print jobs.

### checkPropertiesAccess

```
public synchronized void checkPropertiesAccess()
```

Stubs can only access properties that have been explicitly allowed stub access. These properties are tagged in the checkPropertyAccess() method.

### checkPropertyAccess

```
public synchronized void checkPropertyAccess(String key)
```

This method will check if a stub has access to the property associated with the given key. The property that corresponds to the key must be set to the Boolean value "true" if the stub is to have access. For example, the property java.home is accessible only if the java.home.stub property is set to "true."

### checkRead

```
public synchronized void checkRead(FileDescriptor fd)
```

Stubs are not permitted to open file descriptors for reading.

### checkRead

```
public synchronized void checkRead(String file)
```

Stubs cannot read files.

### checkRead

```
public synchronized void checkRead(String file, URL base)
```

Stubs cannot read files.

### checkRead

```
public synchronized void checkRead(String file, Object o)
```

Stubs cannot read files.

### checkSecurityAccess

```
public synchronized void checkSecurityAccess(String SecProvider)
```

A stub cannot perform security provider operations.

### checkSetFactory

```
public synchronized void checkSetFactory()
```

A stub cannot set a network factory.

### checkTopLevelWindow

```
public synchronized void checkTopLevelWindow()
```

A stub can create top-level windows with warning. These windows are similar to the top-level windows set by applets with the "Untrusted Applet Window" warning.

### CheckWrite

```
public synchronized void checkWrite(String file)
```

A stub cannot write to a file.

### checkWrite

```
public synchronized void checkWrite(FileDescriptor fd)
```

A stub cannot open a file through a file descriptor for writing.

### GetSecurityContext

```
public Object getSecurityContext()
```

This returns an object that represents the current execution environment in a manner that enables certain checks to be performed. The only variable that affects the stub access is the host that the stub came from.

# Reference B

# The java.rmi.dgc Package

THE `java.rmi.dgc` PACKAGE CONTAINS one interface and one class that are used by the distributed garbage collection system. Garbage collection on distributed systems has some unique needs that separate it from garbage collection in a single memory space.

The interface and class of this package will not generally be used by programmers using the RMI tools, but rather by system implementors who may want to create their own garbage collection algorithms. In this section, I will give a brief description of the various components of the DGC package, but garbage collection is a topic in and of itself that warrants its own book. The goal of this section is to give an understanding of the components in the garbage collection system that is used by RMI.

# Interface

## DGC

```
public interface DGC extends Remote
```

The DGC interface is used for the server side of the distributed garbage collection system. This interface contains two methods that are called remotely by an RMI client. These methods are the `dirty()` and `clean()` methods. A dirty call is made whenever a remote reference is retrieved from a marshal stream. A corresponding clean call is made when no more references to the remote reference exist in the client. If a dirty call fails, a strong clean call is scheduled so that the sequence number of the call can be retained in order to detect future calls received out of order.

In a normal `clean()` call, the virtual machine IDs are removed from reference lists for each remote object specified. The reference lists are generated as references are granted to remote clients. This is all maintained by the garbage collector. A sequence number is used to detect late `dirty()` calls. In the case of a strong clean, there was a previous `dirty()` call that failed, and the sequence number for the virtual machine ID is retained. A `dirty()` call can fail due to network failure or general system failure. Normally, a `RemoteException` will be thrown upon failure.

Remote references are leased by the client. In other words, a request is made for an object lease for a specified amount of time. The lease is renewable but will otherwise expire after the specified time. The lease period starts when a dirty call is received, and the lease will eventually expire if not renewed. It is up to the client to periodically renew leases before they expire by calling the dirty method again. If a lease expires and no more dirty calls are made, the system then has license to assume that the object is no longer referenced and to schedule it for collection. This prevents dead connections from keeping objects in limbo on remote systems. Once a period expires without a lease renewal, the connection is considered dead and the associated object, unreferenced.

## FIELDS
The DGC interface does not define any variables.

## METHODS

### clean

```
public abstract void
    clean(ObjID ids[],long sequenceNum,
    VMID vmid, boolean strong)
    throws RemoteException
```

The clean method tells the server to cancel any leases that were granted for the objects in the ids array to the client identified by VMID. The sequence number is used to detect late (out-of-order) calls. If the strong boolean is set to true, then it is assumed that a dirty call has failed and the sequence ID is remembered for the given virtual machine ID. In other words, the virtual machine reference list is not cleared.

### dirty

```
public abstract Lease dirty(ObjID ids[],
    long sequenceNum, Lease lease)
    throws RemoteException
```

The ids[] array contains a list of object IDs that the caller is interested in obtaining leases for. A call to dirty obtains leases for each of these objects. The Lease object contains a unique identifier for the client's virtual machine and the time that the lease is requested for. A Lease object is returned with the corresponding VMID set, or null. If the lease is accepted, the server adds a lease reference for the given virtual machine ID for each of the objects in the ObjID array. The sequenceNum is used to track late or out-of-order calls for leases. The garbage collector increments the sequence number with each transaction. If the sequence numbers get out of sync, a strong clean() is called. A client needs to obtain only one lease for any object, even if the client has several references to that object. The client is also responsible for renewing leases before they expire. When an object is no longer referenced, the client calls the clean() method for the object so that it can be scheduled for collection.

# Class

## Lease

```
public final class Lease extends Object
```

The Lease object is used as a data structure to record information about a lease—either a lease request (the value passed into the DGC.dirty() method) or a granted lease (the return result of the DGC.dirty() method). The Lease class contains information about the local Virtual Machine and the time the lease is requested for. The Lease object is also used to grant leases that are requested.

### CONSTRUCTOR

```
public Lease(VMID id, long duration)
```

The VMID is the unique virtual machine identifier for the machine requesting a lease on a remote object. The long integer, duration, is the amount of time in seconds that the lease is being requested for. In other words, the lease, if granted, will expire after duration seconds have passed.

### FIELDS
The Lease class does not define any public class variables.

### METHODS
#### getValue

```
public long getValue()
```

The getValue method will return the number of seconds that the lease is valid for.

#### getVMID

```
public VMID getVMID()
```

The getVMID method will return the Virtual Machine ID that is associated with this lease.

# Reference C

# The java.rmi.registry Package

THE java.rmi.registry PACKAGE CONTAINS two interfaces and one class that, together, are used to create, look up, and query a registry server. The class and interfaces in this package can be used to create your own registry services, or to interact with other registry services.

## Interfaces

### Registry

```
public interface Registry extends Remote
```

A Registry is used to locate RMI services. When a client makes initial contact with a service, it must first locate the exported remote objects for that service. The Registry provides a bootstrap mechanism whereby a service running on an anonymous port can register its remote objects with a registry service running on a well-defined port. The server supplies a reference to the remote object(s) and name(s) that are bound to the object(s). Each name in a registry must be unique, so often it is desirable to use fully package-qualified names when binding an object to a registry, such as rmibook.chat.ChatServerImpl.

Once a client has retrieved a reference to a remote object via a registry lookup, subsequent objects can be accessed through other means, namely return values from remote method calls.

### FIELD

```
public final static int REGISTRY_PORT
```

The REGISTRY_PORT contains the well-defined port number that standard registry services will bind to. It is possible to run a registry on another port, just as it is possible to run an HTTP server on a port other than port 80, but this variable holds the standard default port number for registry services, which is 1099.

## METHODS

### bind

```
public abstract void bind(String name, Remote obj) throws
RemoteException, AlreadyBoundException, AccessException
```

Bind is used to bind a name to a remote object reference. The name passed must not already be bound in the registry, or an AlreadyBoundException will be thrown. If the remote operation fails, a RemoteException is thrown, and if the security manager doesn't permit bind access to the caller, an AccessException is thrown. Normally, only services that reside on the same machine as the registry can bind to it. A bind() call must originate from an application that is running on the same machine as the registry. Queries can be made from other machines on the network, but a remote service trying to bind will cause an AccessException.

### list

```
public abstract String[] list() throws RemoteException,
AccessException
```

The list method returns an array of Strings that contain the names of all objects that are currently bound in the registry. If the remote operation fails, a RemoteException is thrown, and if the security manager doesn't permit access to this list, an AccessException is thrown.

### lookup

```
public abstract Remote lookup(String name) throws RemoteException,
NotBoundException, AccessException
```

The lookup is used to query a registry for a remote object reference. The name passed is used to look up the object. It the object is found in the registry, a reference to the remote object is returned. (Note that all remote objects must implement the java.rmi.Remote interface, and so the return value for a lookup() is of type Remote.) If the name lookup fails—in other words, if the name requested is not bound in the registry—a NotBoundException is thrown. Also, a RemoteException is thrown if the remote operation fails, and an AccessException is thrown if the security manager doesn't allow this operation.

### rebind

```
public abstract void rebind(String name, Remote obj) throws
RemoteException, AccessException
```

The `rebind()` method works in much the same way as the `bind()` method. The difference is that `rebind()` will replace an object reference that has already been bound with the same name rather than throwing an `AlreadyBoundException`. The `rebind()` method takes a name `String` and a reference to a remote object and attempts to bind them in the registry. A `rebind()` call must originate from an application that is running on the same machine as the registry. An `AccessException` is thrown if the operation is not allowed by the security manager, and a `RemoteException` is thrown if the remote operation fails.

**unbind**

```
public abstract void unbind(String name) throws RemoteException,
NotBoundException, AccessException
```

The `unbind` method will remove an object reference from a registry. The name `String` contains the name of a bound object in the registry. If the name is bound to an object, the reference is removed; otherwise, a `NotBoundException` is thrown. An `AccessException` is thrown if the security manager does not permit this operation. An `unbind()` call must originate from an application that is running on the same machine as the registry.

A `RemoteException` is thrown if `unbind` is unable to contact the registry.

A `NotBoundException` is thrown if the name requested is not bound with the registry.

# RegistryHandler

```
public interface RegistryHandler
```

A registry uses remote method calls in order to be queried and to return references to remote objects. The implementation of a registry, much the same as the implementation of a remote object, requires stub and skeleton classes in order to marshal the registry requests.

The `RegistryHandler` interface is used as an interface to a private implementation of a registry. It contains methods used to obtain the stub class for a registry and the implementation of a registry.

## METHODS

**registryStub**

```
public abstract Registry registryStub(String host, int port) throws
RemoteException, UnknownHostException
```

The `registryStub()` method is used to obtain the stub class for the registry running on the given host and the given port number. If the host name cannot be resolved, an `UnknownHostException` is thrown. If the remote operation fails for any other reason, a `RemoteException` is thrown. Upon success, a registry stub object is returned.

### registryImpl

```
public abstract Registry registryImpl(int port) throws
RemoteException
```

This method is used to construct and register a registry on the given port. The port number must be valid and not already bound to another service. If the application is unable to create a registry on the given port, a `RemoteException` is thrown.

# Class

## LocateRegistry

```
public final class LocateRegistry extends Object
```

The `LocateRegistry` class is used to locate registry servers and to create new ones. It is used to find registry services given an address or to create new ones given a port number.

### CONSTRUCTORS
The `LocateRegistry` class contains only static methods and does not define a constructor.

### FIELDS
The `LocateRegistry` class does not define any public variables.

### METHODS

#### createRegistry

```
public static Registry createRegistry(int port) throws
RemoteException
```

The `createRegistry` method is used to create a new instance of a registry on the given port. The port must be available, and the effective UID of the application must have permission to bind to the given port. (In Unix, only a user with system privileges can bind to a port that is lower than 1024.) Upon success, a registry object is returned, and remote objects can be bound to this object using the methods described in the `Registry` interface. Upon failure, a `RemoteException` is thrown.

### getRegistry

```
public static Registry getRegistry() throws RemoteException
```

This method will attempt to return an object representing a registry running on the local host and bound to the standard registry port number of 1099. A `RemoteException` will be thrown upon failure.

### getRegistry

```
public static Registry getRegistry(int port) throws RemoteException
```

This method will attempt to return an object representing a registry running on the local host and bound to the given port number. A `RemoteException` will be thrown upon failure.

### getRegistry

```
public static Registry getRegistry(String host) throws
RemoteException, UnknownHostException
```

This method will attempt to return an object representing a registry running on the given host and bound to the standard port number for registry services (1099). If the given host name cannot be resolved to a valid IP address, an `UnknowHostException` is thrown. This can be the result of a misspelled host name, or a problem with your DNS services. Any other failure of the remote operation will result in a `RemoteException` being thrown.

### getRegistry

```
public static Registry getRegistry(String host, int port) throws
RemoteException, UnknownHostException
```

This method will attempt to return an object representing a registry running on the given host and bound to the given port number. If the given host name cannot be resolved to a valid IP address, an `UnknownHostException` is thrown. This can be the result of a misspelled host name or a problem with your DNS services. If the registry cannot be found on the given port number or any other failure of the remote operation occurs, a `RemoteException` will be thrown.

# Reference D

# The java.rmi.server Package

THE java.rmi.server PACKAGE has most of the core classes and interfaces that are necessary to export remote objects. This includes special class loaders, socket factories, and remote object definitions that are subclassed to create your own remote objects.

The java.rmi.server package also contains most of the classes needed for implementing RMI, such as the stub and skeleton interfaces and the calling mechanisms that allow skeletons to communicate with the objects they represent. Many of the classes in the server package are not used directly by programmers working with RMI but are part of the low-level RMI system. The main class in this package that is useful to you as an RMI developer is the UnicastRemoteObject class.

## Interfaces

### LoaderHandler

```
public interface LoaderHandler
```

The LoaderHandler interface is used by implementations of RMI class loaders. It defines methods that are used to load class definitions using URLs and codebase properties.

### FIELD

```
public final static String packagePrefix
```

The packagePrefix String contains the prefix package name for this class loader. It is assumed that the LoaderHandler implementation is in the package named. In Javasoft's implementation, this field is initialized to the value held in the property java.rmi.loader.packagePrefix, and is given the default value "sun.rmi.server." It specifies the name of the package that RMI uses to locate the implementation of the LoaderHandler class.

### getSecurityContext

```
public abstract Object getSecurityContext(ClassLoader loader)
```

This method returns the security context of the given class loader. This is an object representing a subclass of a `SecurityManager`.

### loadClass

```
public abstract Class loadClass(String name) throws
MalformedURLException, ClassNotFoundException
```

This attempts to load the class named from the codebase defined in the `java.rmi.server.codebase` property. If the value of the codebase property is not a valid URL, a `MalformedURLException` is thrown. If the class cannot be found at the given location, a `ClassNotFoundException` is thrown.

### loadClass

```
public abstract Class loadClass(URL codebase, String name) throws
MalformedURLException, ClassNotFoundException
```

This attempts to load the class named, from the URL codebase passed. If code-base is not a valid URL, a `MalformedURLException` is thrown. If the class cannot be found at the given codebase, a `ClassNotFoundException` is thrown.

# RMIFailureHandler

```
public interface RMIFailureHandler
```

The `RMIFailureHandler` interface is used by the `RMISocketFactory` as a call-back mechanism for handling failures when attempting to create `Sockets` or `ServerSockets`. The `RMISocketFactory.setFailureHandler` method takes an `RMIFailureHandler` as an argument. The default failure handler simply returns `false`.

## FIELDS

The `RMIFailureHandler` interface does not define any class variables.

## METHODS

### failure

```
public abstract boolean failure(Exception ex)
```

The `failure` method is called by the RMI run time when the `RMISocketFactory` is unable to create a `Socket` or `ServerSocket`. The `boolean` return value is used to let the system know whether it should retry the operation. A return value of `true` causes the system to retry creating the `Socket`. The exception that was thrown during the attempted socket creation is passed as the parameter.

# RemoteCall

```
public interface RemoteCall
```

The `RemoteCall` interface is used by stub and skeleton classes. It provides an interface for retrieving parameter streams and executing code that is represented by the stub and skeleton proxies.

## FIELDS
The `RemoteCall` interface does not define any class variables.

## METHODS

### done

```
public abstract void done() throws IOException
```

The `done` method is used to perform any necessary cleanup after a call has completed. An `IOException` is thrown if the call fails.

### executeCall

```
public abstract void executeCall() throws Exception
```

This is the interface to the actual method call of the implementation. The `executeCall` method performs whatever actions are necessary to execute the call that the stub or skeleton represents.

### getInputStream

```
public abstract ObjectInput getInputStream() throws IOException
```

Any results or parameters that are received by the stub or skeleton are accessed via the `ObjectInput` stream that is returned by this call. If the stream cannot be created or the call fails, an `IOException` is thrown.

### getOutputStream

```
public abstract ObjectOutput getOutputStream() throws IOException
```

The `getOutputStream` method returns an `ObjectOutput` stream that can be used by the stub or skeleton to post parameters or results. Essentially, a call to a remote method that takes a parameter causes the stub class to open an `ObjectOutput` stream via the `getOutputStream` method. The stub then pushes the parameter class onto the stream for delivery to the skeleton on the server side. The skeleton retrieves the parameter object from the `ObjectInput` stream that it gets from calling `getInputStream`. The object is then used to execute the actual code implementation that the skeleton represents. Upon failure, an `IOException` is thrown.

### getResultStream

```
public abstract ObjectOutput getResultStream(boolean success) throws
IOException, StreamCorruptedException
```

The `getResultStream` method is used by the skeleton class to get an `ObjectOutput` stream that is used to send the results of the execution of a method. The skeleton uses this class after executing the implementation code, to return the results of the method execution. The `boolean` parameter is used to denote normal execution or an exceptional condition. If the parameter is `true`, the method has executed normally. This method is only expected to be called once per remote call. If it is called more than once, a `StreamCorruptedException` is thrown. If the stream fails for any other reason, an `IOException` is thrown.

### releaseInputStream

```
public abstract void releaseInputStream() throws IOException
```

This frees any resources related to the input stream. Upon failure, an `IOException` is thrown.

### releaseOutputStream

```
public abstract void releaseOutputStream() throws IOException
```

This frees any resources related to the output stream. Upon failure, an `IOException` is thrown.

# RemoteRef

```
public interface RemoteRef extends Externalizable
```

The RemoteRef interface is used to tag a remote reference and to define the API that remote references use in the internals of RMI. This reference can be passed via an ObjectStream, since it implements the Externalizable interface and is used as a handle to remote objects. This interface is not normally used by programmers using RMI but rather by programmers implementing their own RMI system. Objects that implement the RemoteRef interface are normally manipulated by the stub and skeleton classes. Each stub instance has a RemoteRef associated with it—the RemoteRef is used to call methods on the remote object that the stub is associated with.

## FIELD

```
public final static String packagePrefix
```

The packagePrefix String contains the prefix for the package that is used to locate the server-related classes of RMI. By default this is initialized to the value of the property java.rmi.server.packagePrefix, or to a vendor-specific string (for instance, sun.rmi.server). Classes loaded from this package include UnicastRef and UnicastServerRef.

## METHODS

### done

```
public abstract void done(RemoteCall call) throws RemoteException
```

If the call has completed and returned successfully, the done method should be called so that the remote method invocation can clean up and release the connection for reuse. A RemoteException is thrown upon failure.

### getRefClass

```
public abstract String getRefClass(ObjectOutput out)
```

This method returns a string that gives the short (unqualified) name of the class that implements the RemoteRef interface.

### invoke

```
public abstract void invoke(RemoteCall call) throws Exception
```

This method invokes a remote method. It passes on any exception not specifically caught by the stub. In other words, application-specific exceptions are thrown to the caller as if they were local invocations as well as RMI-specific exceptions. The RemoteCall object is generated for each remote method call by calling the newCall() method.

**newCall**

```
public abstract RemoteCall newCall(RemoteObject obj, Operation
op[],int opnum, long hash) throws RemoteException
```

All methods that are declared in an implementation of a Remote interface are added to an array of Operations by the stub class that represents the remote object. The operations are referred to via an index into that array. The newCall() method returns a RemoteCall object based on an Object, an array of Operations for the object, and an index into the Operation array. The RemoteCall object can then be used to invoke the method referred to by the Operation. Normally, when a stub invokes a remote method, it first gets a RemoteCall object for the method and then passes the RemoteCall object to the invoke() method to actually cause the method to be invoked. A RemoteException is thrown if the newCall() method fails.

**remoteEquals**

```
public abstract boolean remoteEquals(RemoteRef obj)
```

The equality methods for remote objects work slightly differently than the equality methods of local objects. If the two objects are references to the same remote object, they are considered equal.

**remoteHashCode**

```
public abstract int remoteHashCode()
```

This method returns a hash for the given object. Hash codes for two references to the same remote object are equal even if they are from separate stubs.

**remoteToString**

```
public abstract String remoteToString()
```

This method returns a String that represents the remote object. It adds network information to the standard toString() method, specifying the host name as well as the standard String value representation of the object.

# ServerRef

```
public interface ServerRef extends RemoteRef
```

The `ServerRef` interface extends the `RemoteRef` interface and represents the server-side handle to a remote object implementation.

## FIELDS
The `ServerRef` interface does not define any class variables.

## METHODS

### exportObject

```
public abstract RemoteStub exportObject(Remote obj, RemoteServer
server, Object data) throws RemoteException
```

The `exportObject` method is used to export a remote object so that it may be accessed by a remote client. `ExportObject` finds the `RemoteStub` for the object being exported, generating a new one if necessary. The `UnicastRemoteObject` class implements this method to allow remote access to objects that do not extend `UnicastRemoteObject`. The `Remote` parameter is a reference to the object being exported. The `RemoteServer` object is the server associated with the object, which may be the object itself. Finally, the `Object` sent as the final parameter is used for connection-specific information such as host name or port number.

### getClientHost

```
public abstract String getClientHost() throws
 ServerNotActiveException
```

During processing of a remote method call, `getClientHost` returns the name of the host machine that the client invoking the method is running on. Outside this context, a `ServerNotActive` exception is thrown.

# Skeleton

```
public interface Skeleton
```

The `Skeleton` interface is used by the implementation of a skeleton class that is essentially the server-side proxy for a remote object. This interface declares the methods that are used to actually dispatch remote invocation requests to the implementation code.

## FIELDS
The `Skeleton` interface does not define any class variables.

## METHODS

### dispatch

```
public abstract void dispatch(Remote obj, RemoteCall theCall, int
opnum, long hash) throws Exception
```

The `dispatch` method is used by a skeleton class to call the implementation code of a remote invocation. It is responsible for unmarshaling arguments, invoking the implementation, and marshaling the return values. The `opnum` parameter is used as an index into an array of operations that are returned by the `getOperations()` method. The hash number is generated by the stub compiler and is used to check for interface mismatches and versioning. A generated stub or skeleton class contains an internal field `interfaceHash` that contains the hash value for a given interface. Any exceptions thrown by the implementation code are thrown by the `dispatch` method.

### getOperations

```
public abstract Operation[] getOperations()
```

The `getOperations` method returns an array of `Operation` objects. Each of these represents one of the methods that may be remotely invoked on the given implementation code.

# Unreferenced

```
public interface Unreferenced
```

The `Unreferenced` interface is implemented by remote objects that want to be notified when no more references are pointing to them. Generally, the unreferenced method is called once the reference count to the object reaches zero and the object is set for garbage collection.

## FIELDS
The `Unreferenced` interface does not define any class variables.

## METHOD

### unreferenced

```
public abstract void unreferenced()
```

This unreferenced method is called once there are no remote references to this object. It enables the object to free resources or perform clean-up tasks before being garbage-collected. The unreferenced() method can be called more than once, each time the reference count reaches zero.

# Classes

## LogStream

```
public class LogStream extends PrintStream
```

The LogStream is a PrintStream that is used to monitor server transactions. This stream is used to log transaction and error messages related to RMI server access. It is useful for logging and debugging RMI applications. The log stream can be used as a general-purpose logging device for writing transactional and operational information. This can be "turned on" simply by setting a stream and writing to it. Your methods can get a reference to the stream, once established, by calling the getDefaultStream(), getOutputStream(), or log() method.

### CONSTRUCTORS
LogStream does not define any constructors.

### FIELDS
The three constant variables that follow are used to set the logging level:

```
public static final int SILENT
public static final int BRIEF
public static final int VERBOSE
```

### METHODS

#### getDefaultStream

```
public static synchronized PrintStream getDefaultStream()
```

This method returns the current default stream for new logs.

#### GetOutputStream

```
public synchronized OutputStream getOutputStream()
```

This method gets the current stream that log entries are sent to.

### log

```
public static LogStream log(String name)
```

The log method returns the stream that is identified by the name passed. If a stream with the given name doesn't exist, a log using the default stream is created and the new LogStream is returned.

### parseLevel

```
public static int parseLevel(String s)
```

This method converts a String name identifying one of the logging levels to its internal integer representation.

### setDefaultStream

```
public static synchronized void setDefaultStream(PrintStream
  newDefault)
```

This method sets the default stream to be used by new logs.

### setOutputStream

```
public synchronized void setOutputStream(OutputStream out)
```

This method sets the output stream for this log.

### toString

```
public String toString()
```

This method returns a String representation of the LogStream.

### write

```
public void write(int b)
```

This method writes a byte to the output stream. The bytes are buffered until the value of b is equal to a newline character, at which point the buffer is flushed and the bytes in the buffer are sent to the log's output stream with a log information prefix.

### write

```
public void write(byte b[], int offset, int len)
```

This method passes a subset of a byte array through the write(*int*) method. The offset parameter is the starting index in the array, and len number of bytes are sent.

# ObjID

```
public final class ObjID extends Object implements Serializable
```

The ObjID class is used to uniquely identify objects on a virtual machine.

## CONSTRUCTORS

```
public ObjID()
```

This generates a unique ID.

```
public ObjID(int id)
```

This can be used when an object needs to maintain an ID across different runs of the Virtual Machine. This form of the ObjID constructor is used internally by the RMI mechanisms to create object identifiers representing well-known entities such as the distributed garbage collector and the registry.

## FIELDS

```
public static final int REGISTRY_ID
```

This is a well-known ID that identifies the registry.

```
public static final int DGC_ID
```

This is a well-known ID for identifying the distributed garbage collector.

## METHODS

### equals

```
public boolean equals(Object obj)
```

This returns true if the object passed is an ObjID that has the same contents as this ObjID.

### hashCode

```
public int hashCode()
```

The hash code produced is computed from the object ID number.

**read**

```
public static ObjID read(ObjectInput in) throws IOException
```

This reads and constructs an `ObjID` from the `ObjectInput` stream. If the stream fails, an `IOException` is thrown.

**toString**

```
public String toString()
```

This returns a `String` representation of the `ObjID` object. If the object is from a different address space, an address space identifier is also included in this string.

**write**

```
public void write(ObjectOutput out) throws IOException
```

This writes the serialized version of the `ObjID` to the given `ObjectOutput` stream. If the stream fails, an `IOException` is thrown.

# Operation

```
public class Operation extends Object
```

An `Operation` object is used to identify a method of a remote object. Essentially, this is a wrapper for the method name/signature. The `Operation` object is used by stub and skeleton classes for identifying methods and creating new `Call` objects that are used to invoke remote methods.

## CONSTRUCTORS

```
public Operation(String op)
```

This creates a new `Operation` object with the given method signature.

## FIELDS

The `Operation` class does not define any class variables.

## METHODS

### getOperation

```
public String getOperation()
```

This returns the name of the method that this `Operation` object represents.

### toString

```
public String toString()
```

This returns a `String` representation of the object and method that is represented by this `Operation` object.

# RMIClassLoader

```
public class RMIClassLoader extends Object
```

The `RMIClassLoader` is used to load stubs and classes over a network. Misleadingly, `java.rmi.server.RMIClassLoader` isn't in fact a `ClassLoader` (it doesn't extend `java.lang.ClassLoader`). Instead, it's a utility class that provides a set of static methods used to access the implementation's RMI class loader, to let applications load classes via a URL. It works by first locating a `LoaderHandler` implementation (it does this by looking for a concrete class called "LoaderHandler" in the package identified by `packagePrefix`, which defaults to the value of the property `java.rmi.server.RMIClassLoader`). It creates an instance of `LoaderHandler` if necessary. Finally, it uses `LoaderHandler`'s methods to actually load classes. In Sun's implementation, the `LoaderHandler` implementation works by making an instance of `java.sun.rmi.RMIClassLoader` (which *is* a class loader–it subclasses `java.lang.ClassLoader`) and using this to load classes. Only one class loader can be active, so if your RMI application happens to be an applet, the `AppletClassLoader` is used.

## CONSTRUCTORS
All of the methods in the `RMIClassLoader` are static; it does not define a constructor.

## FIELDS
The `RMIClassLoader` does not define any class variables.

## METHODS

### getSecurityContext

```
public static Object getSecurityContext(ClassLoader loader)
```

The `getSecurityContext` method returns the security context for the given `ClassLoader`. This context is an object that subclasses a security manager.

### loadClass

```
public static Class loadClass(String name) throws
MalformedURLException, ClassNotFoundException
```

This attempts to load the class given in the name parameter. The loader attempts to load the class from the URL that is specified in the `java.rmi.server.codebase` system property. If the value of this property cannot be parsed as a URL, a `MalformedURLException` is thrown. If the class cannot be located at the given codebase, a `ClassNotFoundException` is thrown.

### loadClass

```
public static Class loadClass(URL codebase, String name) throws
MalformedURLException, ClassNotFoundException
```

This attempts to load the class named from the codebase given in the URL. If the URL is not a valid URL, a `MalformedURLException` is thrown. If the class cannot be located at the given URL codebase, a `ClassNotFoundException` is thrown.

# RMISocketFactory

```
public abstract class RMISocketFactory extends Object
```

The `RMISocketFactory` is used to generate sockets for RMI communication. The `RMISocketFactory`, by default, generates standard TCP/IP sockets for use by RMI calls. This class also allows you to replace the default factory with custom implementations that may add compression or encryption algorithms to the sockets that it returns. This layered model allows you to change the lower-level socket implementations without affecting any of the higher-level code that uses it.

## CONSTRUCTOR

```
public RMISocketFactory()
```

This constructor creates an instance of an `RMISocketFactory`. This class is abstract, so the constructor can only be called by subclasses.

## FIELDS
The `RMISocketFactory` does not define any class variables.

# METHODS

### createServerSocket

```
public abstract ServerSocket createServerSocket(int port) throws
  IOException
```

This method creates a ServerSocket on the given port. If port 0 is used, an anonymous port number is assigned. If the ServerSocket fails, an IOException is thrown.

### createSocket

```
public abstract Socket createSocket(String host, int port) throws
  IOException
```

This creates a Socket that is connected to the given host on the given port number. If the connection fails, an IOException is thrown.

### getFailureHandler

```
public static RMIFailureHandler getFailureHandler()
```

This returns an RMIFailureHandler object associated with this RMISocketFailure. The handler is used to handle socket creation failure.

### getSocketFactory

```
public static RMISocketFactory getSocketFactory()
```

This static method returns the socket factory used for generating RMI sockets.

### setFailureHandler

```
public static void setFailureHandler(RMIFailureHandler fh)
```

This sets the failure handler to be used when socket creation failure occurs.

### setSocketFactory

```
public static void setSocketFactory(RMISocketFactory fac) throws
  IOException
```

This enables you to set a socket factory to be used by RMI. A custom socket factory can be used to generate special-purpose sockets that handle data encryption, compression, or other low-level communication operations. You are permitted to call this method only if the current security manager approves of setting socket factories. Otherwise a `SecurityException` is thrown. If the call fails, an `IOException` is thrown.

# RemoteObject

```
public abstract class RemoteObject extends Object implements Remote,
  Serializable
```

`RemoteObject` is the base class for any remote objects. It replaces some of the base methods of the `Java.lang.Object` class with new methods that are modified for the needs of a remote object.

## CONSTRUCTORS

```
protected RemoteObject()
```

This constructor creates a new `RemoteObject`. This is an abstract class, so the constructor can only be called by subclasses.

```
protected RemoteObject(RemoteRef ref)
```

This constructor creates a `RemoteObject` based on the reference passed.

## FIELDS

```
protected transient RemoteRef ref
```

This field holds a `RemoteRef` instance used to communicate with the server-side instance of the object.

## METHODS

### equals

```
public boolean equals(Object obj)
```

This method tests to see of two objects are equal. The objects are considered equal if they are references to the same remote object.

### hashCode

```
public int hashCode()
```

This method produces a hash code for the RemoteObject. Two references to the same remote object have the same hash.

**toString**

```
public String toString()
```

This method returns a string that represents this remote object.

# RemoteServer

```
public abstract class RemoteServer extends RemoteObject
```

RemoteServer is the superclass to all remote server objects (such as UnicastRemoteObject). Subclasses of RemoteServer handle all of the tasks necessary to export, and otherwise make Remote interfaces remotely available.

## CONSTRUCTORS

```
protected RemoteServer()
```

This class is abstract, so the RemoteServer constructor can't be used directly to instance this class but is called by subclasses when they are created.

```
protected RemoteServer(RemoteRef ref)
```

This uses the given reference to create a RemoteServer object.

## FIELDS

The RemoteServer class doesn't define any class variables.

## METHODS

### getClientHost

```
public static String getClientHost() throws ServerNotActiveException
```

During an invocation of a remote method, getClientHost returns the host name of the client calling the method. Otherwise, a ServerNotActiveException is thrown.

### getLog

```
public static PrintStream getLog()
```

This returns the `PrintStream` associated with the server log. The log is used for logging messages and errors and generally monitoring the server.

**setLog**

```
public static void setLog(OutputStream out)
```

This enables you to set the log output stream to the `OutputStream` given. All log entries are added to this stream. If the `OutputStream` is `null`, logging is turned off.

# RemoteStub

```
public abstract class RemoteStub extends RemoteObject
```

The `RemoteStub` class is the superclass to all stub classes for remote objects. The stub class is a client-side proxy for the remote object handling all client-side interaction with the object. A subclass of the `RemoteStub` class that represents a remote object implements all of the same `Remote` interfaces as the object it represents.

## CONSTRUCTORS

```
protected RemoteStub()
```

This constructor creates a new `RemoteStub`.

```
protected RemoteStub(RemoteRef ref)
```

This constructor creates a `RemoteStub` based on the remote reference. `RemoteStub` is an abstract class, so the constructors can only be called by subclasses.

## FIELDS

The `RemoteStub` class does not define any class variables.

## METHOD

**setRef**

```
protected static void setRef(RemoteStub stub, RemoteRef ref)
```

This method sets the stub's `ref` field to the `RemoteRef` instance given.

# UID

```
public final class UID extends Object implements Serializable
```

The UID class is used to create identifiers that are unique on the host they are generated on.

## CONSTRUCTORS

```
public UID()
```

This method constructs a new unique identifier. The identifier is guaranteed always to be unique on this host as long as the system clock on the machine is never set back.

```
public UID(short num)
```

This generates a UID with a well-known identifier number. This number is guaranteed not to clash with the identifiers constructed with the no-argument constructor.

## FIELDS

The UID class does not define any class variables.

## METHODS

### equals

```
public boolean equals(Object obj)
```

This returns true if two UID objects are equal.

### hashCode

```
public int hashCode()
```

This generates a hash code for the object.

### read

```
public static UID read(DataInput in) throws IOException
```

This method reads a UID object from an input stream and returns a UID object. It is used in tandem with the write() method that pushes a UID object onto an output stream. An IOException is thrown if the stream fails.

### toString

```
public String toString()
```

This generates a string representation of the UID object.

**write**

```
public void write(DataOutput out) throws IOException
```

This writes the UID data to a stream, to be rebuilt on the other end of the stream using the read() method. An IOException is thrown if the stream fails.

# UnicastRemoteObject

```
public class UnicastRemoteObject extends RemoteServer
```

The UnicastRemoteObject class is the base class for most user-defined remote objects. It supplies TCP-based point-to-point object references. Remote object implementations that use UnicastRemoteObject are only valid for, at most, the lifetime of the process that creates the remote object. Currently, UnicastRemoteObject is the only supported implementation of the RemoteServer interface, and as such it is the only defined mechanism for creating remote server objects. In early releases of the RMI system, remote objects had to be subclasses of UnicastRemoteObject, but currently, nonsubclasses can be exported as long as they implement a Remote interface and export themselves using the exportObject() method of the UnicastRemoteObject class.

## CONSTRUCTOR

```
protected UnicastRemoteObject() throws RemoteException
```

This method constructs a new UnicastRemoteObject.

## FIELDS
The UnicastRemoteObject class does not define any class variables.

## METHODS
**clone**

```
public Object clone() throws CloneNotSupportedException
```

The clone method is used to create an identical but separate copy of this object.

## exportObject

```
public static RemoteStub exportObject(Remote obj) throws
RemoteException
```

This is used to export remote objects that do not subclass the UnicastRemoteObject class directly. The object must implement a Remote interface. Upon failure, a RemoteException is thrown. This method returns a stub for the exported object.

# Reference E

# The java.io Package

THIS SECTION IS A subset of the `java.io` package. Only those interfaces and classes that are directly related to remote method invocation or object serialization are listed. The `java.io` package contains interfaces and classes that are used for input/output functions in Java. These include basic streams for files or network connections and various tools for manipulating stream and file data.

# Interfaces

## Externalizable

```
public interface Externalizable extends Serializable
```

The `Externalizable` interface is used to provide custom methods for serializing an object. An object that implements `Externalizable` is expected to handle the external representation of the object. It must explicitly coordinate with its superclasses to save its object state. `Externalizable` is used when you need complete control of an object's external representation in a stream.

When an object is serialized, it is first checked to see if it implements the `Externalizable` interface. If it does, the `writeExternal()` method is used to write the object data to a stream; otherwise, the object is checked to see if it implements the `Serializable` interface. If it does, the object is serialized using the default object serialization (that is, all the instance fields except for transient fields are written). Objects that don't implement `Externalizable` or `Serializable` cannot be serialized—attempting to serialize such an object generates a `NotSerializable` exception.

On the receiving end, to read an `Externalizable` object from a stream, first an instance of the object being read is created by a call to the object's no-argument constructor. Then the object's `readExternal()` method is called to rebuild the object data from the `ObjectStream` passed to it.

### FIELDS
The `Externalizable` interface does not define any variables.

## METHODS

### readExternal

```
public abstract void readExternal(ObjectInput in) throws
IOException, ClassNotFoundException
```

When an object that implements the Externalizable interface is retrieved on the other end of an ObjectStream, the object is rebuilt, first through creation of an instance of the object and then by a call to the no-argument constructor for the object. The readExternal method for the object is then called and passed an ObjectInput stream that is used to read the object data and reconstruct the object.

If the object type cannot be found locally or via standard class loader mechanisms, the instantiation fails and a ClassNotFoundException is thrown.

If the ObjectInput stream fails, an IOException is thrown.

### writeExternal

```
public abstract void writeExternal(ObjectOutput out) throws
 IOException
```

The writeExternal method is called when the object is being written to a stream. The object is passed an ObjectOutput object, and it uses the ObjectOutput methods to write any data to the stream that are necessary to rebuild the object on the receiving end. The writeExternal method is responsible for describing the entire external representation of this object including superclasses that the object depends on.

If the write fails, an IOException is thrown.

# ObjectInput

```
public interface ObjectInput extends DataInput
```

The ObjectInput interface is implemented by streams that can read objects that implement the Serializable or Externalizable interfaces. ObjectInput extends DataInput, so the basic DataInput methods for reading raw data and simple types can also be used by objects to read data that form their serial representation.

## FIELDS
The ObjectInput interface does not define any class variables.

## METHODS

### available

```
public abstract int available() throws IOException
```

This returns the number of bytes that are available for reading. If a read is called that requests more bytes than are available, the read is blocked. You can use this method to check whether bytes are waiting to be read.

If the method call fails, an IOException is thrown.

### close

```
public abstract void close() throws IOException
```

This method closes the stream or file associated with this interface. It is called to release any resources being held in connection with this stream. Upon failure, an IOException is thrown.

### read

```
public abstract int read() throws IOException
```

This reads one byte of data from the stream. If the end of the stream is reached, a –1 value is returned; otherwise the value of the byte read is returned. If an error occurs, an IOException is thrown.

### read

```
public abstract int read(byte b[]) throws IOException
```

This reads the number of bytes available up to b.length into the byte array passed to it. If no bytes are available, the method is blocked until data are available. It returns the actual number of bytes read or –1 if the end of the stream has been reached and no data were read. Upon failure, an IOException is thrown.

### read

```
public abstract int read(byte b[], int offset, int len) throws
  IOException
```

This read method reads an array of bytes and inserts them into the byte array that is passed to the method. A total of len bytes are read into the array starting at the index represented by offset. The len parameter is considered a maximum number to read, but it is not guaranteed to return that number. The actual number of bytes read is returned as the return value. This method is blocked until there is an exception or at least one byte is read. If the end of the stream is reached, a −1 is returned. Upon failure, an IOException is thrown.

### readObject

```
public abstract Object readObject() throws ClassNotFoundException,
  IOException
```

The readObject method is used to read an object from the stream. This method first tries to create an instance of the object found on the stream. If it is unable to locate a class definition, locally or via a class loader mechanisms, a ClassNotFoundException is thrown. Otherwise, the object is created, and its readExternal or readObject method is called so that it can recreate itself from the data stream. If an I/O failure occurs, an IOException is thrown.

### skip

```
public abstract long skip(long n) throws IOException
```

This method skips forward n bytes in the stream, returning the actual number of bytes skipped. Upon failure, an IOException is thrown.

# ObjectInputValidation

```
public interface ObjectInputValidation
```

This interface is used to validate an object once the entire graph of objects that it depends on have been deserialized. Validation mechanisms can be used to carry out checks after a whole object has been retrieved from the input stream. To register an object for validation, the object must implement the ObjectInputValidation interface and provide a validateObject method. Furthermore, it must define a readObject or readExternal method that calls the ObjectInputStream's registerValidation method to request validation.

## FIELDS
The ObjectInputValidation interface does not define any class variables.

## METHODS

### validateObject

```
public abstract void validateObject() throws InvalidObjectException
```

The `validateObject` method is called to validate an object after deserialization. If the object is unable to validate, an `InvalidObjectException` is thrown.

# ObjectOutput

```
public interface ObjectOutput extends DataOutput
```

The `ObjectOutput` interface is implemented by streams that write objects. The interface extends `DataOutput`, so an object being written to the stream can use the methods of `ObjectOutput` for writing objects to the stream or the methods of `DataOutput` for writing simple types and raw data.

## FIELDS

The `ObjectOutput` interface does not define any class variables.

## METHODS

### close

```
public abstract void close() throws IOException
```

This `close` method is used to close the stream associated with this interface and free any resources that it may be holding. Upon failure, an `IOException` is thrown.

### flush

```
public abstract void flush() throws IOException
```

The `flush` method is used to flush any data that may be buffered in the stream. Upon failure, an `IOException` is thrown.

### write

```
public abstract void write(int b) throws IOException
```

This writes the value of b, as a byte to the stream. Upon failure, an `IOException` is thrown.

### write

```
public abstract void write(byte b[]) throws IOException
```

This method writes the byte array b to the stream. It blocks until all bytes in the array are written. Upon failure, an IOException is thrown.

**write**

```
public abstract void write(byte b[], int off, int len) throws
  IOException
```

This method writes a subarray of bytes from the array of bytes passed to it. It is blocked until len bytes are written starting at the index off. Upon failure, an IOException is thrown.

**writeObject**

```
public abstract void writeObject(Object obj) throws IOException
```

This method writes an object to the stream. It expects the object to implement either a Serializable or Externalizable interface in order for the object to be pushed onto the stream. Upon failure, an IOException is thrown.

## Serializable

```
public interface interface Serializable
```

The Serializable interface is used to mark any objects that can be serialized and sent along a stream that implements the ObjectInput/ObjectOutput interfaces. Serializable does not declare any methods or define any variables. It is used simply as a flag to mark objects that can be serialized.

# Classes

## ObjectInputStream

```
public class ObjectInputStream extends InputStream implements
ObjectInput, ObjectStreamConstants
```

The ObjectInputStream is used to create streams from sockets, files, or similar stream and storage objects that can hold serialized objects. An ObjectInputStream deserializes objects that have been written using an ObjectOutputStream. Only primitive data types and objects that implement the java.io.Serializable or java.io.Externalizable interfaces can be read from an ObjectInputStream.

## CONSTRUCTOR

```
public ObjectInputStream(InputStream in) throws IOException,
StreamCorruptedException
```

This creates an `ObjectInputStream` based on the given `InputStream`. The `ObjectInputStream` is blocked until a stream header is read. This header contains a magic number and version number identifying the stream. This must be written to the corresponding output stream and flushed before the constructor is returned. If there is a problem with the version or magic number, a `StreamCorruptedException` is thrown. If the stream otherwise fails, an `IOException` is thrown.

## FIELDS

The `ObjectInputStream` class does not define any class variables.

## METHODS

### available

```
public int available() throws IOException
```

This method returns the number of bytes that are available to be read. It enables you to read whatever number of bytes are ready without blocking. Upon failure, an `IOException` is thrown.

### close

```
public void close() throws IOException
```

This closes the stream and frees related resources. Upon failure, an `IOException` is thrown.

### defaultReadObject

```
public final void defaultReadObject() throws IOException,
ClassNotFoundException, NotActiveException
```

The `defaultReadObject` method is used by classes that implement a `readObject` method but want to use the default object reading mechanisms. This method can only be called by a class's `readObject` method, or a `NotActiveException` is thrown. The `defaultReadObject` method only reads nonstatic and nontransient fields. If the class definition cannot be located—locally or via a class loader—`ClassNotFoundException` is thrown. If an I/O problem occurs, an `IOException` is thrown.

**enableResolveObject**

```
protected final boolean enableResolveObject(boolean enable) throws
SecurityException
```

The enableResolveObject method is used to permit the resolveObject method to replace objects in an object stream. If the stream is an instance of a subclass of ObjectInputStream and it is trusted by the SecurityManager, it is permitted to replace objects. When enabled, resolveObject is called for every deserialized object. If the stream is not trusted, or if access is otherwise denied, a SecurityException is thrown. This generally means that the stream has a classLoader associated with it and is not a trusted stream.

**read**

```
public int read() throws IOException
```

This reads a byte from the stream. The integer value for the byte is returned if the read is successful. If the end of the stream is reached, a −1 is returned. The read() method is blocked until data are available. If an I/O error occurs, an IOException is thrown.

**read**

```
public int read(byte data[], int offset, int length) throws
 IOException
```

This reads a series of bytes into a byte array. It attempts to read at most length number of bytes and place them into the given array starting at the offset index. The total number of bytes read is returned, or −1 is returned if the end of the stream is reached. This method is blocked until data are ready to be read. An IOException is thrown upon failure.

**readBoolean**

```
public boolean readBoolean() throws IOException
```

This reads a Boolean value from the stream. Upon failure, an IOException is thrown. If the end of the stream has been reached, an EOFException is thrown.

**readByte**

```
public byte readByte() throws IOException
```

This reads an eight-bit byte from the stream. Upon failure, an IOException is thrown. If the end of the stream has been reached, an EOFException is thrown.

### readChar

```
public Char readChar() throws IOException
```

This reads a 16-bit character from the stream. Upon failure, an IOException is thrown. If the end of the stream has been reached, an EOFException is thrown.

### readDouble

```
public double readDouble() throws IOException
```

This reads a 64-bit double from the stream. Upon failure, an IOException is thrown. If the end of the stream has been reached, an EOFException is thrown.

### readFloat

```
public float readFloat() throws IOException
```

This reads a 32-bit float from the stream. Upon failure, an IOException is thrown. If the end of the stream has been reached, an EOFException is thrown.

### readFully

```
public void readFully(byte data[]) throws IOException
```

This method reads data.length bytes from the stream. It is blocked until all bytes are read, the end of the stream is reached, or an exception is thrown. If an I/O error occurs, an IOException is thrown. If the end of the stream is reached, an EOFException is thrown.

### readFully

```
public void readFully(byte data[], int offset, int size) throws
  IOException
```

This reads size bytes from the stream and places them into the byte array starting at index offset. It is blocked until all bytes are read, the end of the stream is reached, or an exception is thrown. If an I/O error occurs, an IOException is thrown. If the end of the stream is reached, an EOFException is thrown.

### readInt

```
public int readInt() throws IOException
```

This reads a 32-bit integer from the stream. Upon failure, an IOException is thrown. If the end of the stream has been reached, an EOFException is thrown.

### readLine

```
public String readLine() throws IOException
```

This reads a String from the stream that has been terminated by a "\n," "\r," "\r\n," or EOF. If an I/O error occurs, an IOException is thrown. The String read is returned.

### readLong

```
public long readLong() throws IOException
```

This reads a 64-bit long integer from the stream. Upon failure, an IOException is thrown. If the end of the stream has been reached, an EOFException is thrown.

### readObject

```
public final Object readObject() throws OptionalDataException,
ClassNotFoundException, IOException
```

The readObject method reconstructs a serialized object from the stream. The object must implement the Serializable or Externalizable interface. This method attempts to reconstruct the object graph for the object completely and, by default, reads all nonstatic and nontransient data into their corresponding fields. Serializable objects can override default deserialization by defining readObject() and writeObject() methods that take the responsibility of sending and retrieving data that is used to construct a copy of the original object.

Once all of the objects in the object graph have been restored, they are each validated until a copy of the original object is completely restored.

If the class definition cannot be found locally or via a codebase to another machine, a ClassNotFoundException is thrown.

If there are problems with the headers or other data in the stream, a StreamCorruptedException is thrown.

If a primitive data type, rather than an object, is found on the stream, an OptionalDataException is thrown.

If the stream fails, an IOException is thrown.

### readShort

```
public short readShort() throws IOException
```

This attempts to read a 16-bit integer from the stream. If the stream fails, an IOException is thrown. If the end of the file (Stream) is reached, an EOFException is thrown.

### readStreamHeader

```
protected void readStreamHeader() throws IOException,
StreamCorruptedException
```

The readStreamHeader method can be overridden by subclasses. This enables subclasses to read their own stream headers that contain identifying magic numbers and version numbers. It throws a StreamCorruptedException if there is a problem with the stream header, and it throws an IOException if the stream otherwise fails.

### readUnsignedByte

```
public int readUnsignedByte() throws IOException
```

This reads an eight-bit unsigned byte from the stream and returns its integer value. Upon failure, an IOException is thrown. If the end of the stream has been reached, an EOFException is thrown.

### readUnsignedShort

```
public int readUnsignedShort() throws IOException
```

This reads a 16-bit unsigned short integer from the stream and returns its integer value. Upon failure, an IOException is thrown. If the end of the stream has been reached, an EOFException is thrown.

### readUTF

```
public String readUTF() throws IOException
```

This reads a UTF-formatted string from the stream and returns an equivalent String. Upon failure, an IOException is thrown. If the end of the stream has been reached, an EOFException is thrown.

### registerValidation

```
public synchronized void registerValidation(ObjectInputValidation
obj, int prio) throws NotActiveException, InvalidObjectException
```

This is used to register a validation callback mechanism that is used to perform final class validation after the serialized objects in its object graph have been reconstituted. The ObjectInputValidation passed is the object to be notified. The priority integer is used to give an ordering to the validation callbacks; the higher priority validations are made first. If the object is not currently being reconstructed from an object stream, a `NotActiveException` is thrown; if the validation object is null, an `InvalidObjectException` is thrown.

### resolveClass

```
protected Class resolveClass(ObjectStreamClass v) throws
IOException, ClassNotFoundException
```

The `resolveClass` method is used by subclasses to obtain classes from alternate sources. This method is called once per unique class in a stream and returns a `Class` to use for the corresponding deserialized object. If the appropriate class is not found, a `ClassNotFoundException` is thrown.

### resolveObject

```
protected Object resolveObject(Object obj) throws IOException
```

The `resolveObject` method is used to replace objects in a stream. Only streams that are instances of a subclass of `ObjectInputStream` and that are trusted by the `SecurityManager` are allowed to replace objects, and the object replacement must be compatible with the original. The `resolveObject` method can be called only if `enableResolveObject` has been called. Upon failure, an `IOException` is thrown.

### skipBytes

```
public int skipBytes(int len) throws IOException
```

This skips forward n bytes in the stream. The `skipBytes` method is blocked until n bytes have been skipped. Upon failure, an `IOException` is thrown. If the end of the stream has been reached, an `EOFException` is thrown.

# ObjectOutputStream

```
public class ObjectOutputStream extends OutputStream implements
ObjectOutput, ObjectStreamConstants
```

The `ObjectOutputStream` method is used to write primitive types and objects to an output stream, to be reconstituted on the receiving end by an `ObjectInputStream`. `ObjectOutputStream` implements `ObjectOutput`, so it defines the methods necessary for object serialization, but it also extends `OutputStream`, so it has all of the primitive type handling of an `OutputStream`.

Only objects that implement the `Serializable` or `Externalizable` interface can be serialized and sent to an `ObjectOutputStream` using the `writeObject()` method.

## CONSTRUCTOR

```
public ObjectOutputStream(OutputStream out) throws IOException
```

This constructs a new ObjectOutputStream based on the given OutputStream. A stream header is written to the stream buffer. For communications streams, the stream should be flushed after construction so that the receiving end doesn't block for too long waiting for the header. Upon stream failure, an IOException is thrown.

## FIELDS
The ObjectOutputStream class does not define any class variables.

## METHODS

### annotateClass

```
protected void annotateClass(Class cl) throws IOException
```

The annotateClass method allows subclasses to write class-specific data to a stream whenever that class is written to the stream. It is called once for each class written to the stream—and after the class name and type information have already been written to the stream. Subclasses of ObjectOutputStream can override this method to write any additional class data to the stream (for example, the class's byte code). Data that is written to a stream using this technique should be read by using a subclass of ObjectInputStream that overrides the resolveClass method to do the appropriate reading. This subclass is used by trusted streams to enable classes to be replaced on the receiving end by using the resolveClass method. The class representation is up to the implementation; as long as the resolveClass method corresponds on both sending and receiving ends, the class byte code can be written directly to the stream for resolution. Upon failure, an IOException is thrown.

### close

```
public void close() throws IOException
```

This closes the stream and frees any related resources. Upon failure, an IOException is thrown.

### defaultWriteObject

```
public final void defaultWriteObject() throws IOException
```

This is the default method called from the writeObject method of a class being serialized. It serializes all nontransient and nonstatic fields in a class and writes them to the object stream. If it is called from outside the context of an object being serialized, a `NotActiveException` is thrown. If an I/O failure occurs, an `IOException` is thrown.

### drain

```
protected void drain() throws IOException
```

This flushes the object stream buffer without causing the underlying stream to flush. Upon failure, an `IOException` is thrown.

### enableReplaceObject

```
protected final boolean enableReplaceObject(boolean enable) throws
SecurityException
```

The `enableReplaceObject` method must be called before any objects in the stream can be replaced. This call can only be performed by a trusted stream class. If the class is not trusted, a `SecurityException` is thrown.

### flush

```
public void flush() throws IOException
```

This flushes the data buffer and causes it to be sent along the stream. Upon failure, an `IOException` is thrown.

### replaceObject

```
protected Object replaceObject(Object obj) throws IOException
```

This enables trusted subclasses of the `ObjectOutputStream` to replace objects in the stream. The `enableReplaceObject` method must be successfully called before any objects can be replaced. Any classes that are replaced must be replaced with equivalent classes with the same fields. Upon failure, an `IOException` is thrown.

### reset

```
public void reset() throws IOException
```

A `reset` causes the stream to be reset as if it had just been opened, and any objects are written to the stream even if they had previously been written before the stream was reset. Upon failure, an `IOException` is thrown.

### write

```
public void write(int data) throws IOException
```

This writes an integer to the stream. Upon failure, an IOException is thrown. This is blocked until the byte is written.

### write

```
public void write(byte b[]) throws IOException
```

This writes an array of bytes to the stream. The method is blocked until all bytes have been written. Upon failure, an IOException is thrown.

### write

```
public void write(byte b[], int off, int len) throws IOException
```

This writes a subarray of bytes to the stream, starting at the byte at index off. It is blocked until len bytes are written. Upon failure, an IOException is thrown.

### writeBoolean

```
public void writeBoolean(boolean data) throws IOException
```

This writes the given boolean to the stream. It is blocked until the data are written and throws an IOException upon failure.

### writeByte

```
public void writeByte(int data) throws IOException
```

This writes the value of the given integer as a byte. It is blocked until the byte is written and throws an IOException upon failure.

### writeBytes

```
public void writeBytes(String data) throws IOException
```

This writes the given String to the stream as a series of bytes. It is blocked until all bytes are written and throws an IOException upon failure.

### writeChar

```
public void writeChar(int data) throws IOException
```

This writes a 16-bit character to the stream. Upon failure, an IOException is thrown.

### writeChars

```
public void writeChars(String data) throws IOException
```

This writes the given String to the stream as a series of 16-bit characters. It is blocked until all characters have been written to the stream and throws an IOException upon failure.

### writeDouble

```
public void writeDouble(double data) throws IOException
```

This writes a 64-bit floating-point number to the stream. Upon failure, an IOException is thrown.

### writeFloat

```
public void writeFloat(float data) throws IOException
```

This writes a 32-bit floating-point number to the stream. Upon failure, an IOException is thrown.

### writeInt

```
public void writeInt(int data) throws IOException
```

This writes a 32-bit integer to the stream. Upon failure, an IOException is thrown.

### writeLong

```
public void writeLong(long data) throws IOException
```

This writes a 64-bit long integer to the stream. Upon failure, an IOException is thrown.

### writeObject

```
public final void writeObject(Object obj) throws IOException
```

The writeObject method is used for serializing objects and pushing them onto the object stream. Objects that are written to the stream using this method must implement either the Serializable interface or the Externalizable interface. By default, any serializable object has its nonstatic and nontransient fields serialized and reconstituted on the receiving side. An object may override the default serialization by implementing its own writeObject(ObjectOutputStream) and readObject(ObjectInputStream) methods. Upon stream failure, an IOException is thrown.

### writeShort

```
public void writeShort(int data) throws IOException
```

This writes a 16-bit short integer to the stream. Upon failure, an IOException is thrown.

### writeStreamHeader

```
protected void writeStreamHeader() throws IOException
```

This method enables subclasses of the ObjectOutputStream class to append their own headers to the stream. The header contains version and stream ID information that is read on the receiving side with the ObjectInputStream.readStreamHeader() method. Upon stream failure, an IOException is thrown.

### writeUTF

```
public void writeUTF(String data) throws IOException
```

This writes the given String to the stream as a UTF-encoded string. Upon failure, an IOException is thrown.

# ObjectStreamClass

```
public class ObjectStreamClass Object implements Serializable
```

The ObjectStreamClass is used to describe a serializable class. It contains a version number for the class and the name of the class. ObjectStreamClass objects for classes can be looked up with the static lookup() method of this class.

## CONSTRUCTORS
The ObjectStreamClass does not define a constructor.

## FIELDS
The ObjectStreamClass does not define any class variables.

## METHODS

### forClass

```
public Class forClass()
```

This finds the class in the local Virtual Machine to which this class is mapped. If a corresponding class is not found, null is returned.

### getName

```
public String getName()
```

This returns the name of the class that this object describes.

### getSerialVersionUID

```
public long getSerialVersionUID()
```

This returns the serial version ID for this object. A version number is used to identify classes with the same root that have evolved over time.

### lookup

```
public static ObjectStreamClass lookup(Class cl)
```

This looks for an ObjectStreamClass object for the given serializable class. If the class is not serializable, null is returned.

### toString

```
public String toString()
```

This returns a String representation of the class descriptor.

# Reference F

# The java.rmi Exceptions

THIS SECTION LISTS THE exceptions defined in the `java.rmi.*` classes. It is possible for other exceptions to be raised by the system when you are using the RMI and Object Serialization systems, but the exceptions listed here are the common ones you may expect that deal directly with RMI.

Most RMI exceptions include an additional field—the detail field—which may give a reference to the `Throwable` object that caused the RMI exception to be raised. For example, when a run-time exception such as a `NullPointerException` occurs in a server performing an RMI request, the run-time exception is wrapped in a `ServerException`, and the `ServerException` is forwarded to the RMI client involved in the call. The client can use the detail field of the `ServerException` to find out what went wrong in the server.

## java.rmi Package Exceptions

### AccessException

```
public class AccessException extends RemoteException
```

An `AccessException` is thrown when a stub class attempts to access a local resource that it is not permitted to access.

#### CONSTRUCTORS

```
public AccessException(String s)
public AccessException(String s, Exception ex)
```

### AlreadyBoundException

```
public class AlreadyBoundException extends Exception
```

An `AlreadyBoundException` is thrown when an attempt is made to bind a remote object to a registry under a name that is already registered. For example, the call `java.rmi.registry.Registry.bind("Hello", MyRemote)` throws an `AlreadyBoundException` if the name "Hello" has already been bound to an object in this registry. A registered object can be replaced by calling the `rebind()` method instead of `bind()`.

## CONSTRUCTORS

```
AlreadyBoundException()
AlreadyBoundException(String)
```

# ConnectException

```
public class ConnectException extends RemoteException
```

A ConnectException is thrown if a connection to a machine fails. This normally means that the service requested is not running on the port number requested. For example, if you run a registry server on port 1099 and you try to look up an object on this registry using port 1100 instead, a ConnectException is thrown. This exception, of course, is also thrown if the server isn't running on any port for the given machine or if you are denied permission to connect to the given port.

## CONSTRUCTORS

```
ConnectException(String)
ConnectException(String, Exception)
```

# ConnectIOException

```
public class ConnectIOException extends RemoteException
```

A ConnectIOException indicates that an I/O error occurred when you were attempting to connect to a service. This could be due to a socket error or some other problem with the transport layer.

## CONSTRUCTORS

```
ConnectIOException(String)
ConnectIOException(String, Exception)
```

# MarshalException

```
public class MarshalException extends RemoteException
```

Parameters, return values, and application exceptions are all directed between remote implementations and clients that call them via marshal streams. If a stream is corrupted due to a problem with a stub or skeleton, version mismatch, or other network error, a `MarshalException` is thrown. The `MarshalException` is normally directly related to a serialization problem, and if the problem persists, make sure that your serial versions are compiled and up-to-date, and restart your services to make sure that they are using the up-to-date objects; these steps normally correct the problem.

## CONSTRUCTORS

```
MarshalException(String)
MarshalException(String, Exception)
```

# NoSuchObjectException

```
public class NoSuchObjectException
extends RemoteException
```

A `NoSuchObjectException` is thrown if a reference to a remote object is invalid or unreachable. This can happen if the server thinks that a client has died (for instance, because of a timeout), and then it garbage-collects an object that the client was using. When the client attempts to use the object again, the server portion of the object no longer exists, and a `NoSuchObjectException` is thrown to indicate that the object isn't available.

## CONSTRUCTOR

```
NoSuchObjectException(String)
```

# NotBoundException

```
public class NotBoundException extends Exception
```

A `NotBoundException` is thrown from a lookup call to a registry if the name requested is not bound in the registry. This is usually caused when an incorrect name string or URL is used in requesting an object, when the object being requested has not yet been bound with the registry, or when the object has been removed from the registry as a direct result of a call to the `unbind()` method of the registry.

## CONSTRUCTORS

```
NotBoundException()
NotBoundException(String)
```

# RMISecurityException

```
public class RMISecurityException extends SecurityException
```

The RMISecurityException is used to enforce the rules of the RMISecurityManager. In general, a SecurityManager works by defining a set of methods that are called that test whether or not the current application has permission to execute certain types of calls, such as file I/O or access to sockets. If the operation is permitted, the method completes normally; if the application is not allowed, an exception is thrown. In the case of an RMISecurityManager, any time the security manager is set to disallow an operation, an RMISecurityException is thrown to check access when the corresponding method is called.

## CONSTRUCTORS

```
RMISecurityException(String)
RMISecurityException(String, String)
```

# RemoteException

```
public class RemoteException extends IOException
```

This is the root of all RMI exceptions—well, most of them. The RemoteException is subclassed to create most of the RMI-specific exceptions. It is often created with a more specific exception related to the situation that caused the exception to be raised. This detailed exception can normally be accessed via the detail field that contains a Throwable object.

## CONSTRUCTORS

```
RemoteException()
RemoteException(String)
RemoteException(String, Throwable)
```

## FIELDS

```
public Throwable detail
```

This is used to access the detailed Throwable error (or exception) that produced this exception.

## METHODS

```
public String getMessage()
```

This returns the string representation of the current exception, including any nested exceptions if applicable.

# ServerError

```
public class ServerError extends RemoteException
```

A `ServerError` is thrown when an error is produced by the RMI server. The `ServerError` exception is, in fact, a subclass of `RemoteException` (which is in turn a subclass of `java.lang.Exception`), but it contains a reference to a `java.lang.Error` object that was produced by the server. In other words, an instance of a `java.lang.Error` object is held in a reference by a `ServerError` exception.

## CONSTRUCTOR

```
public ServerError(String s, Error err)
```

# ServerException

```
public class ServerException extends RemoteException
```

A `ServerException` is thrown when a `RemoteException` is produced by the skeleton class of an RMI implementation class.

## CONSTRUCTORS

```
public ServerException(String s)
public ServerException(String s, Exception ex)
```

# ServerRuntimeException

```
public class ServerRuntimeException extends RemoteException
```

This indicates that an uncaught run-time exception occurred on the server side of an RMI transaction. Examples of such exceptions are `NullPointerExceptions` and `ArrayIndexOutOfBoundsExceptions`.

## CONSTRUCTOR

```
ServerRuntimeException(String, Exception)
```

# StubNotFoundException

```
public class StubNotFoundException extends RemoteException
```

The RMI environment depends on the stub/skeleton layer in order to function. If a stub for a remote object cannot be found via the local CLASSPATH, or via standard `ClassLoader` mechanisms, a `StubNotFoundException` is thrown. A common mistake that may produce this error is forgetting to run the rmic compiler on classes that declare remote objects before attempting to run them. This error may also be caused by using a bad URL, using the wrong codebase, or class name collisions.

## CONSTRUCTORS

```
StubNotFoundException(String)
StubNotFoundException(String, Exception)
```

# UnexpectedException

```
public class UnexpectedException extends RemoteException
```

The `UnexpectedException` denotes exactly what you would expect: Something unexpected has happened. This is essentially a catch-all for unexpected exception handling. For example, if an exception that is not declared in a method's signature is thrown by that method, an `UnexpectedException` is passed to the client.

## CONSTRUCTORS

```
UnexpectedException(String)
UnexpectedException(String, Exception)
```

# UnknownHostException

```
public class UnknownHostException extends RemoteException
```

An `UnknownHostException` is thrown if your system is unable to resolve a given host name into an appropriate IP address. This is normally due to either a mistyped host name or a misconfigured DNS. (Most systems use a Domain Name Server to resolve names into IP addresses.) In the latter case , try using the IP address instead of the name of the server. For example, `graphics.mrl.nyu.edu` resolves to `128.122.129.64`.

### CONSTRUCTORS

```
UnknownHostException(String)
UnknownHostException(String, Exception)
```

## UnmarshalException

`public class UnmarshalException extends RemoteException`

An `UnmarshalException` is thrown if an object that is expected in a marshal stream is corrupt or otherwise unreadable. This is normally a problem of a corrupt stream header in an object stream; such corruption may result from the stream being left in an undefined state by a crash, a network error, or some other error that occurred during object serialization or deserialization.

### CONSTRUCTORS

```
UnmarshalException(String)
UnmarshalException(String, Exception)
```

# java.rmi.server Package Exceptions

## ExportException

`public class ExportException extends RemoteException`

An `ExportException` is thrown if the system is unable to export a remote object. A common problem that causes this exception to be thrown is an attempt to export an object that does not implement the `java.rmi.Remote` interface or extend `UnicastRemoteObject`, which attempts to implicitly export itself. An `ExportException` can also be thrown if the port number that an object is attempting to bind to is unavailable.

## CONSTRUCTORS

```
ExportException(String)
ExportException(String, Exception)
```

# ServerCloneException

`public class ServerCloneException extends CloneNotSupportedException`

A `CloneNotSupportedException` is thrown if an attempt is made to clone a remote object that does not implement the `Cloneable` interface either directly or implicitly.

## CONSTRUCTORS

```
ServerCloneException(String)
ServerCloneException(String, Exception)
```

## FIELD

`public Exception detail`

The `detail` variable contains a reference to an exception that is the basis of the exception that was raised. In other words, the `ServerCloneException` is the wrapper around the exception that is pointed to by this reference.

## METHOD

`public String getMessage()`

This returns a `String` representation of the exception, including any nested exceptions if they exist.

# ServerNotActiveException

`public class ServerNotActiveException extends Exception`

The `ServerNotActiveException` is thrown when an RMI request is made by a remote object while it is not being operated on via a remote call. For example, a call to `java.rmi.server.RemoteServer.getClientHost()` throws a `ServerNotActiveException` if no client is currently accessing the object.

## CONSTRUCTORS

```
ServerNotActiveException()
ServerNotActiveException(String)
```

# SkeletonMismatchException

```
public class SkeletonMismatchException extends RemoteException
```

A `SkeletonMismatchException` is thrown if the internal `HashCode` for an interface does not match on both the skeleton and stub classes that implement it. This implies that these two objects—the skeleton and the stub—are not referring to the same remote object. Often this problem is the result of changing an interface and restarting a server without removing the remote object from the registry. It can often be fixed by making sure that rmic has generated the stub and skeleton classes for the most recent build of a class, and restarting any server or registry that uses them.

## CONSTRUCTOR

```
public SkeletonMismatchException(String s)
```

# SkeletonNotFoundException

```
public class SkeletonNotFoundException extends RemoteException
```

The `SkeletonNotFoundException` is thrown if a remote object implemetation or registry cannot find the skeleton class of the related object. This can be the result of a misconfigured CLASSPATH or a nonexistent skeleton class. Make sure that you have generated the skeleton class with the rmic compiler and that it is accessible via the local CLASSPATH. This exception can also be thrown because of a bad URL, a wrong codebase, or name collisions.

## CONSTRUCTORS

```
SkeletonNotFoundException(String)
SkeletonNotFoundException(String, Exception)
```

# SocketSecurityException

```
public class SocketSecurityException extends ExportException
```

A `SocketSecurityException` is thrown if an attempt is made to export an object on a port that has been denied socket access by a security manager.

## CONSTRUCTORS

```
SocketSecurityException(String)
SocketSecurityException(String, Exception)
```

# Appendix A

# Miscellaneous Security Issues

WE LIVE IN A dangerous world, where it is not always wise to be trusting, because nasty people are out there who try to steal, cheat, and vandalize your systems, servers, and data. This has lead to the hobbling of many services in the name of security. The only real way to make your system bulletproof is to take it off the network. The next best option is to put it behind a firewall.

## Java RMI Security

Security is always a complicated subject when you are dealing with network computing. In essence, the only completely secure environment is one that is not on a network, and even that can be insecure, depending on who's guarding your machine. With this in mind, you can think of security as an attempt at making it difficult to break into your system without giving up too much functionality or flexibility.

Many properties are built into the Java environment to make it difficult to subvert a system or gain unauthorized access to data. These properties are part of the language as well as the run-time environment. The language has done away with user-controlled memory management and pointer manipulation, making it difficult to access system memory or to change or even read values in the system heap. The run-time environment also has many built-in security features, such as a bytecode verifier that makes sure that the code that it is running is valid, legal code that doesn't break any of the rules imposed by the Java language (such as the rule against miscasting between types).

### Authentication

RMI is chiefly intended to allow you to distribute applications, usually over a network. The network environment opens the door to many more possible breaches of security. Since an object that is fashioned for distribution is essentially registering itself and waiting for clients to access it, it needs to make sure that only authorized clients are in fact accessing it. You can adopt any of a number of approaches to handle authentication. In the "Punch Clock" application from Chapter 4, you implemented a simple password authentication scheme. If a connection was established with a valid password, you allowed the transaction to take place. This was all handled at the application level. In other words, the authentication check was part of your application and not part of the system. This approach provides for a simple and reasonable means of authentication for most applications.

Sometimes, simple authentication isn't enough. Even though you know who is making the transaction, you may not know who is "listening" to the conversation. To prevent such "eavesdropping," you would implement some sort of transport layer encryption such as the Secure Sockets Layer (SSL). This can be handled by swapping out the RMISocketFactory on both your client and server platforms with a version of the socket factory that returns a secure socket rather than a default socket. This solution allows your application to remain unchanged, as a lower-level layer is handling the dirty work. So in other words, the application doesn't change, the underlying system changes.

In order to make such a system change, simply create a custom socket factory based on the SocketFactory class and replace the active socket factory in the system by calling setSocketFactory() and passing it your custom factory. Because you are dealing with a communication level of the application, the sockets produced by this factory must have corresponding or compatible sockets on the client side as well as the server side. Take a look at the reference section on the RMISocketFactory class for more details.

## Browser Security

Because many applications involve Web browsers, it's important to look at the security managers implemented for browsers. First of all, by default browsers are very restrictive in the code they permit to run. Most browsers do not permit an applet to make socket connections to any machines other than the one that the applet was downloaded from in the first place. Fortunately, this behavior can be overridden in many browsers, but it should be used with caution. A malicious applet that has arbitrary network accessibility can connect to mail servers and send nasty e-mail (apparently from you), or it can hack into other computer systems (posing as you).

How do you modify this behavior? In HotJava (and older versions of Internet Explorer), you can set the applet security manager to handle the "Applet Host" protocol, "restricted," or "unrestricted." In the case of Applet Host, the applet can connect only to the machine that it was served from. This is normally the default behavior. The other two options either restrict all network access or grant all network access, respectively. These parameters can be changed in the "options" or "preferences" menus for your browser.

In the case of RMI, an applet that tries to connect to a remote object on a machine generates an exception unless the object exists on the machine that the applet came from, or the security manager has been set to a permissive network state. Because you have no control over how an anonymous user's browser is set, your applets that use RMI will normally only connect to objects on the same server. In order to distribute the connections to other machines, you could implement a "relay" server that relays information that is sent from the host server to other machines. This way, the browser is only allowing connections to a single machine, but that machine is in turn distributing the connections to others.

# Firewall Security

A firewall gives a certain level of protection to a system by limiting the types of transmissions that may traverse the link between the Internet and a local network. This is accomplished in a number of ways, such as permitting only certain types of protocols to pass, such as the Simple Mail Transfer Protocol (SMTP) or the Hypertext Transfer Protocol (HTTP). Other firewalls only permit connections to certain machines and to services running on certain port numbers. This approach enables a site manager to monitor the network traffic and restrict traffic to services that the manager feels are reasonably safe. But unfortunately, these protective limitations often affect your ability to run certain other applications without modifying the firewall.

One reasonable way to traverse a firewall in a relatively safe fashion is through proxy services. An HTTP proxy is essentially a server running on a firewall machine (a machine responsible for routing the traffic over a firewall) that accepts HTTP requests on one side, makes the request on the other side, retrieves the results, and forwards them back to the requester. These types of proxy servers can be used to forward data using HTTP on one side of the firewall and another protocol, such as FTP, on the other (as illustrated in Figure A-1).

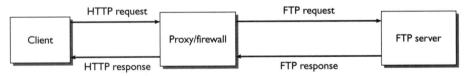

Figure A-1. Using an HTTP proxy to forward an FTP request

So the question is, "how does this affect an RMI session?" Well, actually, this approach has a profound effect on RMI. The most notable and, unfortunately, adverse effect is on performance. RMI transactions that must traverse a proxy server are normally an order of magnitude slower than transactions that use direct connections. Second, the RMI connections must be encapsulated in HTTP for some servers but can be routed directly on others, depending on how the server is configured. In other words, some firewalls can be configured to allow RMI transactions to pass through on some predetermined port number that is established for these transactions, but other firewalls do not permit this type of configuration. Such restrictions arise from either design or policy depending on the site and the comfort level of the site administrators. In the case of a firewall that permits only HTTP transactions, the RMI connections must be encapsulated in HTTP, and only servers can export remote objects (in normal RMI applications, both clients and servers can export objects). This limitation arises from the fact that HTTP is a one-way protocol. A server cannot initiate a transaction. This means that clients will be unable to export callback mechanisms after they register with a server.

## RMI Encapsulated in HTTP

Fortunately, the encapsulation of RMI calls in HTTP is handled by the transport layer. This means that you don't need to change any of your implementation code. The sockets created by the RMISocketFactory are capable of identifying HTTP requests and encapsulating the RMI data in a standard HTTP POST data stream. (The POST method is used in HTTP when data is being sent along with a transaction request, such as an HTML form submission.) When you are using a proxy that will permit connections to pass through to arbitrary ports, the request to invoke a remote method comes in as a standard HTTP POST. The server receives the request and identifies it as an HTTP request. The POST data is decoded and translated to a standard RMI call before being handed up to the remote reference layer for processing. The return data is also encapsulated and sent as the HTTP response.

This picture changes a bit if the firewall doesn't allow connections to arbitrary ports. In this case, the HTTP requests and responses are all ushered through a third application that uses an HTTP server and the Common Gateway Interface (CGI). In this model, the HTTP request that encompasses the RMI call is sent to a CGI application on an HTTP server. This CGI application then runs the Java interpreter, decodes the RMI call data in the POST body of the HTTP request, and forwards the RMI call to the server that is exporting the remote method. The server sends the response data back to the CGI application, which then sends that data up to the HTTP server, which in turn finally returns the data to the RMI client. Pretty messy, huh? Figure A-2 shows a diagram of this interaction.

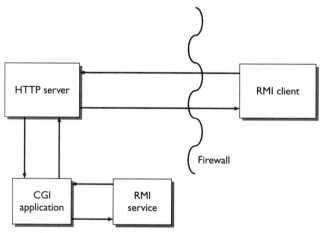

Figure A-2. RMI through a CGI application

# Server Configuration

One of the most important issues is that the server must know what is outside the firewall. On many systems, the relevant property will automatically be set to the proper name, but in order to be safe, you can set this property, `java.rmi.server.hostname`, to the correct value at run time. This can be done with the `-D` flag, followed by the property name and value. For example:

```
java -Djava.rmi.server.hostname=foo.bar.com MyServer
```

Next, you need to have an HTTP server running and listening to the standard HTTP port number (80). This server must be configured to allow CGI access with the standard cgi-bin script alias directory. The RMI call will expect to find the Java-RMI CGI applications to be in this directory or a subdirectory. So, in other words, CGI scripts that you create to forward RMI calls will be available from an HTTP server in the /cgi-bin/ directory.

Finally, you must install a CGI script that can find the Java interpreter and access all of the correct CGI environment variables. Listing A-1 shows the sample script that comes with the standard JDK 1.1 distribution. Notice that a path to the Java interpreter must be defined, and all of the necessary properties are set using `-D` flags. This script will simply be run by an HTTP server whenever a remote client wants to transact with an RMI host. The request will be transferred to this script, which will in turn fire up a Java Virtual Machine (JVM) and forward data to the remote object requested. Any results are then returned to the HTTP server and sent back to the RMI requester.

**Listing A-1. A CGI application that forwards RMI (java-rmi.cgi)**

```
#!/bin/sh
#
# This script executes the Java interpreter, defines properties
# that correspond to the CGI 1.0 environment variables, and executes
# the class "sun.rmi.transport.proxy.CGIHandler". It should be
# installed in the directory to which the HTTP server maps the
# URL path "/cgi-bin".
#
# (Configuration is necessary as noted below.)
#
# This class will support a QUERY_STRING of the
# form"forward=<port>"
# with a REQUEST_METHOD "POST". The body of the request will be
# forwarded (as another POST request) to the server listening on the
# specified port (must be >= 1024). The response from this forwarded
# request will be the response to the original request.
#
# CONFIGURATION:
#
```

```
# Fill in correct absolute path to Java interpreter below. For
  example,
# the "PATH=" line might be changed to the follow if the JDK is
  installed
# at the path "/home/peter/java":
#
# PATH=/home/peter/java/bin:$PATH
#
PATH=/usr/local/java/bin:$PATH
java \
  -DAUTH_TYPE="$AUTH_TYPE" \
  -DCONTENT_LENGTH="$CONTENT_LENGTH" \
  -DCONTENT_TYPE="$CONTENT_TYPE" \
  -DGATEWAY_INTERFACE="$GATEWAY_INTERFACE" \
  -DHTTP_ACCEPT="$HTTP_ACCEPT" \
  -DPATH_INFO="$PATH_INFO" \
  -DPATH_TRANSLATED="$PATH_TRANSLATED" \
  -DQUERY_STRING="$QUERY_STRING" \
  -DREMOTE_ADDR="$REMOTE_ADDR" \
  -DREMOTE_HOST="$REMOTE_HOST" \
  -DREMOTE_IDENT="$REMOTE_IDENT" \
  -DREMOTE_USER="$REMOTE_USER" \
  -DREQUEST_METHOD="$REQUEST_METHOD" \
  -DSCRIPT_NAME="$SCRIPT_NAME" \
  -DSERVER_NAME="$SERVER_NAME" \
  -DSERVER_PORT="$SERVER_PORT" \
  -DSERVER_PROTOCOL="$SERVER_PROTOCOL" \
  -DSERVER_SOFTWARE="$SERVER_SOFTWARE" \
sun.rmi.transport.proxy.CGIHandler
```

# Appendix B

# Thrown-by Index

THIS APPENDIX IS A quick reference to the methods that throw certain exceptions. This is not a complete list of exceptions described in the Java API, but rather a subset dealing specifically with the `java.rmi.*` packages. All exceptions listed are exceptions that are declared in a `throws` clause for methods in the `java.rmi.*` packages. Each exception is followed by a list of methods that throw that exception. Only API-specific exceptions are listed, as well as net system-level exceptions.

| EXCEPTION | METHODS |
|---|---|
| AccessException | java.rmi.registry.Registry.lookup() |
| | java.rmi.registry.Registry.bind() |
| | java.rmi.registry.Registry.unbind() |
| | java.rmi.registry.Registry.rebind() |
| | java.rmi.registry.Registry.list() |
| AlreadyBoundException | java.rmi.Naming.bind() |
| | java.rmi.registry.Registry.bind() |
| ClassNotFoundException | java.rmi.server.LoaderHandler.loadClass() |
| | java.rmi.server.RMIClassLoader.loadClass() |
| CloneNotSupportedException | java.rmi.server.UnicastRemoteObject.clone() |
| Exception | java.rmi.server.RemoteCall.executeCall() |
| | java.rmi.server.RemoteRef.invoke() |
| | java.rmi.server.Skeleton.dispatch() |
| IOException | java.rmi.server.ObjID.write() |
| | java.rmi.server.ObjID.read() |
| | java.rmi.server.RMISocketFactory.createSocket() |
| | java.rmi.server.RMISocketFactory.createServerSocket() |

*continued*

| Exception | Methods |
|---|---|
| IOException *(continued)* | java.rmi.server.RMISocketFactory.setSocketFactory() |
| | java.rmi.server.RemoteCall.getOutputStream() |
| | java.rmi.server.RemoteCall.releaseOutputStream() |
| | java.rmi.server.RemoteCall.getInputStream() |
| | java.rmi.server.RemoteCall.releaseInputStream() |
| | java.rmi.server.RemoteCall.getResultStream() |
| | java.rmi.server.RemoteCall.done() |
| | java.rmi.server.UID.write() |
| | java.rmi.server.UID.read() |
| | java.io.BufferedInputStream.read() |
| | java.io.BufferedInputStream.skip() |
| | java.io.BufferedInputStream.available() |
| | java.io.BufferedInputStream.reset() |
| | java.io.BufferedOutputStream.flush() |
| | java.io.BufferedOutputStream.write() |
| | java.io.BufferedReader.close() |
| | java.io.BufferedReader.mark() |
| | java.io.BufferedReader.read() |
| | java.io.BufferedReader.readLine() |
| | java.io.BufferedReader.ready() |
| | java.io.BufferedReader.reset() |
| | java.io.BufferedReader.skip() |
| | java.io.BufferedWriter.write() |
| | java.io.BufferedWriter.newLine() |
| | java.io.BufferedWriter.flush() |
| | java.io.BufferedWriter.close() |
| | java.io.ByteArrayOutputStream.writeTo() |
| | java.io.CharArrayReader.read() |

| Exception | Methods |
|---|---|
| IOException *(continued)* | java.io.CharArrayReader.skip() |
| | java.io.CharArrayReader.ready() |
| | java.io.CharArrayReader.mark() |
| | java.io.CharArrayReader.reset() |
| | java.io.CharArrayWriter.writeTo() |
| | java.io.DataInput.readFully() |
| | java.io.DataInput.skipBytes() |
| | java.io.DataInput.readBoolean() |
| | java.io.DataInput.readByte() |
| | java.io.DataInput.readUnsignedByte() |
| | java.io.DataInput.readShort() |
| | java.io.DataInput.readUnsignedShort() |
| | java.io.DataInput.readChar() |
| | java.io.DataInput.readInt() |
| | java.io.DataInput.readLong() |
| | java.io.DataInput.readFloat() |
| | java.io.DataInput.readDouble() |
| | java.io.DataInput.readLine() |
| | java.io.DataInput.readUTF() |
| | java.io.DataInputStream.read() |
| | java.io.DataInputStream.readFully() |
| | java.io.DataInputStream.skipBytes() |
| | java.io.DataInputStream.readBoolean() |
| | java.io.DataInputStream.readByte() |
| | java.io.DataInputStream.readUnsignedByte() |
| | java.io.DataInputStream.readShort() |
| | java.io.DataInputStream.readUnsignedShort() |

*continued*

| Exception | Methods |
|---|---|
| IOException *(continued)* | java.io.DataInputStream.readChar() |
| | java.io.DataInputStream.readInt() |
| | java.io.DataInputStream.readLong() |
| | java.io.DataInputStream.readFloat() |
| | java.io.DataInputStream.readDouble() |
| | java.io.DataInputStream.readLine() |
| | java.io.DataInputStream.readUTF() |
| | java.io.DataOutput.write() |
| | java.io.DataOutput.writeBoolean() |
| | java.io.DataOutput.writeByte() |
| | java.io.DataOutput.writeShort() |
| | java.io.DataOutput.writeChar() |
| | java.io.DataOutput.writeInt() |
| | java.io.DataOutput.writeLong() |
| | java.io.DataOutput.writeFloat() |
| | java.io.DataOutput.writeDouble() |
| | java.io.DataOutput.writeBytes() |
| | java.io.DataOutput.writeChars() |
| | java.io.DataOutput.writeUTF() |
| | java.io.DataOutputStream.write() |
| | java.io.DataOutputStream.writeBoolean() |
| | java.io.DataOutputStream.writeByte() |
| | java.io.DataOutputStream.writeShort() |
| | java.io.DataOutputStream.writeChar() |
| | java.io.DataOutputStream.writeInt() |
| | java.io.DataOutputStream.writeLong() |
| | java.io.DataOutputStream.writeFloat() |
| | java.io.DataOutputStream.writeDouble() |

| Exception | Methods |
|---|---|
| IOException *(continued)* | java.io.DataOutputStream.writeBytes() |
| | java.io.DataOutputStream.writeChars() |
| | java.io.DataOutputStream.writeUTF() |
| | java.io.Externalizable.writeExternal() |
| | java.io.Externalizable.readExternal() |
| | java.io.File.getCanonicalPath() |
| | java.io.FileInputStream.read() |
| | java.io.FileInputStream.skip() |
| | java.io.FileInputStream.available() |
| | java.io.FileInputStream.close() |
| | java.io.FileInputStream.getFD() |
| | java.io.FileInputStream.finalize() |
| | java.io.FileOutputStream.FileOutputStream() |
| | java.io.FileOutputStream.write() |
| | java.io.FileOutputStream.close() |
| | java.io.FileOutputStream.getFD() |
| | java.io.FileOutputStream.finalize() |
| | java.io.FileWriter.FileWrite() |
| | java.io.FilterInputStream.read() |
| | java.io.FilterInputStream.skip() |
| | java.io.FilterInputStream.available() |
| | java.io.FilterInputStream.close() |
| | java.io.FilterInputStream.reset() |
| | java.io.FilterOutputStream.write() |
| | java.io.FilterOutputStream.flush() |
| | java.io.FilterOutputStream.close() |
| | java.io.FilterReader.read() |

*continued*

| Exception | Methods |
|---|---|
| IOException *(continued)* | java.io.FilterReader.skip() |
| | java.io.FilterReader.ready() |
| | java.io.FilterReader.mark() |
| | java.io.FilterReader.reset() |
| | java.io.FilterReader.close() |
| | java.io.FilterWrite.write() |
| | java.io.FilterWrite.flush() |
| | java.io.FilterWrite.close() |
| | java.io.InputStream.read() |
| | java.io.InputStream.skip() |
| | java.io.InputStream.available() |
| | java.io.InputStream.close() |
| | java.io.InputStream.reset() |
| | java.io.InputStreamReader.getCharacterEncoding() |
| | java.io.InputStreamReader.read() |
| | java.io.InputStreamReader.ready() |
| | java.io.InputStreamReader.close() |
| | java.io.LineNumberInputStream.read() |
| | java.io.LineNumberInputStream.skip() |
| | java.io.LineNumberInputStream.available() |
| | java.io.LineNumberInputStream.reset() |
| | java.io.LineNumberReader.read() |
| | java.io.LineNumberReader.readLine() |
| | java.io.LineNumberReader.skip() |
| | java.io.LineNumberReader.mark() |
| | java.io.LineNumberReader.reset() |
| | java.io.ObjectInput.read() |
| | java.io.ObjectInput.skip() |

| Exception | Methods |
|---|---|
| IOException *(continued)* | java.io.ObjectInput.available() |
| | java.io.ObjectInput.close() |
| | java.io.ObjectInputStream.ObjectInputStream() |
| | java.io.ObjectInputStream.readObject() |
| | java.io.ObjectInputStream.defaultReadObject() |
| | java.io.ObjectInputStream.resolveClass() |
| | java.io.ObjectInputStream.resolveObject() |
| | java.io.ObjectInputStream.readStreamHeader() |
| | java.io.ObjectInputStream.read() |
| | java.io.ObjectInputStream.available() |
| | java.io.ObjectInputStream.close() |
| | java.io.ObjectInputStream.readBoolean() |
| | java.io.ObjectInputStream.readByte() |
| | java.io.ObjectInputStream.readUnsignedByte() |
| | java.io.ObjectInputStream.readShort() |
| | java.io.ObjectInputStream.readUnsignedShort() |
| | java.io.ObjectInputStream.readChar() |
| | java.io.ObjectInputStream.readInt() |
| | java.io.ObjectInputStream.readLong() |
| | java.io.ObjectInputStream.readFloat() |
| | java.io.ObjectInputStream.readDouble() |
| | java.io.ObjectInputStream.readFully() |
| | java.io.ObjectInputStream.skipBytes() |
| | java.io.ObjectInputStream.readLine() |
| | java.io.ObjectInputStream.readUTF() |
| | java.io.ObjectOutput.writeOutput() |
| | java.io.ObjectOutput.write() |

*continued*

| Exception | Methods |
|---|---|
| IOException *(continued)* | java.io.ObjectOutput.flush() |
| | java.io.ObjectOutput.close() |
| | java.io.ObjectOutputStream.ObjectOutputStream() |
| | java.io.ObjectOutputStream.writeObject() |
| | java.io.ObjectOutputStream.defaultWriteObject() |
| | java.io.ObjectOutputStream.reset() |
| | java.io.ObjectOutputStream.annotateClass() |
| | java.io.ObjectOutputStream.replaceObject() |
| | java.io.ObjectOutputStream.writeStreamHandler() |
| | java.io.ObjectOutputStream.write() |
| | java.io.ObjectOutputStream.flush() |
| | java.io.ObjectOutputStream.drain() |
| | java.io.ObjectOutputStream.close() |
| | java.io.ObjectOutputStream.writeBoolean() |
| | java.io.ObjectOutputStream.writeByte() |
| | java.io.ObjectOutputStream.writeShort() |
| | java.io.ObjectOutputStream.writeChar() |
| | java.io.ObjectOutputStream.writeInt() |
| | java.io.ObjectOutputStream.writeLong() |
| | java.io.ObjectOutputStream.writeFloat() |
| | java.io.ObjectOutputStream.writeDouble() |
| | java.io.ObjectOutputStream.writeBytes() |
| | java.io.ObjectOutputStream.writeChars() |
| | java.io.ObjectOutputStream.writeUTF() |
| | java.io.OutputStream.write() |
| | java.io.OutputStream.flush() |
| | java.io.OutputStream.close() |
| | java.io.OutputStreamWriter.getCharacterEncoding() |

| Exception | Methods |
| --- | --- |
| IOException *(continued)* | java.io.OutputStreamWriter.write() |
| | java.io.OutputStreamWriter.flush() |
| | java.io.OutputStreamWriter.close() |
| | java.io.PipedInputStream.PipedInputStream() |
| | java.io.PipedInputStream.connect() |
| | java.io.PipedInputStream.receive() |
| | java.io.PipedInputStream.read() |
| | java.io.PipedInputStream.available() |
| | java.io.PipedInputStream.close() |
| | java.io.PipedOutputStream.PipedOutputStream() |
| | java.io.PipedOutputStream.connect() |
| | java.io.PipedOutputStream.write() |
| | java.io.PipedOutputStream.flush() |
| | java.io.PipedOutputStream.close() |
| | java.io.PipedReader.PipedReader() |
| | java.io.PipedReader.connect() |
| | java.io.PipedReader.read() |
| | java.io.PipedReader.close() |
| | java.io.PipedWriter.PipedWrite() |
| | java.io.PipedWriter.connect() |
| | java.io.PipedWriter.write() |
| | java.io.PipedWriter.flush() |
| | java.io.PipedWriter.close() |
| | java.io.PrintStream.write() |
| | java.io.PushBackInputStream.read() |
| | java.io.PushBackInputStream.unread() |
| | java.io.PushBackInputStream.available() |

*continued*

| Exception | Methods |
|---|---|
| IOException *(continued)* | java.io.PushBackReader.read() |
| | java.io.PushBackReader.unread() |
| | java.io.PushBackReader.ready() |
| | java.io.PushBackReader.close() |
| | java.io.RandomAccessFile.RandomAccessFile() |
| | java.io.RandomAccessFile.getFD() |
| | java.io.RandomAccessFile.read() |
| | java.io.RandomAccessFile.readFully() |
| | java.io.RandomAccessFile.skipBytes() |
| | java.io.RandomAccessFile.write() |
| | java.io.RandomAccessFile.getFilePointer() |
| | java.io.RandomAccessFile.seek() |
| | java.io.RandomAccessFile.length() |
| | java.io.RandomAccessFile.close() |
| | java.io.RandomAccessFile.readBoolean() |
| | java.io.RandomAccessFile.readByte() |
| | java.io.RandomAccessFile.readUnsignedByte() |
| | java.io.RandomAccessFile.readShort() |
| | java.io.RandomAccessFile.readUnsignedShort() |
| | java.io.RandomAccessFile.readChar() |
| | java.io.RandomAccessFile.readInt() |
| | java.io.RandomAccessFile.readLong() |
| | java.io.RandomAccessFile.readFloat() |
| | java.io.RandomAccessFile.readDouble() |
| | java.io.RandomAccessFile.readLine() |
| | java.io.RandomAccessFile.readUTF() |
| | java.io.RandomAccessFile.writeBoolean() |
| | java.io.RandomAccessFile.writeByte() |

| Exception | Methods |
| --- | --- |
| IOException *(continued)* | java.io.RandomAccessFile.writeShort() |
| | java.io.RandomAccessFile.writeChar() |
| | java.io.RandomAccessFile.writeInt() |
| | java.io.RandomAccessFile.writeLong() |
| | java.io.RandomAccessFile.writeFloat() |
| | java.io.RandomAccessFile.writeDouble() |
| | java.io.RandomAccessFile.writeBytes() |
| | java.io.RandomAccessFile.writeChars() |
| | java.io.RandomAccessFile.writeUTF() |
| | java.io.Reader.read() |
| | java.io.Reader.skip() |
| | java.io.Reader.ready() |
| | java.io.Reader.mark() |
| | java.io.Reader.reset() |
| | java.io.Reader.close() |
| | java.io.SequenceInputStream.available() |
| | java.io.SequenceInputStream.read() |
| | java.io.SequenceInputStream.close() |
| | java.io.StreamTokenizer.nextToken() |
| | java.io.StringReader.read() |
| | java.io.StringReader.skip() |
| | java.io.StringReader.mark() |
| | java.io.StringReader.reset() |
| | java.io.Writer.write() |
| | java.io.Writer.flush() |
| | java.io.Writer.close() |
| | java.net.ContentHandler.getContent() |

*continued*

| Exception | Methods |
|---|---|
| IOException *(continued)* | java.net.DatagramSocket.send() |
| MalformedURLException | java.rmi.Naming.lookup() |
| | java.rmi.Naming.bind() |
| | java.rmi.Naming.unbind() |
| | java.rmi.Naming.rebind() |
| | java.rmi.Naming.list() |
| | java.rmi.server.LoaderHandler.loadClass() |
| | java.rmi.server.RMIClassLoader.loadClass() |
| | java.net.URL.URL() |
| NotBoundException | java.rmi.Naming.lookup() |
| | java.rmi.Naming.unbind() |
| | java.rmi.registry.Registry.lookup() |
| | java.rmi.registry.Registry.unbind() |
| RemoteException | java.rmi.Naming.lookup() |
| | java.rmi.Naming.bind() |
| | java.rmi.Naming.unbind() |
| | java.rmi.Naming.rebind() |
| | java.rmi.Naming.list() |
| | java.rmi.dgc.DGC.dirty() |
| | java.rmi.dgc.DGC.clean() |
| | java.rmi.registry.LocateRegistry.getRegistry() |
| | java.rmi.registry.LocateRegistry.createRegistry() |
| | java.rmi.registry.Registry.lookup() |
| | java.rmi.registry.Registry.bind() |
| | java.rmi.registry.Registry.unbind() |
| | java.rmi.registry.Registry.rebind() |
| | java.rmi.registry.Registry.list() |

*continued*

| Exception | Methods |
|-----------|---------|
| RemoteException *(continued)* | java.rmi.registry.RegistryHandler.registryStub() |
| | java.rmi.registry.RegistryHandler.registryImpl() |
| | java.rmi.server.RemoteRef.newCall() |
| | java.rmi.server.RemoteRef.done() |
| | java.rmi.server.ServerRef.exportObject() |
| | java.rmi.server.UnicastRemoteObject. UnicastRemoteObject () |
| | java.rmi.server.UnicastRemoteObject.exportObject() |
| ServerNotActiveException | java.rmi.server.RemoteServer.getClientHost() |
| | java.rmi.server.ServerRef.getClientHost() |
| StreamCorruptedException | java.rmi.server.RemoteCall.getResultStream() |
| | java.io.ObjectInputStream.ObjectInputStream() |
| | java.io.ObjectInputStream.readStreamHeader() |
| UnknownHostException | java.rmi.Naming.lookup() |
| | java.rmi.Naming.bind() |
| | java.rmi.Naming.unbind() |
| | java.rmi.Naming.rebind() |
| | java.rmi.Naming.list() |
| | java.rmi.registry.LocateRegistry.getRegistry() |
| | java.rmi.registry.RegistryHandler.registryStub() |

# Appendix C

# Defined-in Index

THIS IS AN ALPHABETICAL list of methods that are defined in the classes of the `java.rmi.*` packages. Each method is followed by a list of the classes and interfaces that define the methods.

| METHOD | DEFINING CLASS(ES) AND INTERFACE(S) |
| --- | --- |
| bind | java.rmi.Naming, java.rmi.registry.Registry |
| checkAccept | java.rmi.RMISecurityManager |
| checkAccess | java.rmi.RMISecurityManager |
| checkConnect | java.rmi.RMISecurityManager |
| checkCreateClassLoader | java.rmi.RMISecurityManager |
| checkDelete | java.rmi.RMISecurityManager |
| checkExec | java.rmi.RMISecurityManager |
| checkExit | java.rmi.RMISecurityManager |
| checkLink | java.rmi.RMISecurityManager |
| checkListen | java.rmi.RMISecurityManager |
| checkMemberAccess | java.rmi.RMISecurityManager |
| checkPackageAccess | java.rmi.RMISecurityManager |
| checkPackageDefinition | java.rmi.RMISecurityManager |
| checkPrintJobAccess | java.rmi.RMISecurityManager |
| checkPropertiesAccess | java.rmi.RMISecurityManager |
| checkPropertyAccess | java.rmi.RMISecurityManager |
| checkRead | java.rmi.RMISecurityManager |
| checkSecurityAccess | java.rmi.RMISecurityManager |
| checkSetFactory | java.rmi.RMISecurityManager |

*continued*

| Method | Defining Class(es) and Interface(s) |
| --- | --- |
| checkTopLevelWindow | java.rmi.RMISecurityManager |
| checkWrite | java.rmi.RMISecurityManager |
| checkWrite | java.rmi.RMISecurityManager |
| clean | java.rmi.dgc.DGC |
| clone | java.rmi.server.UnicastRemoteObject |
| createRegistry | java.rmi.registry.LocateRegistry |
| createServerSocket | java.rmi.server.RMISocketFactory |
| createSocket | java.rmi.server.RMISocketFactory |
| dirty | java.rmi.dgc.DGC |
| dispatch | java.rmi.server.Skeleton |
| done | java.rmi.server.RemoteCall, java.rmi.server.RemoteRef |
| equals | java.rmi.dgc.VMID, java.rmi.server.ObjID, java.rmi.server.RemoteObject, java.rmi.server.UID |
| executeCall | java.rmi.server.RemoteCall |
| exportObject | java.rmi.server.ServerRef, java.rmi.server.UnicastRemoteObject |
| failure | java.rmi.server.RMIFailureHandler |
| getClientHost | java.rmi.server.RemoteServer, java.rmi.server.ServerRef |
| getDefaultStream | java.rmi.server.LogStream |
| getFailureHandler | java.rmi.server.RMISocketFactory |
| getInputStream | java.rmi.server.RemoteCall |
| getLog | java.rmi.server.RemoteServer |
| getMessage | java.rmi.ServerCloneException, java.rmi.RemoteException |
| getOperation | java.rmi.server.Operation |
| getOperations | java.rmi.server.Skeleton |
| getOutputStream | java.rmi.server.LogStream, java.rmi.server.RemoteCall |
| getRefClass | java.rmi.server.RemoteRef |
| getRegistry | java.rmi.registry.LocateRegistry |

*continued*

| Method | Defining Class(es) and Interface(s) |
| --- | --- |
| getResultStream | java.rmi.server.RemoteCall |
| getSecurityContext | java.rmi.RMISecurityManager |
| getSocketFactory | java.rmi.server.RMISocketFactory |
| getVMID | java.rmi.dgc.Lease |
| getValue | java.rmi.dgc.Lease |
| hashCode | java.rmi.dgc.VMID, java.rmi.server.ObjID, java.rmi.server.RemoteObject, java.rmi.server.UID |
| invoke | java.rmi.server.RemoteRef |
| isUnique | java.rmi.dgc.VMID |
| list | java.rmi.Naming, java.rmi.registry.Registry |
| loadClass | java.rmi.server.LoaderHandler, java.rmi.server.RMIClassLoader |
| log | java.rmi.server.LogStream |
| lookup | java.rmi.Naming, java.rmi.registry.Registry |
| newCall | java.rmi.server.RemoteRef |
| parseLevel | java.rmi.server.LogStream |
| read | java.rmi.server.ObjID, java.rmi.server.UID |
| rebind | java.rmi.Naming, java.rmi.registry.Registry |
| registryImpl | java.rmi.registry.RegistryHandler |
| registryStub | java.rmi.registry.RegistryHandler |
| releaseInputStream | java.rmi.server.RemoteCall |
| releaseOutputStream | java.rmi.server.RemoteCall |
| remoteEquals | java.rmi.server.RemoteRef |
| remoteHashCode | java.rmi.server.RemoteRef |
| remoteToString | java.rmi.server.RemoteRef |
| setDefaultStream | java.rmi.server.LogStream |
| setFailureHandler | java.rmi.server.RMISocketFactory |
| setLog | java.rmi.server.RemoteServer |

*continued*

| Method | Defining Class(es) and Interface(s) |
| --- | --- |
| setOutputStream | java.rmi.server.LogStream |
| setRef | java.rmi.server.RemoteStub |
| setSocketFactory | java.rmi.server.RMISocketFactory |
| showThreadName | java.rmi.server.LogStream |
| toString | java.rmi.dgc.VMID, java.rmi.server.LogStream, java.rmi.server.ObjID, java.rmi.server.Operation, java.rmi.server.RemoteObject, java.rmi.server.UID |
| unbind | java.rmi.Naming, java.rmi.registry.Registry |
| unreferenced | java.rmi.server.Unreferenced |
| write | java.rmi.server.LogStream, java.rmi.server.ObjID, java.rmi.server.UID |

# Appendix D

# What's on the CD-ROM?

The CD-ROM that accompanies this book contains all of the source code that is contained in the text. The source code examples in the book are drawn directly from these source files with only minor modification. (The CD-ROM source code is sometimes more heavily annotated.)

The CD-ROM also contains the Java Development Kit (JDK) versions 1.0.2 for Macintosh and 1.1.4 for Windows and Solaris from Sun Microsystems.

The CD is structured as follows:

♦ The **src** directory contains all of the source code in subdirectories that map directly to the package names of a particular application. For example, to find the source code for the ChatApplet application, first take the package name given in the example—in this case, rmibook.chat—and prefix "src" to the path. In other words, the ChatApplet.java source file can be found in the CD-ROM directory src/rmibook/chat.

♦ The **jdk** directory contains the Java Development Kit from Javasoft. This package contains an interpreter, compiler, and assorted tools and documentation that can be used to generate, compile, and run the examples from this book. The JDK contains its own documentation in HTML format.

The Windows 95/NT and Macintosh versions are self-extracting archives, and the Solaris version is a shell file that can be executed from a shell prompt to install. Once the JDK has been unpacked, read the documentation that comes with the JDK for installation specifics.

The simplest way to use the source code on this CD-ROM is to copy the entire rmibook directory to your local system. Then change your working directory to the directory containing the files you are interested in and compile them with the javac compiler. Because the files use package names, the compiled code will emulate the package hierarchy described in the source files. The following steps show you how to compile the chat files; modify them to compile the other files on the CD-ROM. (Note that these instructions use the common Unix forward-slash (/) for directory separators. If you are using Windows NT or Windows 95, replace this with the backslash (\).)

1. Change your working directory to the one containing the source code:

   ```
   cd /src/
   ```

2. Compile the code using the javac compiler. Be sure to use the -d flag to specify a directory into which to build the code:

   ```
   javac -d ./mydir/myclasses ./rmibook/chat/*.java
   ```

   Don't be alarmed if you see any "Deprecated API used" messages; these are due to Java migration. Also, you may need to compile the contents of the util directory first.

3. Generate the stubs and skeletons using the rmic compiler. (All *Impl files must have rmic run on its .class files.) For this to work, it is important to make the directory specified in Step 2 part of your classpath environment variable. Follow filename capitalization precisely.

   ```
   rmic -d ./mydir/myclasses ./rmibook.chat.ChatImpl
   rmic -d ./mydir/myclasses ./rmibook.chat.ChatServerImpl
   ```

   These steps should generate your stub and skeleton classes in the same directory as the other object code for this application.

4. Set your classpath correctly. Be sure to include /jdk114/lib/classes.zip in the classpath or you may get a "class not found" error message.

5. Run the application with the Java interpreter:

   ```
   java rmibook.chat.ChatServerImpl
   ```

These steps must be followed to install any of the source examples supplied with this CD-ROM. You may need to make minor adjustments to your source directories, bin directories, and classpaths settings, depending on how you've set up your particular environment. Use the latest version of Microsoft Internet Explorer (4.0 or greater) or you may get error messages.

The Macintosh version of the JDK on this CD-ROM does not support Remote Method Invocation. If you're using a Macintosh, go to applejava.apple.com on the Web and download MRJ 2.0, which is Apple Computer's implementation of the Java VM and runtime environment, based on Sun's JDK 1.1.3 specification. MRJ 2.0 lets you run Java applets and applications on PowerPC and 68040 computers running System 8.0 or later. It also specifically supports RMI.

Be sure to consult the CD-ROM's root Readme file for any additional information about the contents of the disc.

# Index

**281**

# IDG BOOKS WORLDWIDE, INC. END-USER LICENSE AGREEMENT

<u>READ THIS.</u> You should carefully read these terms and conditions before opening the software packet(s) included with this book ("Book"). This is a license agreement ("Agreement") between you and IDG Books Worldwide, Inc. ("IDGB"). By opening the accompanying software packet(s), you acknowledge that you have read and accept the following terms and conditions. If you do not agree and do not want to be bound by such terms and conditions, promptly return the Book and the unopened software packet(s) to the place you obtained them for a full refund.

1. <u>License Grant.</u> IDGB grants to you (either an individual or entity) a nonexclusive license to use one copy of the enclosed software program(s) (collectively, the "Software") solely for your own personal or business purposes on a single computer (whether a standard computer or a workstation component of a multiuser network). The Software is in use on a computer when it is loaded into temporary memory (RAM) or installed into permanent memory (hard disk, CD-ROM, or other storage device). IDGB reserves all rights not expressly granted herein.

2. <u>Ownership.</u> IDGB is the owner of all right, title, and interest, including copyright, in and to the compilation of the Software recorded on the disk(s) or CD-ROM ("Software Media"). Copyright to the individual programs recorded on the Software Media is owned by the author or other authorized copyright owner of each program. Ownership of the Software and all proprietary rights relating thereto remain with IDGB and its licensers.

3. <u>Restrictions On Use and Transfer.</u>

(a) You may only (i) make one copy of the Software for backup or archival purposes, or (ii) transfer the Software to a single hard disk, provided that you keep the original for backup or archival purposes. You may not (i) rent or lease the Software, (ii) copy or reproduce the Software through a LAN or other network system or through any computer subscriber system or bulletin-board system, or (iii) modify, adapt, or create derivative works based on the Software.

(b) You may not reverse engineer, decompile, or disassemble the Software. You may transfer the Software and user documentation on a permanent basis, provided that the transferee agrees to accept the terms and conditions of this Agreement and you retain no copies. If the Software is an update or has been updated, any transfer must include the most recent update and all prior versions.

4. <u>Restrictions On Use of Individual Programs.</u> You must follow the individual requirements and restrictions detailed for each individual program in Appendix D of this Book. These limitations are also contained in the individual license agreements recorded on the Software Media. These limitations may include a requirement that after using the program for a specified period of time, the user must pay a registration fee or discontinue use. By opening the Software packet(s), you will be agreeing to abide by the licenses and restrictions for these individual programs that are detailed in Appendix D and on the Software Media. None of the material on this Software Media or listed in this Book may ever be redistributed, in original or modified form, for commercial purposes.

5. <u>Limited Warranty.</u>

(a) IDGB warrants that the Software and Software Media are free from defects in materials and workmanship under normal use for a period of sixty (60) days from the date of purchase of this Book. If IDGB receives notification within the warranty period of defects in materials or workmanship, IDGB will replace the defective Software Media.

(b) IDGB AND THE AUTHOR OF THE BOOK DISCLAIM ALL OTHER WARRANTIES, EXPRESS OR IMPLIED, INCLUDING WITHOUT LIMITATION IMPLIED WARRANTIES OF MERCHANTABILITY AND FITNESS FOR A PARTICULAR PURPOSE, WITH RESPECT TO THE SOFTWARE, THE PROGRAMS, THE SOURCE CODE CONTAINED THEREIN, AND/OR THE TECHNIQUES DESCRIBED IN THIS BOOK. IDGB DOES NOT WARRANT THAT THE FUNCTIONS CONTAINED IN THE SOFTWARE WILL MEET YOUR REQUIREMENTS OR THAT THE OPERATION OF THE SOFTWARE WILL BE ERROR FREE.

(c) This limited warranty gives you specific legal rights, and you may have other rights that vary from jurisdiction to jurisdiction.

6. <u>Remedies.</u>

(a) IDGB's entire liability and your exclusive remedy for defects in materials and workmanship shall be limited to replacement of the Software Media, which may be returned to IDGB with a copy of your receipt at the following address: Software Media Fulfillment Department, Attn.: *Java RMI*, IDG Books Worldwide, Inc., 7260 Shadeland Station, Ste. 100, Indianapolis, IN 46256, or call 1-800-762-2974. Please allow three to four weeks for delivery. This Limited Warranty is void if failure of the Software Media has resulted from accident, abuse, or misapplication. Any replacement Software Media will be warranted for the remainder of the original warranty period or thirty (30) days, whichever is longer.

(b) In no event shall IDGB or the author be liable for any damages whatsoever (including without limitation damages for loss of business profits, business interruption, loss of business information, or any other pecuniary loss) arising from the use of or inability to use the Book or the Software, even if IDGB has been advised of the possibility of such damages.

(c) Because some jurisdictions do not allow the exclusion or limitation of liability for consequential or incidental damages, the above limitation or exclusion may not apply to you.

7. <u>U.S. Government Restricted Rights.</u> Use, duplication, or disclosure of the Software by the U.S. Government is subject to restrictions stated in paragraph (c)(1)(ii) of the Rights in Technical Data and Computer Software clause of DFARS 252.227-7013, and in subparagraphs (a) through (d) of the Commercial Computer–Restricted Rights clause at FAR 52.227-19, and in similar clauses in the NASA FAR supplement, when applicable.

8. <u>General.</u> This Agreement constitutes the entire understanding of the parties and revokes and supersedes all prior agreements, oral or written, between them and may not be modified or amended except in a writing signed by both parties hereto that specifically refers to this Agreement. This Agreement shall take precedence over any other documents that may be in conflict herewith. If any one or more provisions contained in this Agreement are held by any court or tribunal to be invalid, illegal, or otherwise unenforceable, each and every other provision shall remain in full force and effect.

# JAVA™ DEVELOPERS KIT VERSION 1.0.2 COPYRIGHT AND LICENSE INFORMATION

JAVA™ Web development products are owned and licensed exclusively by Sun Microsystems, Inc. Copyright © 1992–96 Sun Microsystems, Inc. All rights reserved. Java and all Java-based names and logos, including the Coffee Cup and Duke, are trademarks of Sun Microsystems, Inc., and refer to Sun's Java Technologies. Products bearing authorized "JAVA- Compatible" Logo are based upon Sun's JAVA and technology, and are compatible with the API's for such technology.

Sun grants to you ("Licensee") a non-exclusive, non-transferable license to use the Java binary code version (hereafter, "Binary Software") without fee. Licensee may distribute the Binary Software to third parties provided that the copyright notice and this statement appear on all copies. Licensee agrees that the copyright notice and this statement will appear on all copies of the software, packaging, and documentation or portions thereof.

In the event Licensee creates additional classes or otherwise extends the Applet Application Programming Interface (AAPI), licensee will publish the specifications for such extensions to the AAPI for use by third-party developers of Java-based software, in connection with licensee's commercial distribution of the Binary Software.

RESTRICTED RIGHTS: Use, duplication or disclosure by the government is subject to the restrictions as set forth in subparagraph (c) (1) (ii) of the Rights in Technical Data and Computer Software Clause as DFARS 252.227-7013 and FAR 52.227-19.

SUN MAKES NO REPRESENTATIONS OR WARRANTIES ABOUT THE SUITABILITY OF THE BINARY SOFTWARE, EITHER EXPRESS OR IMPLIED, INCLUDING BUT NOT LIMITED TO THE IMPLIED WARRANTIES OF MERCHANTABILITY, FITNESS FOR A PARTICULAR PURPOSE, OR NON-INFRINGEMENT. SUN SHALL NOT BE LIABLE FOR ANY DAMAGES SUFFERED BY LICENSEE AS A RESULT OF USING, MODIFYING OR DISTRIBUTING THE BINARY SOFTWARE OR ITS DERIVATIVES.

By downloading, using or copying this Binary Software, Licensee agrees to abide by the intellectual property laws, and all other applicable laws of the U.S., and the terms of this License. Ownership of the software shall remain solely in Sun Microsystems, Inc.

Sun shall have the right to terminate this license immediately by written notice upon Licensee's breach of, or non-compliance with, any of its terms. Licensee shall be liable for any infringement or damages resulting from Licensee's failure to abide by the terms of this License.

The JDK 1.0.2 binary release is based in part on the work of the Independent JPEG Group.

Developed by Sun Microsystems, Inc.
2550 Garcia Avenue
Mountain View, CA 94043
Copyright (c) 1994, 1995, Sun Microsystems, Inc.

# JAVA™ DEVELOPMENT KIT VERSION 1.1.4 BINARY CODE LICENSE

This binary code license ("License") contains rights and restrictions associated with use of the accompanying software and documentation ("Software"). Read the License carefully before installing the Software. By installing the Software you agree to the terms and conditions of this License.

1. <u>Limited License Grant.</u> Sun grants to you ("Licensee") a non-exclusive, non-transferable limited license to use the Software without fee for evaluation of the Software and for development of Java@tm compatible applets and applications. Licensee may make one archival copy of the Software and may re-distribute complete, unmodified copies of the Software to software developers within Licensee's organization to avoid unnecessary download time, provided that this License conspicuously appear with all copies of the Software. Except for the foregoing, Licensee may not re-distribute the Software in whole or in part, either separately or included with a product. Refer to the Java Runtime Environment Version 1.1.4 binary code license (`http://java.sun.com/products/jdk/1.1/index.html`) for the availability of runtime code which may be distributed with Java compatible applets and applications.

2. <u>Java Platform Interface.</u> Licensee may not modify the Java Platform Interface ("JPI", identified as classes contained within the "java" package or any subpackages of the "java" package), by creating additional classes within the JPI or otherwise causing the addition to or modification of the classes in the JPI. In the event that Licensee creates any Java-related API and distributes such API to others for applet or application development, Licensee must promptly publish an accurate specification for such API for free use by all developers of Java-based software.

3. <u>Restrictions.</u> Software is confidential copyrighted information of Sun and title to all copies is retained by Sun and/or its licensors. Licensee shall not modify, decompile, disassemble, decrypt, extract, or otherwise reverse engineer Software. Software may not be leased, assigned, or sublicensed, in whole or in part. Software is not designed or intended for use in on-line control of aircraft, air traffic, aircraft navigation or aircraft communications; or in the design, construction, operation or maintenance of any nuclear facility. Licensee warrants that it will not use or redistribute the Software for such purposes.

4. <u>Trademarks and Logos.</u> This License does not authorize Licensee to use any Sun name, trademark or logo. Licensee acknowledges that Sun owns the Java trademark and all Java-related trademarks, logos and icons including the Coffee Cup and Duke ("Java Marks") and agrees to: (i) to comply with the Java Trademark Guidelines at `http://java.sun.com/trademarks.html`; (ii) not do anything harmful to or inconsistent with Sun's rights in the Java Marks; and (iii) assist Sun in protecting those rights, including assigning to Sun any rights acquired by Licensee in any Java Mark.

5. <u>Disclaimer of Warranty.</u> Software is provided "AS IS," without a warranty of any kind. ALL EXPRESS OR IMPLIED REPRESENTATIONS AND WARRANTIES, INCLUDING ANY IMPLIED WARRANTY OF MERCHANTABILITY, FITNESS FOR A PARTICULAR PURPOSE OR NON-INFRINGEMENT, ARE HEREBY EXCLUDED.

6. <u>Limitation of Liability.</u> SUN AND ITS LICENSORS SHALL NOT BE LIABLE FOR ANY DAMAGES SUFFERED BY LICENSEE OR ANY THIRD PARTY AS A RESULT OF USING OR DISTRIBUTING SOFTWARE. IN NO EVENT WILL SUN OR ITS LICENSORS BE LIABLE FOR ANY LOST REVENUE, PROFIT OR DATA, OR FOR DIRECT, INDIRECT, SPECIAL, CONSEQUENTIAL, INCIDENTAL OR PUNITIVE DAMAGES, HOWEVER CAUSED AND REGARDLESS OF THE THEORY OF LIABILITY, ARISING OUT OF THE USE OF OR INABILITY TO USE SOFTWARE, EVEN IF SUN HAS BEEN ADVISED OF THE POSSIBILITY OF SUCH DAMAGES.

7. <u>Termination.</u> Licensee may terminate this License at any time by destroying all copies of Software. This License will terminate immediately without notice from Sun if Licensee fails to comply with any provision of this License. Upon such termination, Licensee must destroy all copies of Software.

8. <u>Export Regulations.</u> Software, including technical data, is subject to U.S. export control laws, including the U.S. Export Administration Act and its associated regulations, and may be subject to export or import regulations in other countries. Licensee agrees to comply strictly with all such regulations and acknowledges that it has the responsibility to obtain licenses to export, re-export, or import Software. Software may not be downloaded, or otherwise exported or re-exported (i) into, or to a national or resident of, Cuba, Iraq, Iran, North Korea, Libya, Sudan, Syria or any country to which the U.S. has embargoed goods; or (ii) to anyone on the U.S. Treasury Department's list of Specially Designated Nations or the U.S. Commerce Department's Table of Denial Orders.

9. <u>Restricted Rights.</u> Use, duplication or disclosure by the United States government is subject to the restrictions as set forth in the Rights in Technical Data and Computer Software Clauses in DFARS 252.227-7013(c)(1) (ii) and FAR 52.227-19(c) (2) as applicable.

10. <u>Governing Law.</u> Any action related to this License will be governed by California law and controlling U.S. federal law. No choice of law rules of any jurisdiction will apply.

11. **<u>Severability.</u>** If any of the above provisions are held to be in violation of applicable law, void, or unenforceable in any jurisdiction, then such provisions are herewith waived to the extent necessary for the License to be otherwise enforceable in such jurisdiction. However, if in Sun's opinion deletion of any provisions of the License by operation of this paragraph unreasonably compromises the rights or increase the liabilities of Sun or its licensors, Sun reserves the right to terminate the License and refund the fee paid by Licensee, if any, as Licensee's sole and exclusive remedy.

# my2cents.idgbooks.com

## Register This Book — And Win!

Visit **http://my2cents.idgbooks.com** to register this book and we'll automatically enter you in our monthly prize giveaway. It's also your opportunity to give us feedback: let us know what you thought of this book and how you would like to see other topics covered.

## Discover IDG Books Online!

The IDG Books Online Web site is your online resource for tackling technology — at home and at the office.

**Ten Productive and Career-Enhancing Things You Can Do at www.idgbooks.com**

1. Nab source code for your own programming projects.

2. Download software.

3. Read Web exclusives: special articles and book excerpts by IDG Books Worldwide authors.

4. Take advantage of resources to help you advance your career as a Novell or Microsoft professional.

5. Buy IDG Books Worldwide titles or find a convenient bookstore that carries them.

6. Register your book and win a prize.

7. Chat live online with authors.

8. Sign up for regular e-mail updates about our latest books.

9. Suggest a book you'd like to read or write.

10. Give us your 2¢ about our books and about our Web site.

Not on the Web yet? It's easy to get started with *Discover the Internet*, at local retailers everywhere.

# CD-ROM Installation Instructions

The CD-ROM that accompanies this book contains all of the source code and object code that is contained in the text. The source code examples in the book are drawn directly from these source files with only minor modification. The class files have all been compiled with the Java Development Kit (JDK) from Javasoft and can be used directly as is. The CD-ROM also contains the JDK versions 1.0.2 for Macintosh and 1.1.4 for Windows and Solaris.

The CD is structured as follows:

♦ The **src** directory contains all of the source code in subdirectories that map directly to the package names of a particular application.

♦ The **bin** directory contains all of the sample classes from the src directory after being compiled. The bin directory contains the same package directory hierarchy as that of the src files.

♦ The **jdk** directory contains the Java Development Kit from Javasoft. The Windows 95/NT and Macintosh versions are self-extracting archives, and the Solaris version is a shell file that can be executed from a shell prompt to install.

Refer to Appendix D for more information about the CD-ROM.